CURRICULUM TECHNOLOGY

CJ Communications in the USA
2nd Edition

CONTRIBUTORS:

Julie Gibson, Karl Johnson, Dave West, and Daryl Davis

EDITED BY:

Marta Justak

CHANNEL CUSTOM PUBLISHING

Table of Contents

About the Contributors

Julie Gibson, MD, MBA, RN *

Julie Gibson, MD, MBA, RN, received her M.D. from Southern Illinois University School of Medicine, where she specialized in forensic pathology and pediatrics. Prior to medical school, she was a registered nurse with seven years experience in a neonatal intensive care unit. Dr. Gibson was a medical examiner in Maricopa County, Arizona (Phoenix) and the Chief Medical Examiner of Mohave County, Arizona. Dr. Gibson held master's degrees in human behavior and business, and bachelor's degrees in psychology and biology.

Dr. Gibson responded to multiple mass fatality disasters as a member of the Federal Disaster Mortuary Operational Response Team (DMORT) and was a member of DMORT-WMD, a specialty hazmat team responsible for recovering and decontaminating bodies following weapons of mass destruction incidents.

Dr. Gibson was an active instructor at several universities, teaching courses in criminal justice, forensic nursing, and medicine. She was Arizona POST certified in handguns and shotguns, went through the citizen's police academy, and volunteered as an armed posse member for the Maricopa County Sheriff's Office. She was a member of the National Criminal Justice Board, as well as a member of the Commission for Forensic Education.

* deceased 2011

Karl Johnson, POST, SWAT

Karl Johnson spent 12 years in corrections and law enforcement in California. His police experience includes patrol, jail operations and prisoner transportation, as well as SWAT operations and training. After the 9/11 attacks he became a contractor to the U.S. State Department and other government agencies providing personal security services to diplomats and others. He has also trained local security and police agencies in several countries in the Middle East and Central Asia. He currently lives in North Carolina.

Dave West, BS, CPP, SWAT

Dave West is the Director of International Security Operations with a Virginia-based firm that specializes in providing law enforcement, security advisory, and training services to the U.S. Department of State and U.S. Department of Defense. Originally from Memphis, Tennessee, he attended Memphis State University and received his B.S. in education. He also holds a certificate in project management from the University of Tennessee, and a master's certificate in business administration from Heriot-Watt University. He is a certified protection professional (CPP) through the American Society for Industrial Security (ASIS) and has been a member of the ASIS Council on Business Practices since 2009.

A former law enforcement officer, he worked assignments within his agency's Fugitive Apprehension Squad and Special Weapons and Tactics Team (SWAT). He holds over twenty law enforcement instructor and master instructor certifications from a variety of state, federal, and private organizations including, but not limited to the FBI, Tennessee POST, Arkansas POST, and the NRA.

Daryl Davis, BS, POST, CIT

Daryl Davis is a Sergeant in the Protective Services Department of the Santa Clara Valley Health and Hospital System in Santa Clara County, California. Originally from Chicago, Daryl attended Stanford University and earned his bachelor's degree in political science. His law enforcement career includes stints in patrol, corrections, court security, investigations, personnel & training, crowd control, and search & rescue.

Daryl is a POST-certified Field Training Officer and holds instructor certifications in firearms, baton, arrest control techniques, and OC Spray. He is certified as a Terrorism Liaison Officer, an instructor in incident response to terrorist bombing and prevention and response to suicide bombing incidents, and the crisis intervention team (CIT). He has a background in computer systems, network support and cyber security. He is married and the father of twin daughters.

Enrich Your Criminal Justice Learning with Curriculum Technology's

CT²Learn
EVOLVED LEARNING SYSTEM

- Criminal Justice Students now have access to the latest information in their chosen field of study

- The ELS brings an incredible variety of quality content to users with an easy to navigate, easy to use, multi-platform access

- For instructors, the ELS includes ongoing support from CT2Learn's team of professional instructional designers, enabling rapid development or revision of dynamic course experiences for students

CT²Learn Features at a Glance:

- Learning labs and activities

- Managed web content

- Current events

- Classroom and online teaching tools

- Complete etexts, elearning, and industry publications*

- Instructional design pros to assist with online or on ground course development*

- Learning community featuring nationally respected subject matter experts*

- Choose a Free "Basic" membership or a *Premium membership to access the entire spectrum of ELS content

For more information and to register:
www.ct2learn.com

MODULE 1

Human Communication Basics

Key Module Concepts:

- The three components of human communication

- Voice intonation and body language

- Clues to explain if an individual is lying

- Types of lying

- Reasons for lying

- Methods of active listening

- The effects of cultural diversity on communication
  and detecting deception

Introduction

Human communication is just the words that people say to each other, right? Not exactly. Human communication is the way in which humans exchange meaningful ideas with one another. Depending upon the study involved (percentages vary slightly), research states that only about 10% of communication involves the actual words people say, but 30% of communication is the way in which people say those words, called **voice intonation**. All the rest of our communication, about 60%, is done **nonverbally**.

This module discusses the complexities of human communication. It looks at perceptions, words, and overall communication – not just the spoken words that people say. You'll learn just what is meant by voice intonation. You'll see how people lie and some of the reasons that they lie. In addition, you will examine non-verbal communication, also called **body language**, and learn how to interpret nonverbal clues (also called cues). Nonverbal communication is extremely important in the criminal justice system because it's the way that officers determine whether or not persons they are questioning are being honest with them, whether they are hiding something, and whether or not they are actually lying. This skill is vital to anyone working in the criminal justice world.

Listening is also an important component in communication. A criminal justice professional must be a good listener and an active listener, as well as a very observant listener. Your listening skills will help you ask better questions of your witnesses to get more information about crimes. Listening and observing are key elements in determining whether or not a suspect is lying, as shown in Figure 1.1.

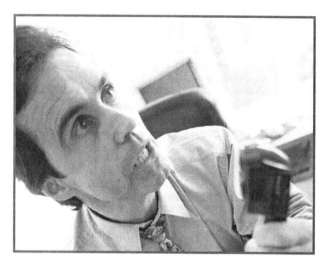

FIGURE 1.1: *Most human communication is conducted through body language and facial expressions, rather than through words.*

Ask Yourself

- *Are there times you knew someone was lying to you? How did you know?*

- *Are there times you knew someone was not listening to you? How did you know?*

- *Can you tell when someone doesn't really know what he or she is talking about, even though they claim they know? What told you they were uncertain?*

Verbal and Non-Verbal Messages

If only 10% of communication involves the words we speak, then obviously we need to learn more about the other 90%. Listening to voice intonation and observing body language will help you understand what others are trying to communicate to you. For example, if the words you are hearing from someone are inconsistent with the voice intonation and body language, then that person might be lying. Inconsistencies in the spoken words and the voice intonation and body language are termed "**leakage.**" (You can remember this because they are leaking their honest thoughts through their dishonest voice intonation and body language.) In other words, the words being spoken convey one message, but the way the words are said or the way the person moves or acts when speaking conveys something entirely different than the meaning of the words alone.

Learning about voice intonation and body language will enable you to become a more effective communicator with others, particularly when questioning witnesses and suspects. It will also provide the foundation for how you determine when you are being lied to, called **detecting deception**.

Voice intonation is the way that words are spoken. Speech may be fast, slow, hesitant, loud, or soft. Speech may reveal a foreign accent or a regional accent. For example, most Americans speak English as their first language; however, the English spoken by someone from Boston compared to someone from South Carolina is very different sounding. The accents are different and so is intonation. People who are speaking with uncertainty may make a statement, yet raise the pitch of their voice at the end of the statement so that it sounds like a question. Or they may make the statement with a quiet voice. Contrast this with a person who is very certain about a statement he is making. He may speak loudly, have no hesitation in his voice, and no raise in pitch at the end of the statement. He conveys his certainty and conviction in his voice.

Body language is everything your body does. The messages you receive from another person's body language are called *cues*. The body communicates something even when an individual is not speaking. To observe how the body communicates, begin watching people in public places. See if you can determine what people's body language is communicating by the way they walk and move. Who is happy? Who is sad? Body language is complex. It involves eye contact, eye movements, head movements, posture, hand gestures, arm and leg positions, and movements that the feet make. Look at how far apart people are when they speak to each other. Body language includes involuntary actions of the body like skin color (pale or flushed) or sweating.

Culture and ethnicity play a big role in voice intonation and body language. Most of the body language we will consider in this module is for Americans. If you are dealing with a person from a different culture, the body language and voice intonations must be looked at differently.

Both voice intonation and body language cues are simply clues to help examine the entire situation. As a criminal justice professional, if these clues confuse you or make you suspect the person is not being honest, you must continue to question the person (see Figure 1.2). Interpretation of voice intonation and body language is an art that must be practiced and always interpreted with caution and in the context of the situation.

FIGURE 1.2: *Interviews and interrogations are conducted professionally and without duress.*

1.5

Listening to Voices

First, let's look at voice intonation alone without the additional body language cues. Picture yourself as a criminal committing a home invasion in the dark. You're putting valuables in a bag when suddenly, a person (male or female) yells, "STOP RIGHT THERE!" The voice issues a command and gets your attention. The voice is stern and sounds mean. As the bad guy who hears only the voice, you don't know whether or not this commanding person has a gun pointed at you or not, but the voice indicates the person means business. You want to run, but are afraid that this person may hurt or kill you.

Now, let's pretend that you are the same bad guy in the same situation. A person sees you and gasps or screams, making a sound you interpret as fearful. He or she has a quavering voice that reveals their fear, and quietly says, "Stop......right....there." You are in the dark and cannot see the person. What are you thinking? You can run out, or you can punch the person first and then run. They sound so scared; they will be easy to get past to make a clean get-away.

In this example, the words are identical. The way they are said is very different. You, as the listener, make very different assessments of the person you cannot see in the dark, based only upon the way they said the same words. The voice intonation is different: commanding versus hesitant. Loud versus quiet. Quavering versus stern.

Voice intonation is usually taken in context with the associated body language, and is much more difficult to interpret alone. In the dark, body language does not add to the voice intonation. Another situation where body language cannot contribute to communication is over the phone.

Let's look at another example. Have you ever had to call a computer technical support person? It's not uncommon to make a call like this and get a technician in a foreign country (see Figure 1.3). Let's say you have to call for technical support, and you get a man who is happy to help you. He speaks English, but has a heavy accent that may be difficult for you to understand. You have no idea about where he is or what his background is. He may be sitting in a high-tech building, and he may have a Ph.D. specializing in the computer system you have a problem with – but based solely on his accent, you may have made some assumptions that have no validity at all. His accent brings out cultural diversity issues. You think that because he is foreign, he will not understand you or your problem, and will not be of much help to you. Would the situation be any different for you if you were a native Chicagoan, and you got a tech support person in Tennessee?

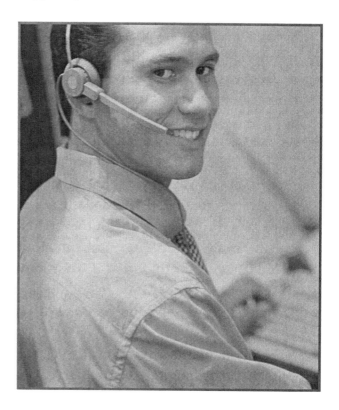

FIGURE 1.3: *Cultural and language differences, without body language, facial expressions, and gestures, make telephone communication difficult.*

Move forward several minutes. Your technical support person speaks quickly and knowingly, and walks you through the problem and fixes it. He has convinced you he knows his stuff. But what if he speaks slower and has an upward pitch of his voice at the end of each sentence? You may decide prematurely that he does not know what he is doing, and if he fixes your problem, he was probably just lucky – he did not really know what he was doing. Over the phone, you have only voice intonation to go by, and when you cross cultural boundaries, it becomes very difficult to interpret voice intonations. The technical support person may have purposefully spoken more slowly so you could understand his accent. He may have been speaking down to you, thinking that you were the dummy here. He may have had the upward intonations to question you, rather than asking, "Are you with me?" "Do you see that on your screen?"

Voice intonation must be interpreted in context. It is difficult to consider by itself, as in the examples of a person in the dark or over the telephone. Cultural diversity also plays a role. Our culture shapes the way we speak. In some non-American cultures, men speak very loudly because it is normal in their culture. In some non-American cultures, women are subservient and speak quietly. This is the norm in their culture, so you cannot use standard American norms to interpret their voice intonation.

As you begin to question a witness, talk to that person about non-threatening topics before you begin to ascertain what happened. This process allows you to establish a baseline of their voice intonations. Look at how fast he or she usually talks. Listen to how fluid his or her voice sounds. The baseline of their relaxed language is important. If they begin to lie or become anxious, they might speak faster or slower, or louder or softer than usual. They may lose the fluidity of their voice if it becomes shaky, which is another indicator of possible dishonesty. The pitch of the voice may change with lying.

Voice intonation is important. Keep voice intonation in mind as you consider body language. Body language and voice intonation are clues that work well together to help you assess honesty versus dishonesty.

Resource - Here is a website that has some good explanations concerning vocal communication. This will help you understand more about the importance of intonation and interpreting what is being said.

http://www.nidcd.nih.gov/health/voice/Pages/whatis_vsl.aspx

Body Language

Body language represents the majority of our communications – it is what people do with their entire body while communicating with other people. It consists of eye contact and eye movements, and all the movements and posturing that people do with their body while they communicate. It includes things their body does without their control, such as sweating. Body language can speak volumes when the person says nothing. For example, how do you know your friends are angry when you see them, before they even tell you? What are their postures that indicate anger?

You must first get to know someone in a relaxed and more normal setting before you begin questioning that person. This is when you "chit-chat" with the person to make them feel more comfortable with you. You discuss nonthreatening topics. Establishing rapport serves multiple purposes. It allows the witness or other person to feel you are more of a friend, and will probably make him open up to you more. Establishing rapport allows you to examine the baseline communication of the individual. This baseline enables you to look at the person's voice intonation under relaxed circumstances, as previously discussed. Does he speak loudly, softly, hesitantly, or quickly? It lets you observe his body language when relaxed. How much eye contact does he make? Does he make hand gestures? Does he kick or move his feet? How far away does he sit or stand when he speaks with you?

After you have observed the baseline of voice intonation and body language, you can begin asking your real questions about the incident that required your intervention. Watch the person closely. Does his pattern of speech change? Does her voice intonation change? Do his gestures and amount of eye contact change? These can be indications of dishonesty or anxiety. Establishing the baseline is key, and changes from the baseline are suspicious. Body language and voice intonations are all subject to change due to cultural diversity, so they must be interpreted with caution. If there are suspicious changes, ask more questions. Body language and voice intonations are clues to help you learn when to go further in questioning or in an investigation.

Before you learn more about body language, it's important to understand some basic details about dishonesty. Knowing the types of lies and the reasons that people lie will help you evaluate body language cues better.

Lying

We all know what lying is. We've all been kids who snuck chocolate cookies, who when confronted by our mother, lied and said, "I never took any cookies." Our mother knew we were lying. We looked down and didn't make eye contact (body language), and we made our statement quietly and hesitantly (voice intonation). Our mother did not have to be a criminal justice professional trained in reading body language to know we were lying. We also had the physical evidence all over us: chocolate on our faces and hands, and crumbs on our clothes!

Lying in adults is a bit more complex than in children. The goal of interpreting voice intonation and the body language of nonverbal communication is to determine if someone is lying or trying to hide the truth. Let's begin our exploration of the communication of dishonesty and deception with how people lie and the different types of lying.

There are many reasons that people lie. Obviously, in the criminal justice world most people lie to keep from getting arrested, so their reason for lying is to avoid punishment. Actually, that is the most common reason that people do lie, but there are other reasons as well. After you learn how and why people lie and understand the perceptual and cultural differences in individuals, you will learn how to unravel lies by observing the witness or suspect, listening to his or her story, and questioning that person.

Types of Lying

There are several types of lying that we are going to examine. They include the following:

- Omission
- Minimizing or exaggerating the truth
- Denial
- Fabrication

The easiest way to lie is by **omission**. This situation occurs when the basic story is true, but a key point is left out purposefully. This kind of lying is the most difficult to detect by examining body language, because the liar is basically being honest. He or she is simply purposefully leaving out a part of the story. Let's look at an example of omission:

"I was at the bar with my buddies. We were having some beers, and watching the hot babes. I had to work the next day, and had only planned to stay out until 10 p.m., but it was such a great time! We closed the place down, and I went home at 2 a.m."

Here, we've added the key point that was omitted:

"I was at the bar with my buddies. We were having some beers, and watching the hot babes. I had to work the next day, and had only planned to stay out until 10 p.m., but it was such a great time that we wanted to stay later. We were out of cash, so I went to the john where I saw a drunk and followed him outside. I punched him in the head, knocked him out, and took all the cash out of his wallet; then we could afford to party the rest of the night! We closed the place down, and I went home at 2 a.m."

The first story was not an example of lying by stating untrue words. All the words uttered by the suspect were true. You will learn as we go through this module that certain things stimulate the autonomic nervous system to trigger our bodies to do things that become visible as nonverbal cues and begin to raise suspicions of lying. Omission allows the suspect to override his autonomic nervous system fairly well because he does not speak false words. He omits words to create a false impression of what actually happened.

Children often lie by omission. Usually, when confronted with the truth, people who lie by omission will state they "forgot" to tell you the omitted truth.

Changing the story by **minimizing** or **exaggerating the truth** is another way to lie. In minimizing the truth, the liar basically tells the truth but plays down or minimizes key parts of the story. In exaggerating the truth, the liar blows up a part of the story and makes it seem to play more of a role in what happened than was really true. Both of these techniques serve to change the tone of the story and distract from the reality of what honestly occurred.

Denial is another way to lie. It is simply denying knowledge about something the liar actually knows. Some common examples include the following:

"I don't know anything about it."

"I don't know him."

"I don't know what you're talking about."

Sometimes, people really don't know something. That is okay. Denial is classified as lying when the liar really does know what you are talking about, really does know about the incident you are asking about, or really does know who you are asking about, but lies and says he knows nothing.

Fabrication is another way to lie. A fabrication involves making up a false story or set of events, and it is the typical lie that people thinks about when asked to think about what makes up a lie. Fabrication is common, and is the easiest form of deception to detect when examining body language while using good interview and interrogation techniques. If a single person commits a crime, he may need an alibi or someone to lie for him to say he was with that person when he was actually out robbing a bank. If two people work together to commit a crime, they must collaborate on their story as to why both are innocent. Because fabrication often involves more than one person agreeing on a false story, this collaborated fabrication can also help reveal the lie.

Resource - Most criminals are not sophisticated liars. Some may be smarter than others. There are websites designed to teach people to become better liars. Knowing what these "educational" websites contain may help you spot liars more easily. Check out this Web article on the art of persuasive lying:

http://www.soyouwanna.com/soyouwanna-lie-persuasively-1629.html

Why Do People Lie?

People lie for a variety of reasons. The most common reasons are the following:

- To avoid punishment
- To keep from being hurt
- To intentionally hurt someone else
- To gain something
- To avoid embarrassment
- To improve their image

Psychologists who study liars say that the avoidance of punishment is the most common reason that people lie. People may also lie to protect other people whom they don't want to get into trouble and to avoid punishment for them.

People sometimes lie out of fear, believing that they or someone they care about will be hurt physically or emotionally if they tell the truth. Children who are victims of sexual abuse or molestation commonly lie about what the perpetrator does to them because the perpetrator tells them he will hurt or kill their parents if they tell anyone what is happening.

Conversely, people maliciously lie with the intent to purposefully hurt other people. A jealous teen-age girl may hate her ex-boyfriend's new girlfriend, so she may tell the new girlfriend he has come back to her, when he has not. This is a lie to deliberately hurt the new girlfriend or break up the relationship.

Self-serving liars tend to help themselves gain something or to get ahead in some way, especially for financial gain. "This 1974 Pinto is in great shape – only driven to church by the original owner," which is a lie told by a used car salesman regarding an obvious battered old car in an attempt to make his sales commission.

Often as a result of low self-esteem, some people lie to appear better or more important than they really are – to improve their image. They lie to try to please others by telling them what they think the other person wants to hear to gain acceptance.

Avoiding embarrassment will motivate some to make false statements if they feel the truth will shame them in some way.

Lying can become a habit or a game to some people, while other people lie as a sign of underlying mental illness. Some people tell the truth from their standpoint, but it is clearly not true. This type of lying is often seen in mentally ill people, especially when they are describing hallucinations.

Interpreting Body Language: Body Position

You can interpret a lot about a person when you look at his body language or his body position. For example, the honest person usually faces you with his body. The dishonest person may lean away from you, or lean to one side or turn his head to avoid facing you directly. The honest person usually has good posture and sits or stands quietly. The dishonest person may slump or change positions frequently, looking fidgety.

The Body in General

Here are some general observations to follow when looking at a potential liar. First, observe the witness for signs of anxiety. Perspiration may indicate tension and dishonesty (if the environment is not hot). Skin may look pale if the witness is afraid or shocked. A witness may get flushed, red skin because lying can trigger the **autonomic nervous system**. Second, observe the general state of the witness: clean or dirty, groomed or unkempt, healthy or sick or injured. Make note of whether their appearance matches the story of what they were doing when the criminal justice professionals arrived.

Third, notice the breathing pattern of the witness. Anxiety and lying can cause an increased rate of breathing or shortness of breath, which may cause the person to sigh often or take frequent deep breaths. Extreme stress and anxiety can cause difficulty breathing. A dishonest person may have smooth, regular breathing until he lies, when his breathing may become irregular. If the witness coughs or yawns frequently, notice the pattern. Coughing and yawning can be distracters used while the witness thinks of his next lie. If you can see a pulse in the neck of the witness, watch it to see if it becomes faster with certain questions, because the pulse often quickens with lying.

The Face

Watch the facial movements and expressions while you establish rapport, so you can establish a baseline of facial expression. In addition, pay attention to the small muscles around the mouth and eyes. They should move naturally, indicating the person's emotions. If the natural movements of these mouth and eye muscles stop when you question the witness, this may indicate dishonesty. If the witness suddenly makes more facial expressions when you question him, becoming more animated, this may also indicate dishonesty.

Eyes

Make eye contact with your witness and notice his or her eyes. Red eyes may indicate crying, intoxication, illness, eye infection, or eye injury. Large, small, or irregularly shaped pupils may indicate poor or bright lighting, fear, drug use, eye disease, or previous eye surgery. Notice how much eye contact the witness makes with you. In our American culture, it is normal to make eye contact about half the time during a conversation, or 40-60% of the time. If the witness makes eye contact about half the time while you chitchat and then makes far more or far less eye contact when you question him, be suspicious of dishonesty. While it is common for a dishonest person to avoid eye contact when lying, some people know this and will make more than normal eye contact when they lie in an effort to convince you of their honesty. People often look away when asked a question that is very emotional for them. They are trying to maintain composure and put their emotions into words. It may be an indicator of dishonesty if the person continues eye contact with you when you ask an emotional question.

Emotions show in the eyes. An honest person will show joy or grief in his eyes. A dishonest person will have a more flat look in his eyes. His face may smile or show grief, but his eyes will remain flat. Watch the pupils. If the lighting is constant, the pupils should remain constant. If the pupils dilate when the person makes a statement, and then the pupils return to normal, this may indicate dishonesty. The autonomic nervous system knows the person is lying, and the pupil dilatation is a response to autonomic nervous system stimulation.

Hands

Watch the hands of the witness while you establish rapport. Notice what he does with his hands when he speaks. Some individuals will cover their eyes or mouth with their hands when they lie, and this may indicate deception. Watch the finger movements, even if the hands are kept relatively still. Some people tap or drum their fingers when they talk, and the movements may change during a lie, becoming slower or more rapid. Continual tapping may indicate anxiety or dishonesty, so try to observe the level of anxiety of the person to decide if he is lying or just upset.

Witnesses may manipulate objects in their hands to distract you. Nervous people may pick at their clothing or groom their hair with their hands, which can also indicate lying. The autonomic nervous system is stimulated with lying, which may cause the hands to sweat or the skin to tingle or itch. Watch for a witness who tries to dry his hands on his clothing or who scratches himself as an indication that he is being dishonest.

Watch the pattern of any hand movements. If the witness is quiet when nonthreatening questions are asked, but his hands move in response to certain questions, this may indicate lying. Normal people have smooth hand movements, and if they make hand gestures while talking, they usually keep their hands within the area of their chest. Dishonest people may gesture wildly with their hands outside of their chest area. Dishonest people also might have shaky hands, or keep their hands unusually stiff or still. Shaky hands can also be due to excitement, medication, or medical problems that cause tremors. Rubbing the hands together rapidly is usually an indication of honesty, while rubbing the hands together slowly tends to indicate dishonesty.

Arms

Arms may be crossed against the chest or abdomen. This pose could be interpreted as a body barrier, which is an indication of dishonesty or a closed attitude toward you. However, this action could also mean that the person is chilly or grieving.

Some cultural or family styles of communication may involve excessive hand gestures or arm waving. This may indicate passion for a subject, an excited state, or some other motivation. Any analysis of gestures and movement should include a period of observation during which the interviewer analyzes the subject's body language usage in general conversation before drawing conclusions.

Feet and Legs

If the witness is sitting, watch his legs and feet. Resting the feet flat on the floor indicates a cooperative, open position that indicates honesty. Holding the knees apart is an indication of openness and honesty. Tapping the feet or circling the feet may represent anxiety and possible dishonesty. As with the hands, watch the foot movement with certain questions. If the feet are quiet with nonthreatening questions and then suddenly begin moving with other questions, this reflects dishonesty. If the legs and feet are kept under the chair with only the toes on the floor, this is called the starting block position, and is a sign of anxiety or fear as though the person is ready to run out of the room. Crossing the legs stiffly may show dishonesty, but if the crossed legs appear relaxed, this may be interpreted as openness and honesty.

As you can see, reading body language and voice intonation is not an exact science. Many witnesses are stressed, and stress can cause people to appear dishonest when they are actually telling you the truth All of the subtle changes in voice intonation and body language are clues in the science of nonverbal communication, and they must be put together to form an interpretation of whether or not the person is being honest.

Resource - Body language, its use and interpretation, has been shown to be a successful tool in advancing any career. Learn more about body language in this article designed for those interested in leadership roles and career enhancement.

http://www.mindtools.com/pages/article/Body_Language.htm

CASE STUDY

Body Language Solves the Crime

Mr. Tanner lived in a dilapidated neighborhood. He was known to be a grumpy old man who didn't like anyone. Police knocked on his door to interview him, after the couple living next door was found bludgeoned to death.

Mr. Tanner opened the door as far as his chain lock would allow.

He just said gruffly, "Whaddya want?"

"Police. We want to ask you some questions about your neighbors."

"Don't know any of them. All a stuck-up bunch."

"Open the door. We just want to get a feel for the neighborhood."

Mr. Tanner opened the door and let Officers Martin and Wood inside.

He was dirty and had messy gray hair and facial stubble. He walked in front of the officers, and indicated they sit on the couch, while he sat in a wooden rocker located at one end of the couch in the corner, facing the front of the room. He stared straight ahead, not facing the officers, and not looking at them. Officers made small talk to establish rapport. Mr. Tanner spoke slowly, and was cooperative but not cordial. He sat very still with his hands on the arms of the rocker, his knees together, and his feet flat on the floor. The officers began to ask about the neighbors. Mr. Tanner put both toes on the floor behind the chair seat, and began to move one knee up and down.

"Don't know them," he said, putting his hand in front of his mouth when he spoke, with his knee moving faster.

"Did you ever see them or talk to them?"

Mr. Tanner coughs, then said, "No," in a quieter voice that quavers. He began tapping the index finger of one hand. Officers noticed his face getting red, he developed perspiration on his forehead, and he began to scratch his chest.

The officers continued to ask questions, while Mr. Tanner seemed more anxious and agitated. He finally exploded and gestured wildly with his arms, shouting with a shaky voice, "I never knew them. I never saw them. I just know the blonde had a nasty little mutt that never shut up."

Mr. Tanner was taken to the police station for further questioning.

What were Mr. Tanner's body language and voice intonation clues to officers that he was a person of interest who needed more questioning? What did he say in words that indicated more knowledge of the neighbors than he admitted?

Active Listening

Listening is a key component in communication. Passive listening is the act of hearing the spoken words. Passive listeners may not make eye contact. They may not acknowledge the speaker. They may be daydreaming, thinking about something else, or planning what they want to say next, rather than actively listening and interpreting what is being said to them.

Active listening is a skill. It must be practiced. Active listening shows the speaker you care about what is being said, and this will encourage the speaker to tell you more. It shows the speaker that you consider that person to be important. Active listening means your complete focus is on the person who is speaking. You, the listener, face the speaker and make eye contact. If you must take notes, look up often to make eye contact. Nod and use facial expressions to indicate that you are listening and following the conversation by smiling or frowning in context to what is being said. If more than one person is speaking, shift your focus and body toward each speaker when he talks. Make small acknowledging comments like, "Uh-huh," "sure," or "okay."

There are tactics to use while engaging in active listening. These tactics will show that you care about what is being said. Some tactics may even help shape the speaker's emotions. The tactics are designed to help the speaker open up more to you and tell you more about what is on his or her mind – and encourage the speaker to think that you care about him or her, and that are interested in what is being said.

Active Listening Tactics

Mirroring is one active listening tactic. It involves using the same body language as the person to whom you are speaking. Studies have shown that the speaker tends to "like" the listener better if the listener mirrors his or her body language and behaviors. If the speaker is crossing her legs, you cross yours. When she uncrosses her legs, so do you.

You can use your body with mirroring to help control the person who is speaking to you. Many people unconsciously mirror others. Have you ever spoken with someone who is really angry and tense, and then later noticed how you felt at the end of the conversation? Were you tense? Were your muscles stiffer than when the conversation began? You were probably unconsciously mirroring the angry person and reflecting their angry tenseness back toward them in your body posturing.

You should become conscious of your own use of mirroring and learn to use it while you listen to someone. If your witness is tense and angry, mirror what you want their behavior to be. For example, if you want them to calm down, then consciously relax your body and keep your face relaxed. As you speak with the witness, he may begin to unconsciously mirror you and become more relaxed.

A witness or suspect may act indifferent and bored and then later get belligerent. If you hold your body in a stern, tense, no-nonsense commanding way, the person may change his attitude to become more respectful, as he or she begins to understand the seriousness of the situation.

Another method of active listening is reflecting back what someone has said to you in the exact words. For example, "She is the most wicked woman in the world!" So you repeat, "She is the most wicked woman in the world."

You can also paraphrase what the person said – reflecting back what the person has just said, but in different words. "She is the most wicked woman in the world." You say, "She is one mean lady."

You can often reflect emotions or state a deeper meaning in different words (see Figure 1.5). Reflecting emotions means you respond to the witness with the feelings you think he is expressing. Stating a deeper meaning is when you suspect there is something deeper beyond the statement's face value, so you voice this. These methods show that you are actively listening, and also serve to encourage the witness to

FIGURE 1.5: *The interviewer must not get caught up in the emotional state of the person they are interviewing. Calm and impartial demeanor is necessary to make accurate observations.*

clarify what he means. "She is the most wicked woman in the world." When you reflect emotions back, you might say, "You seem very hurt and angry with her."

When the witness says, "She is the most wicked woman in the world," if you want your response to reflect a possible deeper meaning, you might say, "I hear that you must have had a past relationship with her."

If the witness does not say more after any of your active listening comments and you feel there is more that the witness wants to say, or is hiding something or holding back and not saying something, you can always say, "Tell me a little more about her. You say she is wicked. Why?"

R **Resource** - This Mind Tools article gives a great synopsis of how to hone your active listening skills.

http://www.mindtools.com/CommSkll/ActiveListening.htm

Cultural Diversity

Cultural diversity reflects the differences that people have based upon their background, upbringing, country of origin, and ethnicity. Americans typically embrace cultural diversity. Cultural diversity must be considered when voice intonation and body language is studied, because culture has a large impact on how people speak and use their body language.

Voice intonation is even more difficult if cultures differ among speakers. If you have ever taken a foreign language, you probably noticed that the emphasis of your training was on verbs, feminine and masculine nouns, and sentence structure. Were you ever taught the voice intonation that was appropriate for a conversation in that language? People for whom English is not their first language have the same problem. They may speak English very properly. They understand spoken words in English, but may take the words at face value, missing the context of the words, because they do not always understand the implications of English voice intonations. Likewise, their voice intonations may be difficult for you to interpret because they use the intonations of their native language. They may also have an accent that makes their intonations sound different to you.

The same is true in dealing with regional English accents and regional voice intonation differences. If you are a native of California, you may have difficulty understanding and interpreting a person from Georgia or Boston, because the regional English is much different in other parts of the United States than the English spoken in California.

This discussion of body language and voice intonations has assumed that you are conversing with Americans and has been explained with the standard American culture in mind. Keep in mind that if you are speaking to someone from another culture, or even another region of the United States, you must be sensitive to the cultural differences. All interpretations of voice intonations and body language must be used with caution.

Cultural Similarities and Differences

Some forms of body language are cross-cultural, like smiling, but many aspects of body language are unique to a particular culture. For example, eye contact in our culture is a sign of honesty, while in some Asian cultures, it is a sign of rudeness. In our culture, the motion of holding up the hand with the thumb touching the index fingers and the rest of the fingers extended means, "Okay!" This, however, is an obscene and offensive gesture in some European cultures. The American nodding and shaking of the head for yes and no are reversed in other countries, so that nodding means "no" and shaking the head side to side means, "yes."

In some cultures, women still are second-class citizens and are "owned" by their husbands, so the wife may be treated with disregard and disrespect, which is typically abnormal in our American culture. A woman from this culture may use few words, little or no eye contact, and speak in a quiet voice. Voice intonations are more difficult to interpret in persons for whom English is not their first language, as previously discussed. Voice volume may be culturally different, too. Body space, or the distance between individuals speaking with each other, varies in different cultures. Keep cultural differences in mind when interpreting body language and voice intonations. You must become familiar with a culture to really be able to interpret the body language and voice intonation of someone from that culture. You will, however, be able to determine if the voice intonation and body language changes from a baseline in any culture, even if you are confused about the meaning of these changes.

The distance that people stand or sit from each other varies from culture to culture, and is even different in different areas of the United States. It is important to notice this distance while establishing a rapport as a baseline of body space, so that you can later notice changes in this distance when the questions and conversation become more threatening to the witness or suspect.

FIGURE 1.6: *This criminal street gang member is communicating through subculture sign language often called "throwing gang signs."*

An example of American cultural differences may be seen in typical gang cultures. For an American gang member, eye contact may be disrespectful. Gang members may have a closer body space with their own gang members. If they use the same body space with opposing gang members, this action is considered to be disrespectful or threatening. They might use hand signs with different meanings so that other opposing gang members will not understand them, much like the hand signs used in professional baseball (see Figure 1.6). Hand signs are a purposeful use of body language.

Resource ▪ Be sure to read this Web article on different aspects of cross-cultural communication. The explanations of these differences will help you communicate with persons from other cultures throughout your criminal justice career.

http://www.beyondintractability.org/essay/cross-cultural_communication

Other Cultural Differences

When questioning witnesses, you expect to get facts that you understand. However, people from other cultures may perceive things differently than you do, and their answers might seem vague or frustrating to you.

Time and space are perceived differently by different cultures. You may ask what time something happened and get an answer in relation to sunset or sundown, with a refusal to be more specific with clock hours. Time, in some cultures, is measured in relation to the sun rather than the clock. You may arrange to meet someone from another culture at a specific time and be frustrated when they don't show up and you are unable to reach them. They may call you hours or days later and ask you where you were because they were at the meeting place and you were not there. Time is seemingly meaningless to some cultures; at least time as the average American views it.

Pride and respect is very important to some cultures. You must be careful to preserve this respect. Some cultures bow to each other rather than shake hands. To people from some cultures, the way they are treated in front of their peers and the way they respond to you in front of their peers is important for maintaining their social standing within their cultural group. This is called *saving face*. These people must be separated from their peers for questioning and also taken to a location where their peers cannot see the interview, even at a distance, in order to get the most information from them. People from some cultures prefer silence while others are loud and interrupt you frequently. Or you may find people of another culture to be very stoic, showing few facial expressions, regardless of the circumstances. You will notice this in your baseline rapport-building conversation, and the absence of facial expression will be unlikely to change throughout your questioning.

Americans are generally very open to questions about any topic. But certain topics are taboo in other cultures, such as discussing money, sex, or sexual preferences. People from some cultures will not discuss their personal lives with you at all. Others only want to discuss themselves and boast, and you will have problems learning any information about anything relevant outside of their personal lives.

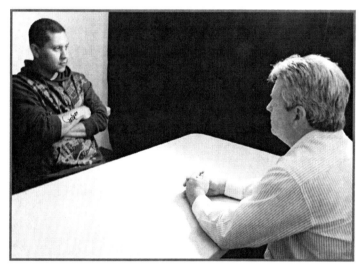

If you know you must question a person from another culture, and you have the time, take a moment to learn about their culture so you can better plan your line of questioning (see Figure 1.7). You want to avoid offending them inadvertently,

FIGURE 1.7: *Criminal justice professionals must be comfortable communicating with persons from a wide variety of cultures.*

and you want to learn the most sensitive way to approach topics that their culture considers taboo. If you have a coworker from that culture, ask for tips or have your coworker actually conduct the questioning. You must be sensitive to cultural differences, but you must still conduct an investigation by gathering all the information you need.

CASE STUDY

Be Aware of Cultural Differences

A series of brutal sexual assault homicides were occurring in the Asian neighborhood of a large American city. The city police were investigating the crimes. Initially, the murders did not appear to have any connections. One victim was a female adult. One was a male teen. Another was an elderly male. The commonalities were that all victims were Asian, and all had been brutally sexually assaulted. Detectives decided these were serial crimes because they were happening more frequently, and they feared more victims would be found.

A task force was formed, and a larger group of investigators began to question possible witnesses. The link between the victims was finally found: all were homosexual. The crimes were determined to be hate crimes that were targeting the Asian gay and lesbian population. The link was discovered so late because none of the original detectives wanted to ask this cultural population any sexual questions because sex was a taboo topic, in spite of the fact that these were sexual assaults ending in homicide.

How would you approach a culturally taboo topic in a case where the taboo topic was vital to the investigation? Is it right or wrong to neglect a sensitive topic? Explain.

In another large city, a problem arose when a skilled forensic child interviewer disappeared. She worked as a civilian at a child abuse advocacy center that worked closely with police. The police needed her to interview and videotape child victims, and occasionally child crime witnesses. It was soon learned that the interviewer was in jail.

This shocked the interviewer's coworkers and the police who needed her for their cases. The interviewer helped police, and was a nice person who seemed to be a law-abiding citizen. The problem was a cultural one. The interviewer was a Native American. In her culture, the belief was that no one person owned land (land was owned by the gods), and therefore the city had no right to control or restrict parking. She had nine outstanding parking tickets. She had not paid the fines and had ignored orders to appear in court. She was picked up with a warrant for her arrest. Her cultural beliefs were so strong that she pled guilty but would not pay for bail, choosing instead to stay in jail until released. To her, time and money were meaningless. Parking restrictions were against her cultural beliefs, and she felt that sitting in jail upheld her beliefs better than paying for her freedom.

What does this case study demonstrate about cultural beliefs?

Summary

Human communication is a complex combination of words, voice intonation, and body language. Body language represents the majority of our communication, or approximately 60% of our nonverbal language, while 30% of our communication is the way we say words or voice intonation. Only 10% of our communication is in the content of the words we speak.

Witnesses, suspects, and victims commonly lie to criminal justice professionals. Understanding voice intonation and body language, the differences between baseline speech and activity, and the inconsistencies of the spoken words will help criminal justice professionals become more alert to dishonesty.

Knowledge of voice intonation and body language, the more subtle forms of communication, will help officers be more effective in questioning witnesses to gather more information about crimes. Officers must keep cultural differences in mind and use voice intonation and body language interpretations with caution when speaking with a person from another culture. Interpretation of these cues, even in American culture, is an art that must be practiced, and all cues must be interpreted together in the context of the situation. Body language and voice intonation interpretation are simply clues to help guide the questioning of witnesses, which may, in turn, help with the investigation.

Criminal justice professionals must also demonstrate active listening skills to help witnesses speak more freely to them. Communication is vital to all people in all walks of life, but is even more important to those who work in the world of criminal justice

Discussion Questions

1. Read the Web article in the Resources box. What aspects of cross-cultural communication surprised you? What do you commonly do that is normal in American culture but may offend someone from another culture? What might they do that you would have found offensive before you learned more about other cultures?

2. What kinds of body language indicate honesty?

3. Discuss ways an officer can use all the types of active listening to get more cooperation and information from witnesses.

4. What are all the reasons that people lie? Give examples.

5. Discuss a variety of voice intonations and what they indicate to you. Have others in the classroom comment to see if other students would interpret them differently.

Key Terms

Autonomic nervous system (ANS): Part of the nervous system that controls certain body functions that are involuntary; the ANS is stimulated during lying, and this stimulation causes observable changes in a person that indicates dishonesty.

Denial: A type of lying where the liar states he or she knows nothing about something he or she really does know something about.

Detecting deception: The art of putting together many complex clues to determine when an individual is lying.

Exaggerating the truth: A type of lying where a part of the story is blown up to seem more important than it was to deceive someone.

Fabrication: A type of lying where the liar makes up a phony story that did not actually happen.

Leakage: Inconsistencies between spoken words, voice intonation, and body language that indicate deception.

Minimizing the truth: A type of lying where part of a story is downplayed or minimized to deceive someone.

Mirroring: Using the same body language as the person to whom you are speaking.

Nonverbal communication (body language): Facial expressions, body movements, and behaviors that communicate with others independent of words.

Omission: Telling the truth but purposefully leaving out part of the story to deceive someone; a type of lying.

Rapport: Talking to an individual about nonthreatening topics to make that person feel more comfortable, and reveal their baseline communication, or their normal, way of communicating.

Voice Intonation: The pitch, speed, fluidity, and sounds of the voice when a person speaks; the way a person says words.

MODULE 2:

Report Writing in Law Enforcement

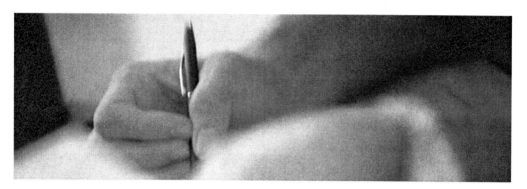

Key Module Concepts:

- The value of writing high quality reports

- Using clearly understood language in written reports

- Writing in the first person, avoiding jargon and overly technical terminology

- The "Five W's" plus "how" in telling a story

- The definitions and uses of Observations and Inferences in report writing

Introduction

The most common complaint heard in department squad rooms and coffee shops frequented by working police officers is that they have far too many reports to write. Generally, people become police officers because they like to be active. Certainly, cops on TV don't appear to spend much time writing, so the reality of the job can be disappointing.

The truth is that, after officer safety concerns, writing excellent reports is the most important skill an officer can develop. Far from being wasted time, carefully written reports result in convictions and appropriate sentencing of dangerous criminals, and they protect good officers from false charges of abuse or brutality. Almost every experienced cop has a story about a colleague whose reports were so useless in court that the district attorneys simply would not file charges on any case that particular officer handled. The officer's reputation for indefensible reports made him completely ineffective on the street because even if he was a human bloodhound at sniffing out crimes, if the suspects weren't turned into defendants and convicts, then the officer's work was wasted. Concise, timely, accurate, and grammatically correct paperwork is a job requirement for a 21st century law enforcement officer.

FIGURE 2.1: *Officers spend a lot of time writing reports.*

Although formats and reporting requirements will differ slightly in each department, police reports everywhere contain the same basic elements. Whether filed electronically from a terminal in a cruiser, dictated over the phone, or written by hand on paper, the report is the proof of the quality of an officer's work. Each piece of written **documentation** that an officer produces reflects back on that officer's capabilities, and the impression that document leaves on superiors can make or break an officer's career (see Figure 2.1).

Ask Yourself

• *Why does police work seem to require so much writing?*

• *Who will be reading my reports?*

• *How good do I really have to be at writing?*

Write Clearly

Fortunately, it does not require a degree in English to write good reports. With a little effort and practice, anyone can learn to write effective reports. Remember that the initial police report is crucial to a successful prosecution. It provides a clear, chronological description of the "who, what, where, when, and why" of an event, and poor grammar can quickly turn that clarity into confusion. Grammar is a dirty word to many officers, and unfortunately our high schools have not been as thorough at teaching it as a police administrator or prosecuting attorney might like. But there is good news! The basics of grammar and punctuation are very important tools for cops, but mastering the obscure details of English grammar are not necessary to write good police reports.

A safe practice for all report writers is to use short, simple sentences. Complex sentences with multiple clauses and parenthetical phrases make for entertaining novels, but factual reports are best served with clear, simple statements. Reports are written to pass on information, not to entertain or impress an audience.

Use Everyday Language

Report writers have to remember that their work is not written for other police officers to read. Unfortunately, many officers write reports in a stilted and unnatural way.

Consider the following two report excerpts:

> **This officer initiated a routine vehicle stop by activating the marked patrol vehicle's emergency equipment. The suspect vehicle came to a halt in an unlighted portion of the highway's shoulder. This officer instructed the driver to pull to the lighted off ramp using the patrol vehicle's public address system. Two men were then observed exiting the suspect vehicle. The men ran into the wooded area adjacent to the marked highway. This officer began a foot pursuit, which he terminated after losing sight of the suspected perpetrators in the unlighted area. This officer then communicated the perpetrators' descriptions and direction of travel via hand held radio.**

This paragraph is perfectly understandable to other officers, but members of the jury who might have this read to them years later will probably be confused. Remember that police reports are not written for police to read, so using normal, correct everyday language is important.

> **I initiated a car stop on the white Prius using the patrol car's red light. The Prius stopped in a darkened part of the highway shoulder, so I called over my car's loudspeaker for the driver to pull to a lighted area ahead. I saw two men get out of the Prius and run into the woods to the south of the road. I followed them on foot until I lost them in the dark, and called dispatch with their descriptions and direction of travel.**

This version gives more information in fewer words, and it is also clearer to the average reader. Normal people drive cars, not vehicles. Normal people do not refer to themselves in the **third person** as "this officer" always does. They use the **first person** forms I and me to refer to themselves. Using the **passive voice** as in, "Two men were observed," is far less clear than the **active voice**, "I saw two men." Also, the passive voice requires the reader to fill in exactly who did the observation, while the active voice makes it obvious instantly.

Jargon is specialized language used by those working in specific fields. The medical world is famous for overusing jargon. For example, a patient who goes to the doctor for a nosebleed might be terrified to hear that he has epistaxis! Hopefully, a kind nurse will tell the poor patient that epistaxis is doctor jargon for a nosebleed. However, the members of a jury might not have a convenient interpreter nearby. Overuse of important sounding words such as *vehicle* and *perpetrator* can be potentially confusing to jurors. It's also critical to avoid using street words like "crank" or "hubba," which are slang words for methamphetamine or crack cocaine. The only time to use these words is in a direct quote when they are defined by the writer.

Writing in everyday language also gives the defense attorneys less chance to discredit an officer's testimony or to use confusion to sow doubt into the jury's minds. While defense attorneys provide a necessary service in ensuring that their clients' rights are respected, some will do that by aggressively attacking the reporting officer's integrity, ability, and training through extremely close examination of the original report. A clear and complete report written in simple sentences using easily understood language is the best protection an officer can have against this common tactic.

Be Complete and Accurate

Police reports are usually filled out using forms that provide fill-in boxes or multiple choice check boxes for basic information. This form is often called a "**face sheet**," because it is the first page of the report. No matter how well the **narrative**, or the story of the event, is written, if the forms are not complete and correct, the case may still be lost.

While each department will use a different version of these forms, they all ask for much the same information as the examples provided. First, the identifying information for each suspect, victim, and witness is collected. This information includes their names, addresses, and other contact information, and frequently their physical descriptions. The need for the suspects' physical descriptors is clear when the suspects have not been identified, but the victim's description may also be important if a major difference in their size, for example, is an important part of the specific charge. In some jurisdictions, a suspect who is considerably larger than a victim may be open to a more serious charge.

Once those involved are identified to the officer's best ability (suspects are not always known at first, of course), other items of information such as location, vehicles used, and generalized details of the type of incident are collected. Although many of these details will have to be written into the narrative as well, these details allow for statistical analysis of the incident and may help identify similar incidents and trends. Given the number of agencies that are using computer-aided reporting systems, these small pieces of information can be collected into a much bigger picture of the local crime situation. This information can be used to coordinate crime prevention and targeted enforcement efforts, and also to identify suspects known to have committed similar crimes in the past.

Because the narrative is the portion that many officers find so intimidating to write, the temptation is to rush through the seemingly easy part. However, taking that shortcut can lead to leaving out important information or even putting inaccurate information into the report. Imagine a form with check boxes listing different physical descriptors. Although the boxes are intended to ease the officer's task of describing an involved person, a check mark intended to indicate brown hair that is near the box for blonde hair might cause the wrong information to be given out and the right suspect to go unfound – or at the very least, give the defense attorney an opening to attack the arrest.

Sometimes, when the initial report is written, the officer might not have all the information necessary to completely fill in the report. In this case, it is far better to put an indication of this in the box rather than to leave it empty. If requested information is unknown, then "unknown" can be put instead, or if the information is not appropriate to this case, then "not applicable" can be filled in. The preferred wording changes between various agencies, but both "unknown" and "not applicable" actually provide information and increase the report's clarity, compared to leaving the space empty. A future reader will not know if that space was left empty on purpose because the information was not known, or if the officer simply forgot to fill it in.

Use the Five W's

The Journalists and storytellers refer to the five W's as their guide to telling a complete story. Who, what, when, where, and why are the questions that have to be answered to explain what happened at any event. The first four are obvious, and the forms that police departments use ensure that those questions are at least minimally answered by having boxes in which that information is listed. *Why* is often more difficult to explain, and sometimes the *why* is never really known.

The five W's and "how" are useful analytical tools to make sure all questions are asked and all information is documented. Frequently, the report writer may assume that the reader has the same underlying information and will gloss over details in the report.

Any information left off of the report, for all intents, is non-existent to the supervisor or prosecutor who later reviews the case file. There is always a who, what, when, where, why, or how that seems to be left unanswered. If you are the reporting officer on the witness stand, you can rest assured that the opposing attorney will ask you why you added information to your report after you submitted it. They will view it as an attempt to lead the jury. Perhaps you were hiding something or were careless in your investigation.

One method of testing the level of detail of your report is to test each name, place, time, and occurrence against a series of five W-type questions.

For example, rather than just writing in the report that Joe Jones was a witness and listing what he told you, include information from the five W's, such as:

- The background on *who* the witness is

- *What* the witness was doing there

- *When* the witness arrived at the scene

- *Where* the witness was when he saw the incident

- *Why* the witness was there

- *How* did the witness perceive the incident?
  Did the witness hear it or see it?

For each answer you develop, try to think of more questions to refine this information. Using this approach will lead to a more thorough and robust collection of information and result in a more complete report.

Form Types

Besides crime reports, police agencies have large numbers of specialized forms. Some of these are **administrative forms**, which officers use for internal memos, to request time off or to report extra duty worked, or to report equipment malfunctions or damage to request maintenance. Usually, the form used for documenting information for a criminal investigation is called an **incident report**, or a **crime report**. In general, forms are designed to ease the officer's job of gathering and reporting information, and to provide a standard format that can be searched and referenced easily.

Some counties use standard forms across several local departments in hopes of standardizing the way information used by the courts, probation departments, and other agencies is presented, but most police departments use forms designed to fit that department's specific needs.

Event Date (s)			Time (s)			
Event Type (s)			Case #			

VICT or COMP LOC.

Last	First		MI
Address			
City	State		Zip

Subject

Race	Sex	Age D.O.B.	Phone: Page# / Bus. / Cell		
		Last	First		MI
		Address			
		City	State		Zip
		D.L.#	SSN or Other ID#		

Race	Sex	Age D.O.B.		Hgt	Wht	Hair	Eyes

Vehicle

☐ Theft ☐ Rec'd ☐ Susp ☐ Vict	Year Make & Model	Tag#
	VIN	State
Additional Vehicle Description		

For example, while a small, rural department might use a generalized incident report form for every event, state highway patrol officers spend so much of their time working car accidents and making drunk driving arrests that they nearly always have forms specifically designed for those tasks (see Figure 2.2).

FIGURE 2.2: *Specialized forms are used for common reports, such as traffic violations and car accidents.*

Computerized Report Writing

More and more departments are utilizing computers for report writing. Some agencies simply use their computers as word processors, and the forms are merely computerized versions of the old handwritten forms. This practice does ensure that a report written by an officer with difficult-to-read handwriting is easily read, and also adds a **spell check** feature that can be useful, but it does not really make the best use of the computer's strengths.

Computers are very good at sifting through large amounts of information, even if technology has not yet made them able to interpret that information as well as a human officer or department analyst. Computerized information can be sorted in any number of ways to help plan crime prevention programs or to identify areas where enforcement resources targeting specific problems are best used. New York City has successfully developed integrated databases that collate information from many sources over time, including information from first-line police reports, in order to predict future crime trends. More immediate uses might include comparing an unidentified suspect's description with the crime's details and location, which could provide enough information for the system to compile a list of likely suspects (along with recent booking pictures and last-known addresses). Criminals tend to do the same crime over and over, so this information gives detectives following up on the case a starting point in their investigation.

No matter what the capabilities of the specific computer system are, it cannot turn a poorly written report into a good one or identify inaccurate information that is carelessly written. If anything, computers require officers to write more precisely and carefully to ensure that the information is usable for more than just the immediate prosecution needs. Fortunately, the generation of officers starting their careers now is generally very comfortable using computers, and those computers are far more reliable and durable than in the past, even if they cannot write the reports themselves.

CASE STUDY

Reporting Skills

Practice your report writing skills by filling in the information on the forms provided from a mock crime scene scenario. Your teacher may have scenes prepared, or you can use the one found at

http://www.wadsworth.com/criminaljustice_d/templates/stripped_ features/WADCJ_StHelpCtr_Report.html

When you read the narrative provided, consider which words are not "everyday language" and whether some might actually be jargon. Think of ways to simplify the story while maintaining all the meaning and information. As you fill information into the face sheet, be systematic and make sure not to leave any important information off. It's easy to miss a box or two on these busy and compact forms. Remember that neatness counts if you are filling them in by hand.

Making the Narrative Flow

The story being told is that of the event, but even more it is the story of how the officer conducted the investigation to learn about the event. Events should be written in the order they occurred so that future readers get a clear picture of the entire investigation and its outcome.

Many officers feel insecure about their report writing ability when it comes to writing the narrative, but it is actually one of the easiest pieces to write. If you remember that you are telling a true story to a jury, it should seem much easier. Every good story has a beginning, middle, and end, and this particular true crime story is no different.

There are many traditional elements in police work, some of which relate to writing reports. For example, some academy or field training officers still require reports to begin with a restatement of information that is already written into the boxes on the report's face sheet.

Consider this report's beginning paragraph:

> **On 10/12/2010 at 1925 hrs I, Ofc B. Smith #1716, was conducting a routine uniformed vehicle patrol. I received a call from dispatch to respond to 1234 Maple Ave for a report of an automobile theft. Upon arrival, I was met by the victim, Bill Johnson, who stated that he had last seen his vehicle at 1900hrs...**

Nearly all of this information was already written into the face sheet, and while it is not wrong to include it in the narrative, it is unnecessary. Modern police officers already spend more time than they would like writing reports. Why add to that time? In the past, officers traditionally used an opening sentence in which they identified themselves as police officers and explained what they were doing before the call. However, the report writer's occupation is obvious from the fact that the report was written, and the writer is already identified by name, badge number, and title on the bottom of nearly every form included as part of the report. The story is about the crime that was committed, not about what the writer was doing before being notified of it, so that usually doesn't add any useful information. There are times when explaining whether the officer was in uniform or driving a marked car is important for demonstrating the elements about the crime charged, but generally it is assumed to be the case.

The Beginning

This report could be stated more efficiently in this manner:

> **Victim Johnson stated that he left his car parked on the street in front of his residence when he returned home at 1900 hrs, but when he looked out of his window at 1915 hrs, the car was no longer there. He pointed to shards of safety glass at curbside where his car had been parked.**

In two sentences, the story's beginning has been told without restating the address or victim's full name. Identifying the individuals referred to in the report as victim, suspect, or witness is a useful aid in keeping a reader from becoming confused, especially in cases where there are several of each. Some jurisdictions might identify Johnson as (V) Johnson or as (V1) Johnson if there were another victim also listed, and they might identify suspects as (S) and witnesses as (W). While shorthand is usually best avoided because the report should be written for a jury, this information is easily enough understood with minimal explanation.

The previous two sentences sum up the victim's experience of the theft and provide an easily understood beginning to the story, but they are hardly enough to tell the story as is. The beginning of the report is also where the elements of the criminal act are described. Each crime has a definition in the state's law codes. For example, typically robbery would require the theft of property from a victim directly, as opposed to theft that involved taking property from a victim without their being there. This means that taking a car while the victim is driving it is *robbery* and taking it when it is parked and unattended is *theft*. The writing officer has to ensure that the story specifically includes each element of the crime that is being charged.

The Middle

The middle of the story remains to be told, and that middle includes all the investigative efforts the officer makes to solve the crime. Interviewing victims is an art form that good officers learn early. While some victims are uninterested in assisting the police, most want those responsible for the crime to

FIGURE 2.3: *A witness attempts to recall information to help solve the crime.*

be captured and prosecuted. When an officer shows some basic concern for the victim's plight, it can open up an unexpected floodgate of information, particularly since the victim often may not realize how much he or she actually knows. Some officers will accept a victim's "I don't know" statement without attempting to follow up and establish useful information. It's important to realize that even a cooperative victim has come under stress due to having a crime inflicted upon them, which makes their inability to come up with a coherent description understandable. If a victim cannot estimate a suspect's height, for example, ask him (or her) whether the suspect was taller or shorter than the victim or than the reporting officer. Raising and lowering a hand to what seems about right to the victim can narrow it down further. Although the suspect's estimated height will be listed on the face sheet, describing the process used to establish that estimate demonstrates the estimate's reliability, and so becomes a useful part of the middle of the story.

In this case, the victim did not see the car stolen, but you can ask him if he saw anyone nearby when he parked the car. Has he seen anyone in the neighborhood lately who does not live there? The conscientious officer canvasses the immediate neighbors in case one of them saw someone who did not seem to belong in the neighborhood, or who may have seen the thief because they heard the car's window break and looked outside. The middle of the story assists investigators who follow up on the crime by telling them with whom the officer spoke and what they said at the time, which may suggest further lines of inquiry the detective can use (see Figure 2.3).

After taking the victim's statement, I canvassed the immediate neighborhood for possible witnesses. Most of the homes were unoccupied and I left business cards with requests for information and contact information for the auto theft unit on their doors.

Jones, Robert (W1) told me that he had heard glass breaking while working in his back yard at about 1910 hrs. The yard's fence kept him from seeing where the vehicle was parked, and by the time he looked out from inside his house, the vehicle was already being driven away from the curb. He could not describe the driver beyond that he was male, white, and wearing a dark blue baseball cap.

Smythe, Mary (W2) approached me as I attempted to contact neighbors to tell me she might have information. She said she had been out walking her dog at 1900 hrs when she saw the victim return home. Even though she lives around the corner on 5th, she knows the victim by sight as they have both lived in the neighborhood for some time. As she was returning home after her walk, she saw a man get out of the passenger side of a white van she had seen before in the neighborhood. The van had a company name and logo painted on its side, but she could not recall any details. She is sure she has seen it several times in the area and believes it to belong to a handyman business. She described the man as white, 5' 10", about 200 lbs. He was wearing dark pants, a green plaid shirt and a blue baseball cap. She did not see his face well as he walked away from her position, but she did see him carrying some sort of tool in his right hand. She said that she turned the corner and lost sight of the man, but felt that it was unusual for the van to leave a handyman with one tool.

Seeing my police car in the neighborhood, she decided to come forward with her information. I gave her a business card with contact information to the auto theft unit, and asked her to call if she remembered any more information about the van, or if she saw it again.

The End

The end of the story should include the outcome of the investigation as of the time the report was written.

> **I contacted Det. Brandon at the auto theft unit to alert them about this theft. He will follow up with the victim and witnesses in the next several days. At his request this report will be cc'd to the unit**

Often, the initial report will be the final report, and it will end with the arrest and booking of a suspect with no follow-up needed. Sometimes, especially with complex crimes or those in which a suspect is not immediately identified, the initial report is simply the first part of a long investigation that might include many officers from several agencies.

(R) **Resource** - Investigation is a science, and the concept of observations and inference that we are going to learn next are used in science experiments as well.

See the PowerPoint presentation at
http://www.slideshare.net/gbbantay/observations-and-inferences-26284428

This powerpoint provides examples of inferences and observations.

Observation and Inference

Those who enjoy reading detective stories will be familiar with heroic investigators whose amazing powers of observation allow them to see and identify the most subtle clues and pieces of information, thereby solving the nearly perfect crime. Edgar Allan Poe's *The Murders in the Rue Morgue* is generally considered to be the first detective story, and he wrote that the detective makes "in silence, a host of **observations** and **inferences**. So, perhaps, do his companions; and the difference in the extent of the information obtained, lies not so much in the validity of the inference as in the quality of the observation."

Of course, observation is one of the police officer's main investigative tools, but investigators are expected to be more than just cameras recording their observations. They must also be able to make logically sound inferences from those observations. If observation is the "what" of an event, inference is the "why."

Observation involves using one or more of our five senses to describe something. For example, the appearance, smell, feel, sound, or taste of some object. These are facts about an object that do not involve judgment, guessing, or opinion. Rather, the types of observations police officers are expected to include in their reports are often divided into quantitative and qualitative.

Here is a simple statement:

   Two people left the room.

The example shows a **quantitative observation**. The observer saw two, and only two, people leave the room. We often think of scientific experiments as being concerned with quantitative observations that can be objectively proven and precisely compared to other observations, but actually we use quantitative observations in our everyday lives. For example, when shopping, we compare the price of one item to the price of another item. When driving, we compare the number of cars at one tollbooth to that in the next lane to determine which one we should use.

Police reports frequently involve quantitative observations such as the following:

- There were five bullet holes through the car's windshield.

- The car came to a stop 33 feet from the intersection's northwest corner.

- A plaster cast of a footprint taken at the scene was later measured to be 3.2 inches across and 10.5 inches long.

The second type of observation that police officers use is called **qualitative observation**.

These are observations that describe an object by using adjectives and adverbs, as shown in this statement:

The man's hair was brown.

Qualitative observations are valuable, even if they are not as obviously objective and comparable. In the example of the man's hair color, an honest observer in low light or who had poor eyesight might identify the color as black, but never as blonde or bald.

Examples of qualitative observations that might be found in police reports include the following:

The suspect's car is blue.

The neighbor reported a strong chemical smell.

The witness stated, "I heard a really loud crash and looked out the window to see what happened."

Inferences are the explanation for observations. They are based on past experience and prior knowledge, which help make sense of the isolated observations that our senses collect. An example is that when we enter a classroom, we infer that the person standing in the front of the room is the teacher. Over time, if that person sits down with the students and another person enters and begins writing on the blackboard, our inference might change to match our new observations.

A police officer dispatched to investigate the burglary of a home might arrive and see that the door was locked, but there was a broken window with a stepladder beneath it. The immediate inference would be that the window was where the burglar entered the home. Inference is the logical thought process that takes into account the officer's previous experience and applies it to current observations.

Police officers are expected to be able to make rational inferences from their observations and to document them in their reports when they are useful. When it is appropriate to write an inference, it is important to also give the observations that led to the inference so that readers can evaluate whether the inference really did follow logically from the known information.

CASE STUDY

Police Work

Officers sometimes engage in incompetent police work, false reporting and other illegal and unethical acts. Every police officer working has an interest in seeing these few "bad apples" caught. Defense attorneys often attempt to make police misbehavior seem much more common than it is in order to cast doubt into the minds of jury members, in an attempt to avoid their client's conviction.

Recently, in California, a police officer's arrest reports were carefully searched after he got in trouble off duty. When an officer exhibits poor behavior off duty, his on-duty life has to be investigated as well, and, in this case, his department's investigators found enough problems in his reports that they could no longer stand by his work. The department filed for dismissal of 79 cases after finding several questionable drunk driving reports.

It is certain that most of the arrests this troubled officer made were legitimate and correct, but even a small handful of questionable reports created enough doubt that the department had to reinvestigate hundreds of arrest reports spanning years, and the courts had to throw out any that might have been tainted. This behavior affected conscientious officers by casting doubts on their work--doubts that may last for years.

Remember that you may be called to testify years later about the report you wrote your first day on the job. If your report is clear, complete, and accurate, you will be able to testify to the events even if you can't remember that particular investigation or arrest. Using commonly understood, everyday language whenever you can leaves less opportunity for the defense to attack, and it keeps the jury confident that they understand what really happened and that they aren't being misled by one of those "bad cops" they've seen in the movies and on the news.

Summary

Communicating through writing is not something that comes easily to many people, but it is a skill that police officers must have to do their jobs well. Well-written reports put criminals in jail and protect officers from accusations of wrong doing. Answering the five W's in simple, everyday language and with a basic knowledge of grammar helps

FIGURE 2.4: *Well-written reports provide the story and facts that help put criminals behind bars.*

guarantee clear, effective reports, no matter how complicated the event. Police forms are designed to assist officers in documenting events completely and accurately, whether those events are administrative or criminal.

Telling the story of the event and the investigation is not as difficult as it may seem at first. Maintaining the timeline and telling about events in the order they occurred helps officers organize their reports and helps future readers follow the story as it unfolds. The report should document the observations made by the officer during the investigation and what inferences were drawn from those observations.

Discussion Questions

1. Who are police reports written for?

2. Why do you think police officers have to document events so completely?

3. Why is accuracy so important? Give some examples of what could happen if incorrect information is included in a report.

4. How do you feel about your ability to write a complete and accurate narrative report? What has prepared you to write well, and what can you do to improve your capability in the future?

5. How is an inference different from an assumption?

Key Terms

Documentation: The written reports and completed forms that describe a situation or event.

First person: The point of view shown by the use of "I" and "we" to refer to one's self.

Third person: The point of view shown by the use of "he" "she" or "they" and similar pronouns to refer to one's self.

Active voice: Indicates that the subject of the sentence is performing the action the verb refers to. The boy threw the ball.

Passive voice: Indicates that the subject is the recipient of the verb's action. The ball was thrown by the boy.

Jargon: The specialized language or technical words used by a certain profession or trade.

Face sheet: The first page of a police report. It contains the basic identification information of crime suspects and victims.

Narrative: The written portion of the report, as contrasted with the pages requiring filling required information into boxes.

Administrative forms: Forms used to track equipment, repairs, work schedule changes etc.

Incident report: All the pages of a report documenting an event; often the same as a crime report.

Crime report: All the pages of a report documenting a crime, or suspected crime.

Spell check: A word processing program's built in feature for finding common spelling mistakes.

Observations: The act of recognizing objective facts or occurrences.

Inferences: Logical conclusions derived from premises known or believed to be true.

Quantitative observation: An observation of something that can be measured, such as weight, distance or speed.

Qualitative observation: An observation describing the character of a thing, such as round, green or soft.

References

Fawcett, Martin A. "Field Notes and Report Writing."
Protection Officer Training Manual. Seventh Ed.
Amsterdam: Butterworth-Heinemann, 2003. 40-45.

Morley, Patrick. *Report Writing for Criminal Justice Professionals.*
New York: Kaplan, 2008.

MODULE 3:

Communication in Law Enforcement

Key Module Concepts:

- Techniques for being a good conversationalist

- Active listening skills

- Using empathy as a tool for gaining a person's confidence and trust

- Differentiating between confrontation and conflict

- Techniques to defuse confrontation

- Tactical language to gain compliance, cooperation, and collaboration from others

Introduction

Whether officers realize it or not, their ability to communicate properly with the public directly affects every other action they perform while on duty. Effective **communication** with fellow officers, witnesses, arrestees, or any other person contacted requires an understanding of the dynamics of sending and receiving both **verbal** and **nonverbal** messages (i.e., not only what people say but also the way that they say it). The tone of voice that officers use, their inflection, pitch, and choice of words all send strong messages to the public. Whether conducting a simple traffic stop interview or when engaged in a complex confrontational situation with multiple offenders, knowing how to communicate well is one of the primary tools that law enforcement officers can use to control situations. Effective communication keeps officers and the communities they serve safe (see Figure 3.1).

FIGURE 3.1: *Effective communication keeps everyone safe.*

This module addresses verbal communication typically used in law enforcement, but it is also appropriate for any of the four criminal justice areas (enforcement, the courts, corrections, and social services). You'll learn how to handle polite, as well as stressful, conversational situations that you might encounter as an officer.

Ask Yourself

• *How does the way a police officer communicates with others affect his or her ability to do their job?*

• *Do communication skills influence other people's perceptions of professionalism?*

• *How does an individual's ability to communicate reflect upon the organizations that he or she represents?*

• *How can communication skills help a police officer to obtain compliance, cooperation, and collaboration from the people he or she interacts with while at work?*

Talking to People

The majority of law enforcement citizen contacts occur face-to-face. These contacts can happen in both formal and informal settings, and are typically one-on-one meetings or involve small groups of people. Whether they occur during a traffic stop, an interview, or any other scenario, the manner in which officers present themselves has significant impact on their individual images and also affects the public's view of their agency, as well as its attitude toward law enforcement in general. Therefore, it is essential that officers learn the vital components of verbal communication and understand how to conduct conversations properly, know the difference between hearing something and actually listening, and learn how to use empathy in their speech in order to talk to people effectively.

Talking to people involves much more than the use of simple words. Effective communication requires an understanding of the dynamics of sending and receiving verbal *and* nonverbal messages, which includes not only what the officers say, but also how they say it.

By learning to be more effective communicators, police officers can achieve the standards of conduct expected of them by the public without surrendering authority, responsibility, or discretion.

Conversations

Good conversational skills are learned traits and are essential to success in the law enforcement career field. Understanding the art of conversation allows an officer to put others at ease in his or her presence, or can assist the officer in maintaining control of confrontational or hostile situations.

The type or mood of a conversation depends greatly on whom the participants are, the topic being discussed, the relationship between or among the participants, and many other factors. In this regard, it is important to always consider with whom the conversation is being held and the circumstances that have led to the conversation. With these factors in mind, the conversation should be adjusted accordingly.

If being a good conversationalist can be learned, then how do you start? Here are some tips.

- **Learn to be interested in people.** If you have a sincere interest in people you will find that you have much less of a problem in striking up a conversation with anyone, whether it is someone you have never met before and are just beginning to deal with on a scene, or someone you work closely with on a daily basis.

- **Maintain eye contact during the conversation.** It is commonly considered to be a sign of sincerity in North America to maintain eye contact. In some cultures however, it can be interpreted as rudeness.

- **Always be polite.** Even in a confrontational situation, there is no reason for you to be hostile or to act rudely. Politeness can cool heated tempers and de-escalate violent behavior. Ask for things in a pleasant way, not as if you are investigating.

- **Ask proper questions.** Questions and replies to questions being asked of you should be related to the topic. Changing topics mid conversation can be frustrating to the other party and inhibits both your focus and the other person's.

- **Learn to listen.** Listening skills are equally, if not more important, than speaking skills when conducting a conversation.

- **Be knowledgeable.** If you know nothing about the topic, then you will have little to offer the other person involved in the conversation. Learning in law enforcement doesn't end upon graduation from the police academy. Commit yourself to learning everything you possibly can about your job.

- **Learn to read and interpret body language.**

- **Act confident (even when you are not).**

Listening Skills

Hearing simply means the ability to perceive sounds. If officers just hear what another person says, rather than actually listening to it, they will contribute nothing positive to the communication process and may cause misunderstandings, mistakes, frustration, and less successful **conflict** resolution.

In contrast, police officers who learn effective listening skills acquire additional facts that allow them to form accurate judgments about incidents or individuals. Armed with more accurate information, officers can respond or act more intelligently and identify better alternatives to resolve situations. Effective listening also demonstrates to others that the officer is aware of and sensitive to their emotions.

Active Listening

Listening is one of the most important skills a police officer can hone. How well people listen has a major impact on their job effectiveness and the quality of their work.

- Law enforcement officers listen to obtain information.

- Law enforcement officers listen to understand.

- Law enforcement officers listen to learn.

Given all of the listening that police officers must do during the course of a day's work, common sense would dictate that most of them would be very good at it. The truth, however, is that most are not. Studies show that people generally remember a rather dismal 25-50% of what they hear.

Not only does remembering such a small amount of what people hear affect their ability to do their jobs effectively, but this also means that when police officers talk to fellow officers, supervisors, witnesses, suspects, and other citizens, they are also only going to retain 25-50% of what is said to them. Can the important parts of a conversation be captured and retained in 25-50% of a message?

Clearly, listening is a skill that all people can improve, but within the law enforcement community that improvement is even more critical. By becoming a better listener, officers will improve their productivity and their ability to influence, persuade, and negotiate. In addition, they can avoid conflict and misunderstandings, all of which are necessary tools for success within the law enforcement community.

One way to become a better listener is to practice "**active listening**." Active listening is done when a person makes a conscious effort to hear not only the words that another person is saying but, more importantly, the total message being sent. In order to do this, it is critical that very close attention should be paid to the other person.

While practicing active listening, police officers cannot allow themselves to become distracted by whatever else may be going on around them. This can be very difficult while working a scene where tempers may flare, or there is activity going on that may cause concern for this individual or another person's safety and security. If possible, it is important that officers speak to people in as controlled an environment as possible to avoid these distractions and safety concerns. While practicing active listening, time cannot be spent forming **counter arguments** that will be made when the other person stops speaking, and focus cannot be lost on what the other person is saying either. All of these barriers contribute to the inability to really listen and understand.

To enhance listening skills, the officer should let the other person know that he is listening to what is being said and to consciously acknowledge them. Acknowledgement may be as simple as a slight nod of the head or saying "uh huh." The intent is not necessarily to be seen as being in agreement with the person, so much as indicating that the officer is listening. Intentionally using body language and other signs to acknowledge listening also helps to remind people to pay attention and not let their mind wander during the conversation.

All responses to the speaker should be made in a way that will encourage that person to continue speaking, so that the information that is needed can be obtained. While nodding and making acknowledgement comments says you're interested, an occasional question or comment to recap what has been said communicates that the message being sent is understood as well.

Becoming an Active Listener

There are five basic rules for effective active listening. These rules ensure that the other person is heard and acknowledged.

Rule 1: Pay Attention
Give the speaker your undivided attention and periodically acknowledge the message being sent. While the other person is speaking, look directly at him or her, and put aside all distracting thoughts. Whenever possible, remove yourself and the person you are speaking with from areas that may be distracting. Do not allow yourself to be drawn into side conversations when dealing with groups. Stay focused.

Rule 2: Show That You Are Listening
Use body language and gestures to convey your attention. Nod occasionally and use facial expressions. Encourage the person you are speaking with to continue by using short comments such as "yes," "OK," or "uh huh."

Rule 3: Provide Feedback
Our personal filters, assumptions, judgments, and beliefs can distort what we hear. As a listener, your role is to understand what is being said. To confirm that you are hearing the person correctly, ask questions of the person with whom you are speaking. You can also paraphrase what has been said already through the use of phrases such as "What I am hearing is…" or "What it sounds like you are saying is…."

Rule 4: Do Not Interrupt
Interrupting is a waste of time. It frustrates the speaker and limits your full understanding of the message. Allow the other person to finish his or her speech.

Rule 5: Respond Appropriately

Active listening is a model for obtaining respect and understanding. The objective is to gain information and perspective. Nothing will be gained by attacking the speaker. Be candid and open in any responses you deliver to the speaker, and treat the person you are speaking with as you would want to be treated.

It takes both concentration and determination to be an active listener. Try to be deliberate with your listening and remind yourself constantly that your goal is to actually hear what the other person is saying. Set aside all other thoughts and concentrate on the message. Ask questions, reflect, and paraphrase to ensure that you understand the message.

Empathy

Empathy is often characterized as the ability to "put oneself into another's shoes." By definition, empathy is the intellectual identification with or vicarious experiencing of the feelings, thoughts, or attitudes of another.

Sympathy on the other hand is defined as the harmony of or agreement in feeling, as between persons or on the part of one person with respect to another.

Resource - Look up the definition of sympathy at dictionary.com. Notice the notes related to its common confusion with empathy and the list of synonyms.

http://dictionary.reference.com/browse/sympathy

While similar, there are some very distinct differences between acting sympathetic toward someone and showing empathy. Law enforcement officers need to understand these differences and utilize the correct tool while communicating with others.

Empathy develops into an unspoken understanding of someone's plight because you, the officer, have experienced something similar to the person you're helping. Sympathy involves having feelings for the person's dilemma, even though you haven't experienced anything like it. In a nutshell, one feels empathy when one has "been there" and sympathy when one hasn't.

Once you recognize who you are speaking to and assume a correct approach for obtaining empathy, the next step is to consider the voice that you will use. Sincerity is of the utmost importance. Someone that is not believable cannot project empathy. Different voices are required for different people. It takes both an earnest effort and experience to develop this skill.

The last step is to be thoughtful about the words chosen. Organize sentences and their content with the intention of connecting with the person whom you are trying to communicate with. The way the Chief of Police at a major metropolitan police agency is normally approached and spoken to is probably very different from the average lower income family man who is working a labor class job in a rural town. Words should be chosen wisely, with the intention of making a connection with the person on the other end of the conversation.

CASE STUDY

Good Conversation Skills

Becoming a good conversationalist can benefit you in almost every aspect of life. Employing conversational tools such as active listening and empathy help people to understand one another better and ensure that the messages sent during verbal communication are the same as the messages received. Not only does this benefit a police officer while at work, but understanding the use of these tools and being able to apply them properly allows parents to communicate better with their children, managers to work more productively with their employees, and doctors to understand their patients more clearly.

Consider how the use of these tools enables you to obtain more out of a conversation, and then think about how having a larger amount of information that is both more accurate and specific helps you solve problems.

Imagine arriving on a scene where you have been called to help a parent deal with a delinquent child that keeps coming in late after curfew. When you arrive at the house, the father and teenage daughter are discussing the evening's events. The father is doing all of the speaking and the daughter is not able to get a word in edgewise, although she is trying very hard to do so. The father makes several statements about how he cannot understand why his daughter cannot follow simple directions and get home on time and that he has now called the police to help him with the problem since he obviously cannot get her to work with him on her own. It is now 12:30 a.m.. The daughter's curfew was 12:00 a.m., and you note that you received the call for service at 12:15 a.m.. The daughter is becoming more and more visibly frustrated.

By the time the father has finished talking, she no longer wants to interrupt and has nothing to say.

How did things go wrong in this situation? Based on this conversation, do you believe there is any hope that things will change at all without your intervention? Even if you intervene at this point, how much change can you hope to make right now?

What if the father had used tools such as active listening and empathy in an attempt to engage his daughter in a conversation about her continually coming in after curfew?

The father could have started the conversation by simply stating: "Your curfew was 12:00, and it's now 12:15. Did something happen tonight that caused you to be late?" and then waited for her to respond. How might things have gone differently? What if he simply started by asking open-ended questions and let her do all the talking for a little while, and followed the five active listening rules. Is it possible that he might have obtained more information or been able to get to the root of the problem a little easier? Could he have shown some empathy in his response by stating something along the lines of "I understand where you are coming from. I was a teenager once, too." At that point, it's possible he might have gotten her to listen to him once he began trying to counsel, rather than to deliver punishment for her actions.

How could the use of proper communication tools benefited the father in getting his daughter's attention and helping her understand and agree to his rules. Perhaps with active listening, a call to the police could have been avoided.

Confrontations

Confrontation is defined as "discord" or "a clash of opinions and ideas." During communication, confrontation is used for many things. It is used to address negative situations, express negative **emotional responses**, allow others to see and feel your anger, and ventilate your anger openly. It can also be used to change other people's behavior; change the things that make people angry; help them stand up for your rights if they feel they are being violated; or clarify what has happened and why it is upsetting and get corrective action taken.

> **Resource** - Look at the FreeDictionary.com definition of confrontation. Notice the many examples of confrontation that are listed.
>
> **http://www.thefreedictionary.com/confrontation**

There are numerous ways for people to confront one another. Acting angry, assertive, direct, accusing, ordering, blaming, belittling, scolding, lecturing, and name calling are all behaviors that indicate that one person is trying to confront another about something. Depending on the situation, these behaviors can be appropriate or inappropriate. It is up to the individual to learn how to analyze conversations, obtain a broad-based view of the entire situation, and then determine if an individual's behavior is acceptable or not.

When properly used, confrontation can be an effective **communication tool** for law enforcement officers. However, first they must be able to recognize the difference between appropriate and inappropriate behavior. Officers must never cross the line and present themselves in an unprofessional or inappropriate manner.

Just as important as understanding how to use confrontation as a communication tool is the importance of learning to eliminate confrontation during a conversation when necessary. Inappropriate confrontation can stir up or cause irrational thinking. Irrational thinking drives confrontation to actual conflict. Conflict then has to be defused, before violence or other inappropriate acts take place.

Defusing Conflict

It's been a long, miserable afternoon. It is over 100 degrees outside, and you have been answering back-to-back service calls for almost six hours straight. Now you have arrived on a scene where a very loud and angry man is arguing with an animal control officer about his pet that has been captured. The pet owner claims that his dog was confined to his fenced-in backyard all day and has not been loose in the neighborhood. The animal control officer states that he received a call about a loose dog in the neighborhood and when he arrived in the area, he found the young mixed breed wandering aimlessly down the street. The tempers of both the pet owner and the animal control officer have already flared and are bordering on getting out of control as you step out of your patrol car.

Is it possible to defuse this conflict and assist both the pet owner and the animal control officer at the same time without further fanning the flames or creating greater conflict?

It absolutely is — even on your worst days. Defusing conflict through communication is rarely easy, and it does take practice, but experts insist that volatile confrontation can be de-escalated by using a series of conflict resolution techniques.

Here are some tips:

- **Aim for empathy.** When it's 100 degrees outside and you have been working at a breakneck pace for hours, it won't be easy to feel someone's pain, but empathizing, even if you have to fake it at first, can be an extremely effective way to short-circuit a blowout.

- **As you practice putting yourself in another person's place, realize that just the act of interacting with a police officer can be stressful for some people.** Whether the person you are interacting with really wants to communicate with you and resolve the problem or not, the mere fact that you are there in the capacity of a police officer may be an obstacle that you will have to help some people overcome.

- **Be a good listener. Listen without judging.** This can be difficult when dealing with someone who is angry and already acting belligerently, but if your goal is to reach a resolution that's truly best for all parties involved, consider listening with warmth and respect, and aim for understanding rather than agreement. Paraphrase people's comments without reacting or blaming and maintain positive, reinforcing body language such as sincere eye contact, nodding your head, and keeping your facial expression friendly and open.

- **Don't take it personally.** That's easier said than done, but if you're trying to calm an agitated citizen, the worst thing you can do is let yourself get sucked in by comments or accusations.

- **Don't fan the flames.** Personalized blaming and accusatory comments only make things worse. Avoid them by keeping communication impersonal. A simple technique is to use "I" instead of "you" whenever possible. For instance, instead of saying, "You're wrong," try "I can see there's been a miscommunication."

- **Take away the stage.** Someone may be adamant about being right in a place where everyone is watching or it is embarrassing to admit the truth. Try to move the conversation to a more private location such as an adjoining unoccupied room or around the corner of a house out of view of neighbors and family members.

- **Stand back and let them rant.** When all else fails, sometimes the best course of action is to let someone just vent. As long as you have already taken away the stage and are out of public view, letting someone simply blow off a little steam for a minute may help. However as a police officer, you cannot allow others to control your scene, and you must consider your safety, as well as everyone else's safety, at all times.

- **Remember the 30-second rule.** Think of an angry person waiting as a pressure cooker building up steam. The longer they wait, the angrier they will become when you have to tell them something that they don't want to hear. If someone is waiting to speak, acknowledge that person within 30 seconds, with a quick nod or quick verbal recognition like, "Let me speak to this person first, and I'll be with you just as soon as I can."

- **Be aware of your filters.** Knowing the facts, unembellished and unencumbered by bias, is critical to handling conflict. Don't allow gut feelings or preconceptions to cloud true perceptions. Whether you're walking into a yard littered with empty beer bottles or interviewing someone with a previous record of complaints, make sure that your attitude isn't hindering your ability to gather facts and deal fairly.

- **Remember your goal.** There are many good reasons to improve your communication style, but the most compelling is this — it's what's best for you, your partners, and the general public, and that's your ultimate goal.

The Tactics of Language

The improper use of words can cause law enforcement officers to be sued, get fired, or in a worst-case scenario can lead to incidents that can get them or their partners injured or killed. It is therefore important to understand the use of **tactical language** as a tool to achieve a police officer's goal of obtaining compliance, cooperation, and collaboration from the people he interacts with while on duty.

Studies show that over 90% of effectiveness in communication comes from the way that messages are delivered or through nonverbal means. This means that it is just as important, if not more so, that people consider their tone, their audience, and the manner in which they present their words as it is to consider the actual content of words in the message. Applying skills already discussed in this chapter, such as active listening and employing empathy, are keys to using language as a tactic for achieving compliance, cooperation, or collaboration, but there is much more to it than that. Officers must also learn how to shape their words into sentences and further shape those sentences into conversations and allow people to understand that they are not only professional, but are also there to help resolve the problem at hand. More importantly, it lets people know that the police officer is in control.

Resource - Notice in the linked article at think8.net how the tactics of language can apply to many career fields and not just law enforcement. These tactics can also be beneficial in any profession where effective communication is critical.

http://www.think8.net/articles_05_effective_comm.php

The first thing to understand is that what people say, and what people mean, are often two completely different things. When police officers arrive on a scene, the people they must engage in conversation are often speaking out of fear, anger, frustration, or other emotions that do not allow them to communicate property. When an officer approaches a home owner who has just been burglarized and he states, "What took you so long to get here? It's been two hours! I could have been killed!" What he likely really meant is "Help me. I feel violated. I am afraid. Can you help me recover my things?" But personal egos have been bruised, emotions are involved, and clear communication is hindered. It is therefore up to the officer to help the home owner think clearly and to encourage the behavior required for the officer to get the job done. Basically, the best way to do this is through the tactical use of language.

Using tactical language is a two-step process. The first step is to use a technique called **deflection** in order to gain the person's attention and springboard past the desire to remain confrontational. As long as a person is confrontational, that person is not accurately receiving the messages that are being sent. If you stop the process, the person being spoken to will begin to receive very clear messages from the officer.

Taking deflection further, another tactic involves simply recognizing the person who is speaking and acknowledging that what they are saying is understood, and then adding a quick "but" to the sentence in order to prepare to push the conversation in a different direction. For example, while trying to interview the same homeowner mentioned above, rather than becoming upset or angered at his attitude, in order to deflect his anger and be able to start communicating properly, the officer might try stating in a calm voice "I hear what you are saying, but...", or "I can see that you are very upset; I might be too under these circumstances, but...".

By using deflection, an officer can springboard past the argument and get to the issue at hand. Once the other party's problem has been recognized and not reacted to in a negative manner, the confrontational person is disempowered and retains no reason to continue to be argumentative. Additionally, remaining calm and acknowledging the other person simply sounds good to witnesses or other people who might be in the surrounding area, and it helps the officer maintain a professional appearance.

The second step is utilization of a technique known as **redirection**. It is important that the person being spoken to realizes that even if the news being brought to them is bad, that the willingness to work with the officer (comply, cooperate, or collaborate) is in their best interest, and that what the officer really wants is to help them. Redirection allows a police officer to refocus another person's energy in a positive way so that the injured party is reasonable to deal with and able to put emotions aside during conversation.

One of the keys to making redirection work for law enforcement officers includes learning to motivate people, which is frequently accomplished by raising expectations. It has been proven that by entering a conversation with negatives first, communication generally stops. No one wants to hear the bad things that sometimes have to be told to them, and they will generally tune out the person trying to deliver the negative message one way or another. Instead of telling the burglarized home-owner that there have been a rash of burglaries in the area and none have been solved yet, the officer might start with something positive such as, "I can see that you are very upset. I might be too under these circumstances, but I am here to help you through this process. I have worked a lot of home invasions in this area, and I am going to see to it that we do everything we can to catch the person that did this and get your things back for you." The homeowner can always be told about the other burglaries and be given an honest opinion on how likely they are to be solved later in the conversation, once he has calmed down and is helping the officers do their job, but the goal is to obtain cooperation at this point. Officers need to stay focused on their goal.

CASE STUDY

Good Conversation Skills

It is six weeks later, and you are called back to the same house with the father and the curfew-breaking teenage daughter. This time when you arrive, it is 1:30 a.m. on a Saturday, and both parties are in the front yard screaming at each other loudly. As you pull up to the scene, you notice that several neighbors have come outside and are beginning to gather and watch the altercation taking place. Several other lights in the neighborhood are starting to come on as well.

As you step out of the patrol car, you notice that the father is red in the face and beginning to clinch his fists in anger. His wife is standing inside of the doorway of the house and is yelling through the cracked door for him to calm down and come inside and telling him that he is embarrassing her. It becomes apparent to you that the father has reached his boiling point and that this attempt at communication between the father and daughter has already passed a simple confrontation and is now in full-blown conflict.

What is the best response to this situation given the information provided?

Understanding that it is likely that you have probable cause to make an arrest for disorderly conduct or disturbing the peace almost immediately upon arriving on the scene, if you chose to make this decision, what benefit could be obtained by trying to defuse the conflict first before making the arrest? Which tools that have been mentioned come to mind that might help you defuse the conflict?

Assuming that you decide that the best course of action is to gain control of the scene, calm the father down, and then put them all to bed for the evening, how could the use of tactical language benefit you in doing so?

Summary

Often a police officer is the first line of communication the public encounters with the criminal justice system. When approaching someone while out on patrol, whether it is his immediate supervisor, someone with an arrest warrant, or just a local citizen looking for directions, it is always important to remember that an officer is always being observed, and that professionalism is paramount to success in the law enforcement field. Learning to communicate verbally clearly promotes a professional appearance and primes the pump for obtaining compliance, cooperation, and collaboration (see Figure 3.2).

Every time a law enforcement officer speaks, he represents himself, his department, his city or county government, and the entire law enforcement community. The way that citizens perceives an officer as an individual affects not only their ability to do their job, but also other law enforcement officers' ability to do their jobs in the future when they interact with that citizen later. Police officers must learn to think and communicate differently than most people because their lives and safety depend on it, as well as the lives and safety of fellow officers and the rest of the citizens of their community.

FIGURE 3.2: *Cooperation is best for everyone concerned.*

Discussion Questions

1. How does word choice affect an officer's ability to communicate? How does word choice influence others that an officer is speaking with? Discuss how word choice can change people's perceptions of an officer and the organizations that the officer represents.

2. Discuss the role of active listening in conversation. Why is active listening important? How does it increase your effectiveness as a conversationalist? Give an example of how active listening can assist a police officer when interviewing a witness of a crime.

3. Discuss the differences in sympathy and empathy and why it is important for law enforcement officers to be able to demonstrate empathy for people in certain situations.

4. Why is deflection such an important technique in the use of tactical language? In what ways might deflection assist a law enforcement officer in de-escalating conflict? Discuss some phrases that could be used to deflect a situation.

5. Discuss diffusing conflict. What are some basic tools for de-escalating a heated conversation rather than fanning the flames? Why is it considered important for police officers to be able to diffuse conflict through conversational skills?

Key Terms

Active Listening: Communication technique that requires the listener to understand, interpret, and evaluate what they hear.

Argument: A discussion involving differing points of view; debate.

Communication: The imparting or interchange of thoughts, opinions, or information by speech, writing, or signs.

Communication Tool: Any of a group of communication techniques and tactics, such as the use of empathy, or delivering feedback, that can be used to control the direction of a conversation.

Conflict: A fight, battle, or struggle, especially a prolonged struggle; strife.

Confrontation: An open conflict of opposing ideas, forces, etc.

Deflection: A tactical language technique that is used to verbally recognize another party and acknowledge a source of conflict without reacting in a negative manner.

Emotional Response: A reaction to a particular intra-psychic feeling or feelings, accompanied by physiologic changes that may or may not be outwardly manifested but that motivate or precipitate some action or behavioral response.

Empathy: The intellectual identification with or vicarious experiencing of the feelings, thoughts, or attitudes of another.

Feedback: A reaction or response to a particular process or activity.

Nonverbal: Expressed in a means other than words.

Redirection: A tactical language technique that is used to bring another person out of confrontation and refocus the conversation in a positive way.

Sympathy: Harmony of or agreement in feeling, as between persons or on the part of one person with respect to another.

Tactical Language: The process of using deflection and redirection to control the direction of a conversation and de-escalate confrontation.

Verbal: Expressed in spoken words; oral rather than written.

Interviews and Interrogations

Key Module Concepts:

- The differences between interviews and interrogations

- The narrative story

- Tactics and techniques for conducting interviews and interrogations

- The goal of interviews and interrogations: finding out the who, what, when, where, why, and how

- How to detect that an interviewee is being dishonest

Introduction

During your career in criminal justice, you will have to talk with many different kinds of people of all ages under many different circumstances. Some may just have a conversation with you, for example, to ask for directions. In other situations, you will be asking them specific questions to learn more about a crime, a complaint, or some other incident you investigate. There are specific ways to get the information you need when you ask these questions. This question and answer session you have with witnesses is called an **interview**. In an interview, the witness is not in custody.

Once the witness is in custody and is now a suspect, the interview is now called an **interrogation.** There are special techniques you can use to get more information from the suspect during an interrogation.

There are even certain ways to set up the room to assist you in gathering more information during the interrogation.

There are techniques to help you with these various types of interviews and interrogations. In this module, we will explore these various techniques.

Ask Yourself

• *How do you get information when the victim is a confused elderly woman who thinks it is still 1956?*

• *How do you interrogate a hostile rape suspect?*

• *How do you interview a witness to an incident who is intoxicated?*

What Is an Interview?

Interviews are one of the main ways that criminal justice professionals get information from people (see Figure 4.1). These persons may be the **complainant** (the person who called to report something wrong), the victim, a witness who saw something happen, or simply a person who lives in the neighborhood where the incident happened. Actually, people who live in the neighborhood may not have seen anything, but they will be interviewed during a neighborhood canvass to ask them about the neighborhood and what normally happens there, just because they live there.

Not all people are cooperative. Some people are confused or have mental deficiencies. There are special techniques for gathering more information from these people who might otherwise seem difficult to interview.

Good interview skills will help you get the information you need in the most time efficient way. Interviewing people can be informative and even fun when you learn the techniques (see Figure 4.1).

The interview is conducted with persons who are not in police custody in contrast with the interrogation, which involves questioning someone who is in police custody.

FIGURE 4.1: *This witness is not in custody and is being interviewed by a law enforcement officer.*

The Location of the Interview

The location and environment for the interview will vary. Many interviews are performed in the field – at the scene or at the person's home. Interviews should be done as quickly as possible after an incident so that the interviewee will remember as much as possible. Make sure that you separate witnesses as quickly as you possibly when you encounter them. You do not want them to collaborate on real facts, which may change what they tell you, and if they are lying, you do not want them to have time to plan out their lies.

Here's an example where collaborating and changing the real facts might occur inadvertently when a group of friends sees a robber running from a bank. They might discuss the robber as follows: "Did you see that guy's purple shirt?" "I just thought it was dark colored." "No, it was black." "No, it wasn't. I distinctly remember it was purple." "Okay then, it was purple." "And that red hair!" "I didn't notice his hair." "I thought it was brown." "No, it wasn't. It was red."

When you interview this particular group of witnesses, you'll get a description of a red-haired man wearing a purple shirt. The witnesses are not lying, but the strongest witness has convinced her friends about what she thought she saw. If you initially separated the witnesses, you would get a less definite but more accurate description of a red- or brown-haired man wearing a dark colored shirt, possibly purple or black. If the suspect does have brown hair and a black shirt, you will miss him if the entire group of witnesses described red hair and a purple shirt, so the less definite but more accurate description is better.

If you have a group of witnesses that you separate, whom should you interview first? There are two theories about whom to interview first. One theory is that the weakest link should be interviewed first. This is the most anxious, timid person. This person may calm down if inter-viewed first, and may be the easiest person from which to get an honest story. The second theory is to interview the strongest person first. The idea behind this theory is that if the other witnesses believe their leader has been honest with you in his or her interview, the others are more likely to be honest. You must decide whom to interview first. You are in control, and you should not just take the first volunteer. Instead, make a conscious choice to choose whether you want to interview the weakest or the strongest person and then begin. Your choice of the weakest or the strongest person may vary at different scenes, depending upon the situation.

Many interviews are done immediately after a crime or complaint, and there may not be much time to plan for them. If you have the time, plan ahead regarding the information you are seeking. Plan the ways to phrase your questions. Make sure that you cover all the goal questions, which will be discussed later in this module.

How to Conduct an Interview

The interview environment may be out of your control. It should, however, be conducted in a private location. No one else should be able to interrupt or listen to the interview. Witnesses should be separated as quickly as possible, so it is best to interview only one person at a time. If there is no private area available and you do not want to take witnesses to the police station, use your vehicle.

Minimize distractions during the interview. The interview setting should be as quiet as possible. Phones and radios should be silenced if possible. Other people should not be allowed to interrupt. The **interviewee** should not be allowed to answer his or her cell phone or send or receive texts during the interview. The interviewee should not be allowed to have any distractions such as small objects to manipulate in their hands.

Sit or stand 3-4 feet away from the interviewee. Placing yourself too close may cause discomfort, and placing yourself too far away may decrease your ability to hear words, voice intonations, or interpret body language. It may also make the interviewee feel that you don't care about him or her if you are too far away.

If two officers conduct the interview, only one should speak at a time. The person not speaking should sit in the background. When you change speakers, change places. The reason for this is to avoid intimidating the interviewee. Intimidation is used only in interrogations.

The interview begins with an initial meeting of the interviewee. Greet the interviewee and shake his hand. (For ease of discussion, we will refer to the interviewee in the male gender.) Note the grip and steadiness of the handshake, and note the temperature of the interviewee's hand. Thank him for cooperating with the interview process.

You must begin by establishing **rapport**, or a common ground with the interviewee. Smile. Introduce yourself and explain who you are and your role in the interview process. If the witness is seated, sit down. You must be at the same eye level with the witness or below him. Clarify who the witness is and allow him to introduce himself. Get the demographic details of the witness: name, date of birth, address, phone numbers and contact information, and the relationship to the incident or persons involved in it.

As you clarify the demographic information, observe the witness. This is where you notice his baseline behavior and speech patterns. Observe these things throughout the interview to determine unexplained deviations from his baseline that may indicate he is lying to you. Make conversation with him as you deal with the demographics. The goal of rapport is to establish some common ground or similarities that you can talk about and that allow you to relate to each other in regards to a topic outside of the incident. If the witness is upset, show concern. Ask him if he is comfortable if you are in a setting you can do something about; for example, ask if they are too warm or too cold if you are where you can adjust the temperature. Ask if he needs a drink of water if water is available.

As you chitchat about common ground topics to establish rapport, such as the weather or sports, make sure that you are honest and genuine. If the witness is a baseball enthusiast, you cannot tell him how much you also love baseball if you know and care nothing about it. It is okay to tell him you do not know anything about baseball, and ask him to explain the basics about it to you. This also helps to build rapport: having the witness educate you about something he is passionate about.

After you establish rapport, ask a broad, general open-ended question to get the interviewee to tell you the narrative story of what happened. You may just ask, "So what happened?" Let him tell the story from beginning to end and do not interrupt, unless you must encourage him to continue by asking, "So what happened next?"

The witness should then tell you the story in his own words. You should listen and indicate you are actively listening by nodding your head or saying, "Uh-huh." Focus your entire attention on the witness, and face the witness so that your body language shows your attention. If you are taking notes, look up frequently and make eye contact. If the witness becomes silent, ask, "What happened next?" Your goal at this step is to get the witness to tell you the story in his own words. You may want to clarify some of the details, but hold your clarifying questions for later. This initial story is called the narrative story as told in the witness's own words.

The Story Unfolds

The honest person usually tells a narrative story in three equal parts: the things that led up to the incident, the incident itself, and the things that happened after the incident. A dishonest person may exaggerate one or two of these parts and minimize the dishonest part. They may, on the other hand, tell a longer dishonest fabricated story in the part they are lying about. A disparity in lengths of these three parts of the story indicates dishonesty. This is a general rule of thumb, because not all witnesses saw all parts of an incident. For example, there may be a witness who came upon a car that had crashed into a tree. She cannot describe what led up to the crash because it had already happened when she discovered it.

Honest witnesses will often include details that are not pertinent to the incident. For example, a woman comes upon a car that was smashed into a tree. She tells you she stopped her car and called 911 and then ran to the driver to see if he was hurt. He was not seriously hurt, so she tells you she called her husband to tell him she would be late, and was so upset she dropped her phone and had to call him again. Calling the husband and dropping the phone is not pertinent to the incident, but it shows you she is telling you everything and is most likely telling you the truth. Dishonest people seldom think to include irrelevant details that might make their fabricated story seem more believable. They tend to stick to the phony facts of only the incident they are lying about.

Honest witnesses may be shocked by an incident they saw. It is normal to have some degree of memory loss about shocking events. On the other hand, some witnesses may remember details with amazing clarity, and they may tell you they watched the incident unfold, almost in slow motion. Both examples tend to indicate honesty. The honest person with partial memory loss will be frustrated by it. "I just can't remember. It just drives me crazy. I noticed his shirt, but I just can't remember what color it was."

A dishonest person will just say he forgot some of the details and be unconcerned that he doesn't remember. Not caring about a loss of memory about certain details indicates dishonesty.

Changing Chronology

After the witness has told the narrative story from the beginning of his or her involvement up to the present time, go back to the details in the story and ask what happened before something happened.

> "Now what did you see just before the man collapsed?"

Asking clarifying questions like this forces the witness to tell the story in a different order than how it happened. The honest witness can do this, and this is one of the **cognitive interview** tactics to help him remember even more. Dishonest people memorize a fabricated, phony story from beginning to end in chronological order, and you will confuse them by asking them to give details out of **chronological order**. They may tell changing stories, particularly if they realize they made mistakes in their answers. Changing the story is an indicator of dishonesty, especially if the story seems to change multiple times. An honest person who has forgotten some of the details may actually remember more details when you ask questions that change the chronology of the story, so their basic story will remain the same, but they may recall more of the details.

To force the person to change the chronology of his or her story, pick out a detail and first ask what happened right beforehand. For your next question, choose a detail and ask what happened right afterwards. When you change whether you are asking about something right beforehand or right after a specific detail, the dishonest person cannot anticipate and mentally rehearse his answers. Let's look at an example.

A man has just finished telling you the narrative story about how he ran his car off the road and crashed it.

"What happened right before you came to the curve in the road?"

"Let me think. Oh, that's right! I remember now! A rabbit was crossing the road, and I could see lights that a car was coming at me in the other lane, so I swerved toward the ditch."

Here is a different man after telling a narrative story about how he ran his car off the road and crashed it.

"What happened right before you came to the curve in the road?"

"I came to the curve in the road and just spun out. Must've been damp out."

"Did you spin out before you came to the curve?"

"Yes. Well, not quite before. I had started into the curve but spun out before the road straightened out."

Which man was telling the truth? In the first story, the skid marks on the road were consistent with a rapid brake application, matching the story of the sudden appearance of the rabbit. The skid pattern indicated a defensive maneuver of the driver towards the ditch. There was a dead rabbit on the opposite side of the road with skid marks on that side of the road. A car pulled up behind the squad car with the driver of the oncoming car. He thought he had noticed lights in the ditch and came back to investigate, confirming the truth of the story.

The second story was felt to be a lie by officers. The roadway was not damp. There were no evasive skid marks to indicate a spin out. Tire tracks went straight when the road curved. Multiple empty cans of Budweiser were found 20 feet east of the crashed car, with three cans that were still cold. The man's blood alcohol was .189, and he was arrested for DUI.

Some witnesses are unable to communicate very well due to existing mental limitations or even from the psychological shock of the incident at hand. It is sometimes difficult to get information from these people. One of the techniques, which seems unusual but is effective, is rather than asking the person what they saw, ask them to describe what someone else present observed. This technique tends to depersonalize the incident as it is easier to tell the story from the viewpoint of another rather than explain what happened " to me." Confused or traumatized witnesses sometimes respond well to this method.

Witnesses may not remember details. Try to place them back in the situation and ask what they felt, heard, or saw. These are cognitive interview techniques – the technique of placing the interviewees mentally back in the incident to examine what they know while mentally back within the situation. Did the suspect remind him of anyone like a celebrity or a friend or relative? Why did the suspect remind him of another person? If the interviewee does not remember colors, try to ascertain if the color was dark or light. If they don't remember numbers, ask if they were low numbers like 1, 2, or 3, or if they were higher numbers like 7, 8, or 9. Were any numbers repeated? Ask about weapons or a bulge in clothing that may have been a weapon. If you determine what the person's overall orientation is, visual, auditory, or kinesthetic, focus on asking details involving the orientation. "What did you hear next?" "What did the gun look like?" "Were his hands soft or rough and callused?"

When the interview is concluded, thank the interviewee and shake his hand again. Compare the handshake to the introduction handshake. Cooler, sweaty hands may indicate the witness has been lying to you. Make note in your report of all the nonverbal cues. Was the interviewee lying, anxious, or anything else? Tell the witness that you will contact him if you have additional questions and be sure to invite him to contact you if he remembers anything else.

The Goal Questions

What do you want to learn from the witness? Everything that person knows about the incident! You need to go back and clarify the story after it is told and actually interview the witness. It helps to begin the interview process with certain goals in mind. Going over the goal questions in every interview after the narrative story will give you nearly all the information you need. Asking about all the goal questions, especially when changing the chronological order of the narrative story, will also help you determine whether or not the person is telling you the truth.

The goal questions to have answered after you hear the narrative story of what happened are who, what, when, where, why, and how? The witness may have answered some of these questions in the narrative story, but always go over these questions again in your interview questions to get more details. Remember to try to notice whether or not the witness is a visual, auditory, or kinesthetic type of person. Ask more details regarding their orientation. Visual people will give you more information about what they saw. Auditory people will give you more information about what they heard, and kinesthetic people will give you more detail about what they felt emotionally or physically touched.

Who

The "who" goal question seeks information about all persons present at the scene or somehow involved with the complaint. Get full names, if possible. Nicknames or partial names are fine if the witness doesn't know the full name. Get physical descriptions including height, weight, eye color, skin color, ethnicity, hair color and style, and presence or absence of facial hair. Ask about skin conditions like moles, acne, freckles, and scars. Ask about tattoos, piercings, and jewelry. Get a description of the clothing and shoes. Ask if another person called anyone else by a name or nickname. Did anyone walk with a limp or speak with an accent? Did they speak English or another language? Which language? What did their voices sound like? Did anyone try to conceal him or herself with any type of disguise? Get a description of the concealment or disguise. Get information about all persons at the scene or who were part of the incident or complaint including witnesses, victims, and perpetrators. Did anyone refer to a person who wasn't there? Get all the information you can about the absent person. Does the witness know anyone else who may know some of these people who may be able to provide additional information?

What

The "what" goal question seeks to clarify all the details of what happened. Your ultimate goal is to find out what happened from the very beginning until the time of your interview. Each witness may have seen different things at different times as the incident unfolded, so getting the details of what happened from each person is more likely to give you the most information about the entire incident.

When

The "when" question seeks information about when, the time and date, something happened. It goes closely with the "what" question. You want to establish a time line of when the incident began, and what happened at each step of the time line. Get dates and times, and years if applicable. One witness may have seen the beginning of an incident, so you can list this at the beginning of the time line. For example, one witness was in a bar and watched one man bump into another man, spilling his beer at 22:00. They began to argue and push each other, then they both went outside at 22:05, and the witness saw nothing else. The men bumping into each other begins your time line, followed by the spilled beer, and then the argument. This part of the time line ends with the parties going outside. Another witness who was outside may begin his or her story of what happened and when it happened at 22:06 when he or she saw two men burst out of the door of the bar and begin fighting. You continue your time line at 22:06 with the men running outside and starting to fight. The "when" question and time line may be much longer than the bar fighting example. For example, you may respond to a shots fired call and find two dead bodies, a male and a female. This appears to be a murder suicide. The house is torn up as though there were a fight before the shooting, and the couple was married, so it appears to be a domestic violence problem. You need to ask witnesses when the couple moved to the neighborhood, when did neighbors begin hearing shouting or fighting, and so on. This kind of time line may go back for many years.

Where

The "where" question seeks to uncover the locations of people and events. Get the exact location of where the incident occurred. If the address or exact location is not known by the witnesses, get descriptions of locations as close as possible, such as at the corner of Kline and Graves Streets, or in the field by the big tree just past the curve, or in the gray two-story house on the north side of 16th Street between Oak Street and the freeway. Keep in mind that the incident or complaint may involve more than one location. Get information on all possible locations involving the situation. If the suspects were seen arriving at the scene, find out from which direction they came. Which way did they go when they left? The second part of the "where" question involves finding out where the other witnesses and suspects were sitting or standing at the scene. Where in the car were different individuals sitting? Where were each of the customers in the store when the suspects ran in and began firing shots? Where were the suspects standing when they began firing shots? If they were mobile when firing shots, where in the store did they go as they fired shots? Where did they seem to be shooting, for example, at customers, the clerk, or at the ceiling?

Why

The "why" question seeks the motive behind the incident. Why did the cars crash? Was one driving erratically beforehand as though the driver were impaired? Did one car disobey a traffic signal to cause the accident? Did a driver swerve to avoid another obstacle such as a dog in the street? The reason something happened might not be obvious to the witnesses, but ask them why they think it occurred. Make it clear in your report that the witness was uncertain, but that this is their opinion about why the incident happened. For example, the motive for a sexual assault is often power and control, but the witness may incorrectly think the motive was sexual gratification. Describe the witness's opinion, even though, as a trained criminal justice professional, you know that the witness's opinion may be incorrect. Ask why John Smith was the target of a shooting. Different witnesses may give you many different opinions such as, "John was a low-life," "John always ripped people off," "John was a drug dealer," and "John was fooling around with Ben Boyer's wife." These different opinions give you leads for the motive of the shooting: revenge, a drug deal gone bad, or a love triangle, or a combination of these things.

How

The "how" question seeks to uncover the logistics and details of how an incident occurred. How did the suspect hold the gun? How did the car leave – slowly or peeling tires and zooming off at a high rate of speed? How did the suspect gain entrance to the house? How did the suspect gain control of a sexual assault victim? How did the argument start? How did the suspect get the knife he used – did he bring it with him or grab it out of the kitchen?

Use all of the goal questions to find out all the details about an incident. Always get all witness contact information so that if you need to ask witnesses something else, you can reach them. Give them your contact information and invite them to contact you if they think of any other details that might be helpful.

Resource - Read the article "Behavioral Mirroring in Interviewing" in the *FBI Law Enforcement Bulletin*, December, 2009.

http://www.fbi.gov/stats-services/publications/law-enforcement-bulletin/2009-pdfs/december2009.pdf

Different Perceptions

It may be frustrating to you, as a criminal justice professional, when you get different stories from different witnesses about the same incident. You are investigating a strip mall jewelry store robbery where the suspect fled in a car. Multiple witnesses noticed the car in question. One person describes a black sedan and another tells you the car was an old red Chevy Nova. One may describe nothing about the car other than it was large and loud. Another may not describe the car very well at all except that it seemed large and powerful.

Who is lying and who is telling the truth? In this example, everyone is being honest. So why do you have so many different descriptions, and what kind of car is the suspect really driving?

The difference lies in the ways that individuals perceive the world around them – their **perceptual orientation**. You can listen to people when they say something and then add a clarifying remark such as, "Do you see what I mean?" or "Do you hear what I'm saying?" or "Do you get a feel for what I mean?" There are three major ways people sense and communicate about the world around them. These ways are visual, auditory, and kinesthetic.

People with a **visual orientation** "see" the world around them in visual pictures, and are best at describing what something looked like. They can "see" it in their mind and describe it to you. You can ask them questions to clarify more about their visual image of the event. This is the person who will tell you something and then end with, "See what I mean?" If you can determine each individual's overall perception type, you will get the best description of what something or someone looked like from the witnesses with a visual perspective.

People with an **auditory orientation** "hear" the world around them. They remember the sounds surrounding an incident, and may have a mental recording of it in their mind. They are the people who will ask, "Hear what I'm saying?" These witnesses are good at describing a foreign accent a suspect used, exactly what wording the suspect used in making robbery demands, what kind of music played when the suspect's cell phone rang, or any other sounds that may be important to the incident.

People with a **kinesthetic orientation** "feel" the world around them. They know the way various events made them feel emotionally, and they have a keen sense of touch. They remember things better if they touch something or hold it in their hands. If you interview a kinesthetic person who was held hostage, they will describe the coldness of the smooth, concrete floor or the splintery wooden walls, or the rough, prickly rope about the size of their pinky finger that was used to restrain them.

Kinesthetic perceptive people will ask, "Get a feel for what I mean?" When interviewing a kinesthetic person, ask about textures and things they touched. Ask them about their emotions. For example, what made them suddenly feel fearful during an incident in what had otherwise been a routine day?

You must communicate with witnesses to get a sense of how they perceive the world around them. Understanding their sense of perception will help you ask better interview questions to determine what they remember in their perception of the incident. You will also learn that people communicate best in the same perceptive voice. In other words, if they can "see" it, you ask what it looked like and they can describe its appearance. If they can "hear" it, you ask what they heard and they can describe its sound. If they can "feel" it, you ask how it made them feel and what it felt like, and they can describe its texture, firmness, and temperature, as well as the emotional feeling it evoked for them.

In the previous example, one witness thought the car was a black sedan and another said it was "an old red Chevy Nova." Are these two different cars? There is more to perceiving the world than the overall perceptive type. There are external influences on our perceptions. One witness may have seen the car in the shadows, but it was in the bright sun for the other. One witness may have forgotten her glasses that day. The other one may have been wearing sunglasses.

What if you were told the witness who saw the car as a sedan was an elderly lady? She may only know two kinds of cars: sedans and compacts. What if you were told the other witness was a 50-year-old classic car enthusiast? He also told you it was a '69 Nova muscle car with a tunnel ram hood scoop, had ladder bars and air shocks, and was a big block motor with headers and glass pack mufflers. We expect an old lady to have a limited knowledge of cars, and likewise, we expect an old gearhead to know his classic cars.

There is a name for the difference in witness knowledge and of our expectations of their knowledge. This difference is due to cultural diversity. We can easily identify that these two witnesses come from different cultures. We expect them to view the world differently. One is male and one is female. This is a gender difference.

The elderly woman lives in a posh retirement community where her usual day consists of eating lunch at the country club, playing bridge or lawn bowling with her lady-friends, and then going shopping. She has dinner at the yacht club and then attends a cultural event like a big band concert or a travelogue.

The man spends his day working as a mechanic and spends evenings restoring his '71 Camero. His favorite TV shows are NASCAR and drag racing events. On weekends he goes to car shows or car races (see Figure 4.2). Both witnesses have very different cultures, and that is evident in their descriptions of the suspect vehicle. People describe things based on their cultural understanding or knowledge of the situation. As a criminal justice professional, we, as officers, also bring our own cultural background and expectations into play. We expect a man to know more about cars than an elderly woman. What would you think if the man described the car as a black sedan and the elderly woman gave you the red muscle car description

FIGURE 4.2: *How would you perceive and describe this car? What is your primary orientation for describing things?*

in detail? Would you recall that mentally ill people might honestly describe their hallucinations? Would you believe the elderly woman, or think maybe she is crazy? Or maybe your grandmother was a top fuel funny car driver until she was 75; if so, your cultural background may make you think nothing of an old lady gearhead.

CASE STUDY

Witness Perceptions – Armed Robbery

Police respond to a call to a convenience store where a man robbed the cashier with a knife. Officers Jones and Romero were close to the store and responded within two minutes. The cashier was shaken but unhurt. She told officers that a man in a black knit ski mask with brown eyes, wearing blue jeans and a black tee shirt came in, held up a big hunting knife, and said, "Give me all your money or you're dead." She took five twenty-dollar bills and three ten-dollar bills from the register and handed the money to him, and he turned and ran. There were no customers in the store. She described him as about 5'8" tall and about 175 pounds. She guessed him to be in his 20's.

A couple entered the store right after the robber left who witnessed a man yanking a hat off his head outside as they entered. The woman, Mrs. Beeler, stated to Officer Jones that she could see the cashier was upset. She ran to the cashier who told her she'd just been robbed, so Mrs. Beeler called 911 to report the crime. She described the robber as 5'10" with dark brown hair, weighing about 200 pounds, and wearing dark clothes. She told Officer Jones that the robber cursed in Spanish as he pulled off his hat. She did not see the knife.

Mr. Beeler told Officer Romero that he noticed a tall, mean-looking Hispanic "guy" run out of the store. He watched him stick something shiny in his pocked and yank off a dark-colored hat. The man said something, but Mr. Beeler did not remember what he said. He said he watched the man run outside to a waiting car, jump in the back seat, and watched the car take off, squealing the tires. Mr. Beeler told the officer he got the feeling the car was fast and "souped up." The car was a larger, dark colored, 4-door. The car had two other people in it. He did not see the driver, but the passenger was a man with dark hair and dark clothes. The car had local license plates, but he did not remember the license number except that there was an "X" in it, two other letters, and three numbers.

Kenny Herrea pulled in to gas up his pickup truck during the robbery. He told Officer Jones that he pulled up to the gas pump with his truck pointing toward the car, and could see inside the door of the store from where he was. He could see a man with dark hair and dark clothes inside the store at the register. The car was a black Buick 4-door, about 15 years old with moon hubcaps. He could see there were two people in it, but could only see the driver who was a local gang member he knew as "Killer Hastings." Killer is 20 years old, 5'7" tall, 175 pounds, and was wearing a dark red tee shirt. Killer went to high school with Kenny until Killer dropped out. Killer was described as a white male, but was known to associate with a Hispanic gang.

Ask Yourself

- *How does each of the witnesses seem to perceive his or her world?*

- *What additional questions would you ask each witness to gather more details, based on their perceptual orientation?*

CASE STUDY

Witness Interview Techniques – Confused or Traumatized Witness

Officer Johnson was interviewing Eunice, a 74-year-old female who was beaten and robbed by an assailant who entered her home by breaking the window in the door and then opening the locked door.

"So what happened," asked Officer Johnson.

"It was all black; then it got blacker. I have a headache and want to go home."

Eunice was in her living room at home. Officer Johnson sensed that Eunice must be a demented old lady who had no business living alone.

"What was black?"

"The night. The room."

"How many people came in and did this to you?"

"None. It was just black."

A cat walked into the living room.

"Is this your cat?"

"Yes, that's Missy. She's been with me 10 years now."

"Okay. I think Missy knows what happened. She sleeps on your bed, I'll bet. What does she know about what happened tonight?"

"Well, she was sleeping so good. She snores a bit, you know. She heard some glass break, and she stopped snoring and jumped up and arched her back and hissed. I felt so sorry for her. Scared her, poor thing."

"What did she see next?"

"She hissed at this man who came in, all dressed in black. She was scared, and she was mad because he came in and punched me in the eye. She attacked him – scratched him good, I'm sure. It was dark, and I couldn't see real good, but she heard my jewelry box jiggle. I heard it too, and then Missy leaped at him – just attacked him. I could hear her yowling, and she got quieter, then a door slammed, and she ran back to me. I need to make sure she's okay."

Eunice was confused, either as a baseline, or as the result of the injuries suffered from her attack, or simply the shock of the attack. She was unable to give a coherent description of what happened to her to police, but she was able to describe accurately what her protective cat had seen. A description of a man dressed in black with evidence of cat bites or scratches, possibly carrying a jewelry box was given to en route backup officers. A man in black with a jewelry box and with scratches on his arms and bites on his face was apprehended. Blood was found in Eunice's bedroom. The DNA of the blood matched that of the apprehended man.

This is an example of success using the third-person interview technique. Eunice could not tell police what happened to her, but she was able to describe what the cat saw and experienced.

Interrogation

An interrogation is an extension of the interview, and the same concepts apply. The goal of the interrogation is the same as the interview: to learn who, what, where, when, why, and how something occurred. There are additional tactics that are used in interrogations. The interrogation is the questioning of a suspect and is used when you expect to learn facts that will incriminate the suspect. The interrogation is used when the suspect is in custody. The suspect may not have been arrested yet, but he does not feel that he is free to leave.

Miranda Rights

The Miranda warning must be read to the suspect prior to the interrogation (see Figure 4.4), and the suspect must understand it. The suspect usually must sign or initial the Miranda rights to indicate his understanding of them. The Miranda rights are a clarification of the 5th Amendment of the Constitution. They inform the suspect that he has the right to remain silent, and that if he does not, the statements he makes may be used against him in court. He is informed that he may have an attorney present during questioning, and that if he cannot afford one, an attorney will be assigned to him without charge.

The Miranda warning does not have to be given if the suspect volunteers information without being questioned. If you are interviewing the person, you do not have to read him his Miranda rights until you reach a point that he becomes a suspect and feels he is in your custody and is no longer free to leave. For example, if a murdered body is found in a house, and you are interviewing the neighbor about the deceased person, you do not have to read him the Miranda warning. During the interview, you may notice blood underneath his fingernails. He may make some suspicious statements, and in your mind, he is a likely suspect. At the point you decide he is not free to leave the interview, and that you will probably have to take him to the police station for more questioning, is the transition into the interrogation, and then he must receive the Miranda warning. If any suspect decides he wants an attorney present at any time during the interrogation, all questioning must stop until the attorney arrives. If a suspect knowingly waives his Miranda rights, this means he will answer interrogation questions without an attorney present, but he may change his mind at any time and request an attorney, even if he originally waived this right. If a suspect changes his mind and asks for an attorney, all questions stop until the attorney is present.

In some cases, suspects are questioned before they are given their Miranda rights in order to elicit incriminating answers. After officers have the incriminating information, they read the suspect the Miranda warning, in hopes that the suspect will repeat the same information after waiving his rights. The original statements are not admissible in court, but the statements given after waiving the 5th Amendment rights will be considered admissible. This technique is called "Beachheading" or the "Question First" technique of interrogation, and it was found unconstitutional by the Supreme Court in 2004 (Missouri v. Seibert), so this technique cannot be used.

MIRANDA WARNING

You have the right to remain silent

Anything you say, can and will be used against you in a court of law

You have the right to speak to an attorney and have your attorney present with you during questioning

If you cannot afford to hire an attorney, one will be appointed to represent you

You may exercise these rights and to answer any questions or make any statements

WAIVER

Do you understand each of these rights as I have explained them to you?
Do you wish to waive these rights

FIGURE 4.3: *Typical Miranda Card as used by law enforcement officers preceding formal custodial interrogation.*

Setting Up the Interrogation

Recall that in the interview, the interviewer tries to sit at the same level or lower than the interviewee to put him at ease. The interrogation is more intimidating than the interview, so the interviewee should be higher than the eye level of the suspect. This may mean a higher chair, or the interrogator may stand at times when the suspect is seated.

Most police stations have interrogation rooms set up for interrogations. They may have audio and video recording devices, because it is best if the interrogation is recorded for use by attorneys and for other officers to review. If the constitutionality of the interrogation comes into question, the recording can prove whether or not the suspect's rights were violated. The interrogator does not have to take as many notes if the interrogation can be revisited electronically before the preparation of the written report about it. The interrogation rooms may have two-way mirrors for observers to watch the interrogation. If you must conduct an interview in a room other than one designed for interrogations, there are some things to prepare.

The room should have a minimum of furniture. There should be a table and a chair for the suspect. There should be a chair for the interrogator. More than one interrogator may be present at the same time during the interrogation. If so, make sure everyone has a chair, even if the interrogator chooses to stand. There should be no windows in the room, and nothing present that will distract the suspect. The suspect's chair should be away from the door, and his back should be facing the door.

The interrogation must be carefully planned before it takes place. The facts of the case must be well known by the interrogator. The techniques to be used in the interrogation should be planned beforehand. The background of the suspect should be known. Interrogations are more likely to be successful if adequate planning is done beforehand.

> **Resource** - This is an article on conducting successful interrogations, written by an attorney. It originally appeared in the *FBI Law Enforcement Bulletin*. It contains many helpful tips on interrogation.
>
> **http://www.au.af.mil/au/awc/awcgate/fbi/interrogations.pdf**

Interrogation Techniques

There are many good interrogation techniques. This section will introduce some of the most commonly used in law enforcement. Keep in mind, different techniques are often combined in any given interrogation. Good interrogation skills require lots of practice!

The suspect is taken to the interrogation room or a room you have set up for the interrogation. The suspect is often left alone in the room to wait for the interrogator. His behaviors are observed while he waits. He often becomes anxious while waiting. He probably has no idea who will interrogate him, which may also increase his anxiety while he worries about the interrogator and what he will be asked.

Enter the room, show the suspect your identification, and introduce yourself. Try to project confidence to show that you are in command of the interrogation. You may either choose to be friendly or to be authoritarian initially. You may change roles and get tougher on him later, or you may see that being hard on him initially is not working and may change roles to be more compassionate by saying something like, "I seem to have been a little hard on you. Let's start this over." You are not committed to play the same role throughout the interrogation.

Just like the interview, regardless of the role you decide to play, you must establish rapport with the suspect. In doing this, you establish some kind of common ground in a non-threatening way. You watch the suspect's baseline behaviors and voice intonations to determine whether or not he is lying to you when you reach more threatening topics. You go over the Miranda warning, and respect his wishes if he wants an attorney, continuing the interrogation later when his attorney is present.

After you establish rapport, you ask the suspect to tell you everything that happened. Again, as in the interview, you want the suspect to tell you the narrative story of what happened with minimal interruption except encouragement to continue. After the story is complete, pick a point in the story and ask what happened right beforehand, then pick another point and ask what happened afterwards. Remember to eventually get to all of your goal questions.

The interrogation differs from the interview in the way that you ask questions. For example, you want someone you interview to be comfortable and ease. However, during the interrogation, you may want to increase the suspect's anxiety. Some of the interrogation techniques are designed to intimidate, control, and manipulate the suspect into telling you the truth. You may ask the same question, phrased in different ways, to detect changes in the story. You may ask questions rapidly to unbalance the suspect and to force him to slip up and tell the truth before he has time to think of a lie. You may be confrontational and aggressive. You can yell at the suspect. You can speak softly to him. You may accuse him of things. You can stand over him or get very close to him and intimidate him by being right in his face. You may use dishonesty and lie to the suspect to get him to talk. Do not use force or threaten physical harm to the suspect.

Another approach to take is to be compassionate. You can express how you understand the suspect's behavior. "So she cheated on you. That must have hurt a lot. I can see why you wanted to teach her a lesson." You may be more authoritarian and sternly say, "So she cheated on you. Are you telling me you never cheated on her, or even thought about it? Is that any way to treat your girlfriend?"

You may use direct or indirect questions. Direct questions imply you know something, and indirect questions do not. For example, a direct question is, "What time did you leave Bill Wilson's house?" This implies that you know the suspect was at Bill's house. An indirect question is, "Have you ever been to Bill Wilson's house?" Asking direct questions are more likely to force the suspect to answer. With the direct line of questioning, you may go on and ask, "So why did you stab Bill Wilson?" even though the suspect has not yet admitted to the stabbing.

Some suspects respond to a line of questioning that gets to their ego. You may do this by minimizing the crime, by referring it blandly as "the incident" or "that thing that happened." This is understating the crime. Criminals with certain personality disorders are proud of their crimes, and are offended by this approach and may eventually correct you by saying, "You mean the shooting." You may also overstate the crime by describing much more property than was stolen, or quote a much higher amount of money than was actually taken. You may describe a "heinous attempted murder." The suspect may correct you and tell you, "I only took $50," or "I only took his TV," or "I only beat him up. I didn't try to kill him."

You may attack the suspect's ego even more directly by either inflating or deflating his ego. You may tell him you know about some brilliant robbery jobs. You could tell the suspect you know he is too dumb to have committed them, but that he might know who did. This is deflating his ego. He may decide to confess to them since you thought it was a brilliant job and try to change your opinion that he is dumb. You may also inflate his ego and imply that you know he committed the robberies, but that you are stunned with his skill and planning in committing them. He may confess or tell you more about how great he is at his job as a robber.

You may choose to rationalize the crime in a way that tells the suspect you understand and empathize with why he did it. "It sounds like your girlfriend really needed to be punished. It sounds like she was just asking for you to stab her, cheating on you like that. Cheating women all need to be punished."

You may also project the blame on the victim. This is particularly effective in sexual assault cases. "I know she was asking for it – with those long legs and cleavage showing. She was asking, so you just gave her what she wanted." This encourages the suspect to elaborate more on how the victim got what s/he "clearly" wanted.

Some interrogators begin with a story to set the stage for the questions, like talking about how bad the economy is and that it is hard to get by on what most jobs pay, and that it is even worse for those out of work to survive. They may go on to say that the economy is what drives people to be forced into crime just to survive. They then ask the suspect if that is what happened to them.

The interrogator may change his or her voice throughout the interrogation. Yelling and acting in a confrontational way, but then alternating with a soft voice and more compassion is confusing to the suspect. He may speak to you and cooperate to keep you compassionate and "nice." An alternative is to use two interrogators in the classic good cop/bad cop technique, where one interrogator is "mean" and confrontational, but the other is kind and compassionate. The confrontation may set the stage for the suspect to confess or give information to the compassionate interrogator. Both may be in the interrogation room at the same time, or may alternate after the other leaves the room.

Unlike the interview, if there are two interrogators in the room, both may ask questions at the same time, and they may both sit next to each other. If the good cop/bad cop technique is used, the good cop may choose to confront the bad cop on his treatment of the suspect in front of the suspect. "Detective Jones, that was not necessary. John is trying to help us here. You don't need to yell at him. Now John, start again and tell us what your girlfriend was doing that upset you." The good cop/bad cop technique may also be used with one interrogator in the room at a time, who then leaves and is replaced by the other interrogator.

The suspect may be left alone for a period of time between interrogators to increase his anxiety.

Using deceit during the interrogation is also a good technique, and is not considered damaging to the case. "So you, John, tell us this. Bruce told a bit of a different story that tells us you had a lot more to do with this than you are saying." You may not have even spoken with Bruce, or if you did, he may not have told you anything, but this tactic makes the suspect nervous and may get him to tell you the truth about what happened because he doesn't know what Bruce said that has incriminated him.

You may use guilt. "Now we have a little 3-year-old girl with no mom. Somebody killed her mom. We don't want this poor little girl to grow up with no mom, and she will never even know who did this. Growing up without a mom will change her life, and not in a good way. She deserves to know."

Interrogations may take hours. The longer the interrogation takes, the better the chance of getting the truth. The chances of getting the truth increase by 25% for each hour the interrogation lasts.

Interrogations require that you develop your acting ability, and they require practice. Study the body language discussed in Module 1. If you use dishonesty in the interrogation, you do not want to project any body language to indicate you are lying. Interrogation techniques are based on psychology, so you are, in effect, playing with the suspect's mind to get him to confess or tell you the truth. You must do whatever it takes with the exception of the use of force or the threat of the use of force to get the information you need.

CASE STUDY

Mixed Approaches – Good Cop/Bad Cop

A suspect was in custody. He was suspected of a series of sexual assaults. A detective came into the interrogation room to ask questions. The detective introduced himself and established rapport, discussing the local pro football team. He suddenly turned on the suspect, and said "Tell me about all these ladies you raped."

"I didn't do nothing."

"No – why does Luke say you did? Why did the ladies describe someone who looks just like you?"

"I don't know."

"So why were you downtown at 5th and Oak Saturday night? Right where Sally, the eighth victim was raped?"

"I was there doing business."

"Business. You are too stupid to do business. You were there to rape women."

"You are the stupidest person. I can't believe you deliver papers."

Another detective enters the room.

"Detective Blake, you are being too hard on Jim, here. He is just a good working man, delivering papers downtown. Go take a break and calm down. I'll talk to Jim."

Detective Blake acts angry and leaves. The new detective continues,

"I'm sorry about Detective Blake. He has a short fuse. I know it is tough when you have to deliver papers in a rough neighborhood. And I know about all the chicks who hang out by that bar there...I forget the name...."

"Ralph's"

"Yeah, Ralph's. Chicks just seem to go there to pick up guys. Bet you saw some down there just asking for it – long legs, short skirts, showing their belly with really low shirts...chicks looking for action."

"Yeah. They were there, and they wanted to hook up."

"Did you help them out?"

"Well, yeah. There was this one who kept looking at me. She was hot for me. I did take care of her. I didn't rape her – she wanted me."

"What was her name?"

"I don't know. But she had on these blue stockings with garters and this short skirt...."

Sally, the eighth victim, was wearing the outfit described by the suspect. All victims had the same DNA, which matched the suspect. Photos were taken of the suspect, and all eight victims identified him as their attacker. The suspect was arrested.

Detecting Deception Through Details

You are a rookie criminal justice professional, and you questioned suspects and are unsure whether or not they are being honest with you. There are additional tactics that can help you determine whether or not they are lying to you. Once you are proficient in these tactics, you can use them as soon as you establish rapport so you can combine your observations of their voice intonation and body language along with the way you ask them about what they saw.

Always ask about the details of an incident, even if they do not seem to be particularly pertinent. This is especially important if you have multiple witnesses and you are interviewing them separately. Witnesses who have agreed to collaborate on a lie will tell you the same basic story. It is unusual for them to have the lie coordinated down to the fine details. For example, groups of people are at a party, sitting around several tables when a man runs in the door with a gun and shoots one of the people. Ask each witness who was sitting by whom, and what each was doing, saying, or wearing. If the witnesses give you a different seating order or give you vastly different information about what each person was doing, saying, or wearing, they may have agreed on the lie about the major incident that occurred, but did not plan on having to provide such detail about each individual who was present. Vastly differing details in a story can indicate dishonesty.

You are asking about the people at the party. Jordan, one witness, tells about a masked gunman who ran in the door, looked at Matt and said, "There!" then shot Matt in the arm. You ask the details of everyone. Jordan tells you that Matt and Eva were sitting at a round table, and then clockwise around the table were Rusty, Jayden, Cheyenne, Ruth, Juan, and Emilio. Sitting at the round table next to Matt's table, clockwise around the table were Laura, Brianne, Cody, Rick, Jason, Wilson, and Catherine. You speak to Emilio, also a witness. He claims a masked gunman ran in the door, looked at Matt, and said, "There!" and then shot him in the arm. When Emilio listed the guests and their seating at the tables, the only two people who agreed with Jordan's story were

Matt and Eva, who were a couple and would logically be seated together. Jordan and Emilio did not have agreement about who was at which table. It is time to discuss the situation in greater detail with all the witnesses, but especially Jordan and Emilio, who appear to have collaborated on a phony story about what happened.

Resource - This article is from the *FBI Law Enforcement Bulletin* on detecting deception.

http://www.fbi.gov/stats-services/publications/law-enforcement-bulletin/june_2011/school_violence

CASE STUDY

Setting Traps to Identify Deception

Mr. Tanner went to the police station with Officers Martin and Wood to discuss his murdered neighbors. During a neighborhood canvass, Mr. Tanner was caught lying and seemed to know more about the situation than he initially admitted, so now he was going to be interviewed in more depth, and depending upon the outcome, possibly taken into custody and interrogated further. Officer Wood confronted Mr. Tanner and told him they knew he was acquainted with the neighbors, Jan and Brian Baker. He asked Mr. Tanner to tell them about what the neighbors had been doing over the past seven days. They did not tell him the neighbors were dead. As he told the narrative story, Mr. Tanner remained nervous and agitated. His face was red and perspiring, although the air conditioning was chilly in the room.

"Those two were trouble. Dealing drugs, I'm sure. Never to me. They came and went late at night. Jan had a little matted mutt that never shut up.

Dog always woke me up. I yelled at her, and she only smiled. She just ignored me. That was three days ago. They just came and went at night all this week. They were always fighting. They banged things around all the time. I never saw them today. I heard some banging over there today, but nothing else. Brian probably killed her. I saw him leave there and drive off this afternoon."

"What did Jan do to you three days ago?"

"Nothing. She ignored me. Well, she yelled at me after I told her dog to shut up."

"When did you see Brian today?"

"I never saw him today."

"When did he drive off today?"

"I don't know."

"What did Brian and Jan do for a living?"

"She was a nurse. He was a chaplain for the fire department."

"Did they work the night shift?"

"Maybe. Sometimes."

"Why do you think Brian killed Jan?"

"Well, she's dead, isn't she?"

Officers confronted Mr. Tanner with the information that they had said nothing about anyone being dead. Mr. Tanner then asked for a lawyer.

Investigation of the crime scene revealed that Brian and Jan were remodeling a bedroom of their house. The murder weapon was a hammer that matched the tools in that bedroom. After a warrant was obtained, Mr. Tanner's house was searched. Bloody clothing was found in a closet, and traces of blood were found in the shower.

Identify the parts of the narrative story. Is there disparity among the parts? Without detailed information about Mr. Tanner's body language and voice, how did officers know he was lying? What types of lies did Mr. Tanner use?

Summary

You have learned many different ways to get information from people. Keep in mind the differences between interviews and interrogations. Remember always to establish rapport. Watch body language.

Use care and compassion when speaking with people you are interviewing. In an interrogation, you may use compassion, or you may chose to be authoritarian, aggressive, and intimidating. Even the setup of the interrogation room is different as you are asserting that you are in charge. All interview and interrogation techniques are skills that require practice!

Discussion Questions

1. Explain the things you can do to put an interviewee at ease during the interview process.

2. Discuss methods to help a witness remember details during the interview process.

3. What types of questions might you ask during an interrogation that are designed to intimidate the suspect?

4. What types of questions might you ask during an interrogation are designed to be compassionate and empathize with the suspect?

Key Terms

Auditory orientation: People who perceive the world through what they hear; they remember things best in terms of sounds.

Chronological order: An order from beginning to end.

Cognitive interview technique: Interview techniques that help the victim remember details by helping the person return to the incident in question mentally.

Complainant: A person who called the police to report something wrong.

Interrogation: The questioning of a suspect who is in police custody.

Interview: A question and answer session you have with a witness.

Interviewee: The person being interviewed.

Kinesthetic orientation: People who perceive the world through what they feel; they remember emotions or feelings, and remember the way things felt to their touch.

Rapport: the establishment of "common ground" and a certain level of trust between the interviewer and the interviewee.

Perceptual orientation: The sense that an individual uses most to view the world and remember things.

Visual orientation: People who perceive the world through what they see; they remember things as visual pictures.

MODULE 5:

Public Relations for Law Enforcement

Photo courtesy of FEMA News Photo

Key module concepts:

- How public relations are used in criminal justice

- Useful procedures for interacting with the media

- The role of a Public Relations Specialist

- Skills needed for presentations

- Special tools required for meetings

Introduction

The effectiveness of the activities undertaken by members of the criminal justice system is often deemed to be a success or failure by the way the activities are perceived by the public. Members of the criminal justice system are constantly in the public eye due to the high-profile nature of law enforcement and the public's interest in crime and punishment.

The most high profile of all the elements of the criminal justice system is law enforcement. Most people in the community know what a police officer does and understand it better than they do a judge or prosecutor and their responsibilities. The police are supposed to reflect the values and ideals of the public they serve. They are the front line of defense for the public in the war on crime, and they are also the most susceptible to criticism and hindsight.

Law enforcement agencies are often deemed to be either effective or ineffective based on the perception the public has developed through the media, through agency public relations efforts, and through other means of communicating informa- tion that is of interest to the public, such as local access cable television and Web pages.

It is not a surprise that law enforcement is susceptible to criticism. After all, police work is typically reactive to situations that have already gone terribly wrong and where the outcomes are not always positive. A bad presentation of the case to the public, or reporters looking for a scoop on police incompetence, can take a case in which the resolution was as good as it could be, to a case in which the media catch phrase "police bungled investigation" comes into play.

The support of the public is critical to law enforcement efforts. If public confidence in their law enforcement agency fails, then the task of enforcing laws and keeping order becomes impossible. That is why it is important for the police to do as good a job in building their image and credibility as they do in protecting the public. It is critical to the success of the law enforcement agency to have a good relationship with the public and to have the support of the media.

Law enforcement agencies try to improve their image in a variety of ways, including developing relationships of trust with the media, presenting information and education to the public, and communicating effectively with government leadership, elected officials, and other agencies.

In this module, you will learn the basics of presentation skills, identify what is needed to develop **law enforcement public relations**, and learn about the complex yet necessary relationship that law enforcement has with the media.

Ask Yourself

- *What advantages does an institution have when there's a positive affiliation with the media?*

- *What are some ways to develop public relations with the community?*

- *What actions would an agency need to do in order to recover from a damaging news story?*

Public Relations and Criminal Justice

As you study criminal justice, you will come to realize that public opinion is a fickle and fairly unpredictable thing. As the most high profile part of the criminal justice system, law enforcement makes significant efforts to manage public opinion and to garner its support.

Law enforcement public relation efforts are generally intended to enhance the level of cooperation with the public, journalists, and elected officials. Of the three of these, journalists, or the media, have the most profound effect on general public opinion.

The relationship between the media and law enforcement is best described as a love-hate affair. The media depends on law enforcement for most of its news content and works diligently to develop "insider" law enforcement sources.

The media business model consists of selling advertising by leveraging the people's interest in news events. The journalists in the media want to write the most dramatic and compelling stories they can. This desire often leads to stories about the rare case of corruption or mistreatment of prisoners rather than the somewhat boring daily life of the majority of the criminal justice professionals.

On the other hand, the media has a responsibility to root out corruption and incompetence.

Law enforcement is somewhat secretive by nature, possibly due to the culture of law enforcement or legal constrictions, so officers are often distrustful of the media. Sometimes the distrust is warranted because the press gives an account of a story that officers know to be different than reported. It's important to remember that the press is constrained by the amount of time or print space they have to convey the news. Also, they have an interest in getting the news out faster than their competitors, often resulting in a lack of depth in their stories. But on the other side, reporters are often frustrated by the lack of information that the police make available to them, so they are not always able to write detailed and accurate stories.

The police know that no matter how hard they try, or how well they handle a situation, someone will find fault with the outcome. The negative aspects of the law enforcement efforts in any community, whether based in truth or not, often find their way into the lead stories of multimedia news. The friction between law enforcement and the press is also healthy. A skeptical and vigilant press prevents corruption and holds law enforcement accountable to the public.

However, positive communication, cooperation, and transparency benefit both law enforcement and the media and both parties recognize this more and more. The relationships between the press and the police have improved over the years through concerted efforts by both parties to better understand each other's perspectives. With the application of evolving technology for accessing records and producing information, as well as more training in press relations at every level of service, the police have greatly improved their ability to meet the needs of a demanding media pool.

Thus, law enforcement agencies are finding ways to protect confidential information while still satisfying the media's appetite for news content. The advent of open-door policies between police administrators and the press has made communication and access much simpler.

The last element in the relationship between the police and the press involves the public (see Figure 5.1). While it is true that there are still a significant number of journalists who may be too quick to slant a story in a way that is demeaning to an official's character, or to overly sensationalize a case, they only exist because of a consumer demand for more stimulating stories. The public demand for compelling stories and scandal has created an environment in which some unscrupulous journalists thrive.

FIGURE 5.1: *The triangle of communication.*

Examining a National PR Scandal

In July 2009, the Cambridge Police Department generated a lot of attention but not the kind it would like. Officers responded to a possible break-in at the home of Henry Louis Gates Jr., but rather than apprehending a burglary suspect, they ended up arresting the resident, Mr. Gates, who happened to be a friend of the President of the United States. The ensuing sensationalism surrounding this case distracted police from their regular duties and caused embarrassment for all parties involved. This incident was appropriately deemed by many as a **"media circus,"** a term used to describe the act of increasing a story's relevance beyond its actual importance, resulting in the coverage of the story being more significant than the story itself.

The temptation to chalk this incident up as a case of racial profiling was something even President Obama could not resist. The actual events, individual actions, and personal perceptions of those people involved were much more complex than the initial reports indicated.

Mr. Gates, a Harvard professor and one of the nation's pre-eminent African-American scholars, arrived home in Cambridge after a trip to China on July 16. He came home to find the front door lock damaged and was unable to open it without force. A likely conclusion was that someone had, in fact, attempted to break in during his absence and caused the door to be jammed.

In a subsequent interview given to the *Washington Post* after the incident, Gates told the reporter that it was his driver who popped the door open with his shoulder and allowed him to enter into the home. At the time the driver was forcing entry, a woman neighbor observed this activity and feared that two men were burglarizing the residence. She reported a burglary in progress to the police.

After the driver opened the door and the two men entered the house, Mr. Gates called the college maintenance staff to have the door repaired.

While he was on the phone with maintenance, the Cambridge police arrived to investigate the "burglary in progress".

Sergeant James Crowley was the first on the scene. Almost immediately, according to reports, Gates became uncooperative while being questioned. He accused Crowley of being a racist police officer. Mr. Gates became loud and confrontational with the officer, eventually resulting in a crowd gathering and a subsequent disruption of the public peace when Gates took the confrontation outside. Crowley then handcuffed Gates for disorderly conduct. The charges were dismissed five days later.

Outside Looking In

Although Mr. Gates is African-American and the arresting officer, Sergeant Crowley, is Caucasian, racial profiling, although initially perceived by Mr. Gates, was probably not a part of this incident. Sergeant Crowley made the arrest after Mr. Gates reportedly yelled and verbally abused him repeatedly. In the aftermath, both parties agreed that the situation escalated unnecessarily. Gates was certainly disorderly, but he was in his own home when the incident started, and he made some inaccurate conclusions about what Sergeant Crowley was trying to accomplish. Crowley, being an experienced officer, should have tried harder to diffuse the situation and refocus the discussion on the previous break-in.

But it did not stop there, as is often the case with mistaken intentions.

The incident started a backlash by African-American students and faculty against the local police for racial discrimination and profiling. Then on July 22, about a week later, President Obama spoke openly at a White House news conference where a journalist questioned the event. That is when the President expressed his opinion that the Cambridge police had "acted stupidly" in arresting his Harvard friend. A media-fueled firestorm erupted.

The members of the Cambridge Police Department did not care for being characterized by the president as "stupid." At stake was their credibility and their efforts to work with the community, particularly at a time of volatility on campus concerning race issues.

Two days after President Obama's statement, a different press conference was held to defend the reputation of the Cambridge Police. Steve Killian, president of the Cambridge Police Patrol Officers Association, said that the President's comments were "disgraceful" and "For this to happen to Sergeant Crowley is wrong. Cambridge police are not stupid...when the time is right they should make an apology to us." Alan McDonald, lawyer for the Cambridge Police Department, added, "There is no evidence whatsoever the arrest was race-based. It was inappropriate of him (Obama) to make the allegation."

As more information came forward about the department and the officer involved, it appeared that some preconceived notions were proven wrong.

For six years, Sergeant Crowley taught a racial profiling class at the Lowell Police Academy in Boston with a black colleague – a role that he was chosen to serve in by a senior African-American officer. A review of his record indicates that when Sergeant Crowley was a young campus police officer he tried unsuccessfully to save the life of African-American basketball star Reggie Lewis by administering mouth-to-mouth re-suscitation. That occurred 17 years prior to the event with Mr. Gates. Sergeant Crowley, although initially characterized as a possible racist rogue officer, was eventually found to be a well-respected professional with an extensive record of service to the Cambridge community at large and absolutely no history of racism.

In fairness to President Obama, he admitted before his notorious remark that he did not know all the facts of the story and that knowing "Skip" Gates made him somewhat biased; he was merely conveying that some police still occasionally treat ethnic groups inappropriately. The Commander in Chief later clarified the remarks he made by stating the following:

"I continue to believe, based on what I have heard, that there was an overreaction in pulling Professor Gates out of his home to the station. I also continue to believe, based on what I heard, that Professor Gates probably overreacted as well. My sense is you've got two good people in a circumstance in which neither of them were able to resolve the incident in the way that it should have been resolved and the way they would have liked it to be resolved."

Damage Control

Three wrongs certainly do not make a right. In hindsight, the controversy could have been avoided had certain **damage controls** been followed:

- Gates thanked the officers for doing their job in protecting his property.

- Crowley had dismissed the charges when it was clear that Gates posed no threat and released a public statement about the case before the President did.

- President Obama answered "no comment" when he did not know all details, even though what he *did* say was clearly an opinion based on the brief information available.

President Obama hosted a "beer summit" at the White House (see Figure 5.2) to allow the three men to meet socially, resolve their differences, and to discuss ways to improve police and community relations.

FIGURE 5.2: *The President, Sergeant Cowley, and Professor Gates resolving their differences at the White House.* Photo by Pete Souza

This case is one in which the media played a large role in escalating events beyond where they should have gone. The sensationalism of stereotyping Sergeant Crowley and Professor Gates, coupled with some unfortunate words from the president whose intent was to defend the character of a personal friend, led to a story that was expanded far beyond its significance.

This was also a case in which the public relations branch of the police department could have been more proactive by rapidly getting accurate information to the press, garnering support from the community, and diffusing the subsequent conflict.

Camaraderie Among Unlikely Forces

Law enforcement is acutely aware that the public they serve is the same as the audience of news outlets. The Police Executive Research Forum (PERF) study showed that an improved media relationship correlates to the positive influence and effectiveness the public views in its agencies. Simultaneously, most departments that were polled believed that their public perception was "basically very good and overwhelmingly said that the media had an impact on its perception," said Larry Jones, the Assistant Chief of Crimes against Property for the Jacksonville Sheriff's Office.

In retrospect, the two adversaries have quite a bit in common because both the media and police agencies serve the public. Both require credibility to sustain the trust of the community.

"If we continue to stereotype all members of the mass media as unfriendly, then any effort we make to influence their behaviors, or products, will be rejected," wrote Edward J. Tully, a former FBI special agent and presently the Executive Director of the Executive Institute Associates.

Even the work environment is similar as journalists have editors breathing down their neck the same way that sergeants watch over their patrol officers. Both groups frequently deal with society at its worst.

Cooperation between law enforcement and the media is not easy, but it can be accomplished. By developing trust and mutual respect prior to a critical incident occurring, both participants will be prepared to focus on the lawful and responsible sharing of information rather than infighting and antagonism. For example, law enforcement often stages a zone at major incidents for news crews to work and assigns an officer to act as a liaison. This area provides access for reporters to work freely, as well as space for first responders to protect sensitive information. Experienced professional reporters respect the secure zones marked by crime scene tape and are familiar with police rules, procedures, and legal restraints.

Cooperation, communication, and trust are critical to any relationship, including the media and law enforcement.

Preparation for the Media

One can virtually guarantee that whenever a disaster occurs, the police will be there to preserve safety and the media will be there to document the unfolding drama. The direct impact that law enforcement has on the community through the mass media can enhance its reputation, credibility, and effectiveness. Thorough coverage by the press on critical topics serves the interests of the public at large. Since neither group is likely to abandon its mission even when their immediate goals may be in conflict with one another, the reasonable approach is to forge a working alliance (see Figure 5.3).

FIGURE 5.3: *Getting information out at a disaster scene requires team-work by the press and emergency managers.*
Photo courtesy of FEMA News Photo

Sometimes the media will arrive at the scene before the responders have been organized. Since journalists are under a strict timetable, they will be eager to interview anyone who can give them insider information. By knowing the agency's guidelines when it comes to communicating with news personnel, the likelihood of disrupting the investigation is reduced.

After a tragedy strikes, usually an **informational briefing** will take place so that all persons are given the same news at the same time. This briefing takes the place of having to have continuous meetings with the media and it also helps to avoid discrepancies or errors in the story that might come from incorrect information. However, because it is normal for a story to develop incrementally as time passes, case continuing briefings are held periodically to disclose new and important details.

Another type of briefing is sometimes formed specifically to address the community, and this meeting often excludes the media. For example, those in attendance might be family members or other loves ones or community members of the victims. This briefing serves as a means to alleviate the stress of the families in a somewhat private environment. During these meetings, disclosures of the cause and effect from the disaster may be relayed, as well as any short- or long-term response plans. Whether it is after the informational briefing or a separate meeting altogether, a question-and-answer session, or a **defusing meeting**, is held to discuss the disaster in further detail.

Public Relations Specialist

For legal and jurisdictional purposes, typically there is a sole person allowed to speak for any agency; it is common to politely direct reporters to this individual when asked. For example, the medical examiner or coroner may speak about the body count in a mass fatality. A representative from the search and rescue team may address questions concerning those people recovered. Depending on the company, this selected person may be referred to by many names, but the general term would be *public relations specialist.*

PR is a constant, developing field with an expected 24 percent increase from 2008 to 2018, according to The Bureau of Labor Statistics. There are plenty of areas of interest, but criminal justice students should focus on government positions. Otherwise known as press secretaries, their job is to keep the public informed of certain activities. To give you a better picture, the public affairs specialist in the U.S. Department of State alerts the public of travel advisories and U.S. positions on foreign issues. A PR representative of Congress informs constituents of its accomplishments.

Whatever degree the job entails, the PR specialist's task is to handle publicity for an individual or institution that requires an enormous amount of research and preparation. In large organizations, the public relations executive (often a high-ranking official) may build plans and policies with other executives. PR specialists also arrange and conduct programs to maintain contact between organization representatives and the people. Part of their job involves setting up public engagements and preparing the speeches for officials. In short, they write, study, respond, prepare materials, and maintain contacts.

A good public relations specialist will study public relations, journalism, marketing, and communications with supporting skills in the firm's business.

Public Information Officer

Law enforcement has its own PR specialist. During emergency situations, police will have a predetermined **Public Information Officer (PIO)**. The PIO (see Figure 5.4) is the designated person to speak to the media; this person is the only agency member with the authority to represent the police position in a crisis. Like other officers, a PIO must work well under pressure and make judgments quickly.

What makes this person exceptional, however, is his or her strong verbal skills and ability to communicate with a crowd in an effective and professional manner.

FIGURE 5.4: *A professional PIO can effectively handle the distribution of information to the press and protect the integrity of active investigations.*
Photo courtesy of FEMA News Photo

A 2000 survey of Police-Media Relations showed that PIOs "perform a wide array of traditional public relations activities and that they have been instrumental in moving law enforcement from a closed to a more open system of communication." As the spokes-person for the police team, the PIO discloses how much information can be released at a given time for a given emergency – usually by the **command staff**. A command staff is a cluster of individuals who retain specific positions with various responsibilities. In this case, the safety officer and liaison officer join the public information officer in reporting directly to the incident commander. So when a reporter asks a question, it should be clear that he will be directed to the official person designated to work with the media and not snubbed from an uncooperative officer. This chain of command is set to draw lines that provide the best media relations.

Providing effective, accurate information to reporters is a job that changes according to the situations. Some of the PIO's responsibilities include the following:

- Scheduling interviews
- Developing and maintaining a media contact list
- Issuing press releases
- Gathering and verifying information
- Becoming familiar with disaster management and the Federal Response Plan
- Knowing the agency's history and capability

Most PIOs know that it is preferable and respectful to keep the names of the victims, injured or deceased, from going public before the families have been notified. Not only is this an ethical decision but also a liability issue. Details of an investigation should remain confidential until the investigation has been determined to be of public importance. It's also important that the PIO never release speculation or opinion about a case, even if it appears harmless at the time. The media might cut the story to meet a set of standards and any false or misunderstood information could lead to a destructive turn of events.

CASE STUDY

Beware of Offering Opinions

Sheriff Clarence Dupnik of Pima County, Arizona gave numerous national press statements declaring that talk radio and political media outlets were somehow to blame for inspiring the suspect to commit the Tucson, Arizona mass murder that involved the wounding of Congresswoman Gabrielle Giffords.

Dupnik admitted that he had no evidence on which to base this speculation other than his opinion of the political climate. In other words, his comments were not based on anything that was discovered during the course of the investigation. This unusual statement by the Sheriff detracted from the investigation and resulted in the media focusing on his speculations rather than the facts of the case. This subsequently caused accusations that the elected sheriff politicized this horrific incident, which harmed the credibility of the agency's investigation and potentially the integrity of the case. An experienced PIO would probably not have made this mistake.

Resource - *Chris Ryan.* Every PIO will have heard this name at least once – and for good reason. Ryan is the president of a communications firm and teaches a course that trains officers how to speak to the media. The four-day boot camp includes writing more effective news releases, preparing for interviews, responding to tough media questions, and much more.

http://www.piobootcamp.com/bootcamp.html

The Softer Side of News

Not every interview will be based upon the reporting of disasters. Good PIOs may help journalists by providing feature story ideas on slow news days. The tales of unsung heroes or charitable events make great stories that serve as interest for both the agency and the community. They also help balance the often-reported tragic news.

In fact, any opportunity a PIO has to shine a positive light on his or her police force, while at the same time helping the members of the media address their own needs, leads to overall better rapport. This bond creates a powerful partnership. Positive leads will give reporters a better understanding of the police team's work and perhaps even lead to better stories.

Tearing down the barriers between the two divisions can be taken a step further by inviting the media to document training procedures, suggests Chief Edward M. Morley and Sergeant Martin J. Jacobson, (Public Information Officer) of the Stuart Police Department. This exceptional invite gives a unique peak into the law enforcement world. Most beat journalists would be happy to have the chance to impart behind-the-scenes action to the readers. Plus, the community will be proud to know that their public safety officials are trained to react to disastrous incidents.

Training for PIOs varies among agencies; some have no formal training, while others attend courses specifically designed for this trade. Those who are elected are always strong with their public speaking and report writing skills. Far from being shy creatures, a PIO is usually comfortable being the center of attention, but it does help to have some rapport with reporters built up beforehand. It makes work more pleasant when there is a recognizable face here and there among the sea of correspondents when standing in front of a Q&A firing squad. No favoritism is allowed, though.

The Varieties of Public Image

The public image of a law enforcement agency is largely framed on how the news media reports the agency's actions. How the agency interrelates with the media may well be critical to how their activities are reported to the public. The classic example is J. Edgar Hoover who took the Federal Bureau of Investigation (FBI) from a small obscure federal bureaucracy to an internationally recognized law enforcement agency by encouraging the image of the "G-Men," an elite force fighting gangsters in the 1930s. Although they were not often actually involved in the apprehension of gangsters, Hoover's relentless marketing of his fledgling organization created the public image of an unstoppable crime fighting force.

Abraham Lincoln once said, "Public opinion, though often formed upon a wrong basis, yet generally has a strong underlying sense of justice." The media aids in the representation of the police force but it is not their voice. The police as a unit are the most important factor in determining public attitudes.

To further a positive representation, police departments should form **community policing** units that improve visibility and understanding. Educational assemblies or programs in schools are also important for police departments. The relationships they build may help encourage young witnesses, and sometimes victims, to come forward, when they may otherwise have remained silent.

One example occurred at a school presentation in 2010 where police officers were discussing the importance of reporting sexual abuse. A 13-year-old told victim reported an attack that occurred when the student was eight or nine years old. After an investigation, police arrested and charged 30-year-old Christopher Cary Adams for indecency with a child by sexual contact. Because of the school presentation, police were able to apprehend an alleged sexual predator years after he committed his crime.

Before the introduction of the automobile, law enforcement patrols were conducted through walking beats, horseback patrol, and bicycle patrols. Police officers were generally born, raised, and lived in the communities they served. There was a direct, daily personal interaction between the police and the public prior to the evolution of the anonymous patrol car driving through a neighborhood. Community based policing still occurs today – in fact, there are 20,000 registered local Neighborhood Watch Programs in the U.S. Officers have extensive opportunities to meet with and present information to groups of citizens.

Resource - To find or register for a Watch Group, go to
http://www.usaonwatch.org/register/default.aspx
and in five easy steps, you can become involved in your community.

The Effects of Community Policing

How do crime prevention efforts diminish the division that can exist between citizens and police? As the "eyes and ears" for law enforcement, these efforts helps establish or even reclaim an informal control for the public. The National Crime Prevention Council composed a list of the benefits police-community relations brings.

Some include the following:
- Police more effectively
- More trust and respect instilled

- Less tension and conflict
- Safer communities
- Greater resolutions

There are also six factors necessary to improve this dynamic teamwork.

Membership: Members see that collaboration is in their best interest so members develop the ability to compromise.

Environment: The collaborative group is viewed as a leader in the community. Political figures view this trait favorably.

Process and structure: With clear roles and responsibilities, members become invested in the process as well as the outcome.

Communications: Due to the open and frequent interaction among the group, members relieve themselves through venting and learn to listen to other's concerns.

Purpose: A shared vision gives desired results and strategies while creating attainable goals and objectives.

Resources: Staff and volunteer time are a must. The joint effort influences political officials' desire to invest adequate funds.

Community policing is the responsibility of both law enforcement and community members; both have important roles that are indispensable. The rewards of reduced crime and improved safety unites a kinship that improves crime reporting by citizens.

There are many ways to involve residents in crime reduction and problem solving, including community meetings and citizens' police academies. A community involved with a program such as a neighbor-hood watch is another great way to increase the positive publicity for the police force. There are many people who are looking for ways to protect their property and enhance safety and the best way to do it is by volunteering in their own neighborhood. This is also one of the best ways to keep in contact with the people in a neighborhood who know about what goes on in their area. This effort may result in more tips on criminal activity that will lead to arrests.

The development of a Neighborhood Watch Program (see Figure 5.5) does not require a lot of formal procedures, and it provides a safe place for neighbors to confer with police to discuss matters of mutual concern. Remember that the officers do not control the meeting when present at a Neighborhood Watch meeting. Instead, they facilitate the discussion and provide security advice, such as the best methods to secure homes and

FIGURE 5.5: *Neighborhood Watch is an effective tool against crime.*

automobiles, as well as the best way to respond to a variety of threatening situations. The purpose is simply for residents to share in the responsibility and become guardians for their community.

CASE STUDY

A Successful Partnership—Law Enforcement and the Public

There are obviously not enough police officers to ensure the safety of everyone at all times so the National Sheriffs' Association created the U.S. Neighborhood Watch Program in 1972. The idea was that by combining the efforts of law enforcement, private organizations, and concerned citizens, residential crime could be reduced. The notion helped serve as a bridge between law-abiding residents and the police so that police could receive help in surveying areas of the community.

Usually, residents know what is deemed out of the ordinary in their immediate neighborhood. For example, when tips trickled in to the Alton Police Department in Illinois that there were numerous people coming and going to a particular house, officials began surveillance and conducted undercover drug buys for two months. In December 2010, officers found four adults and three juveniles occupying the house and seized cocaine, cannabis, and several thousands of dollars in cash.

Because Police Chief David Hayes and several representatives from the agency attended monthly Neighborhood Watch meetings, they had an advantage in arresting the suspects. "The best information we received was from Neighborhood Watch meetings during the past year," said Hayes in an interview. Cases such as this are just one of the many examples of community programs doing their part to reduce crime. Crime Reports' statics show that neighborhoods with a Neighborhood Watch program have crime rates 40 percent lower than neighborhoods without such a program.

Meetings also make the police appear more humanized to the public. Police are sometimes not regarded as local citizens within their community. These personal encounters at Watch meetings often serve to demonstrate that officers, like anyone else, have families, financial stress, and personal interests and concerns. People begin to recognize officers as much more than just a uniform and a badge.

Presenting and Sharing Information

Verbal communications, whether with the public or within the department, is a secondary job of law enforcement. Officers talk about what procedures need to be taken, stage conferences to inform the public of important news, and introduce new tactics to their fellow officers that are beneficiary.

If the job of an officer is communicating and sharing information, then the first step to being effective at this skill would be to become familiar with how to produce an excellent presentation.

The formality of presentations may differ today slightly from those given decades ago, but the intent has never changed. A great presentation engages an audience through to the very end, while achieving the desired communication goal. It requires a great deal of preparation to communicate ideas effectively. Well-researched and rehearsed statements, spoken aloud from a person brimming with enthusiasm, attract listeners and get their attention and support

Research is not limited only to the objectives in mind. A great presenter is familiar with his or her audience, as well. Greeting the guests beforehand establishes a direct connection and makes them feel welcomed; discussions afterward create rapport and trust that lasts long after the speech is over.

Preparation Makes Perfect

First, begin a presentation by building an outline. It needs to flow and cover the points that will be highlighted. Ask yourself "What, exactly, do I want people to remember?" and build from there. Some presenters like to start with the conclusion first and then expand their ideas outward. Be aware that most people do not remember more than a few key points, so cleverly worded summaries can leave a better impact on the audience's long-term memory. Effective repetition, without sounding like you merely said the same thing twice, also triggers a person's brain to "hard wire" information. Another way that humans tend to remember is through emotions, since emotions influence how memory is processed. Be sure to give your audience something meaningful to retain: a powerful quote, a disturbing statistic, or a feel-good story.

Powerful introductions offer the platform for a winning presentation. They work best in two parts: The first is to introduce yourself as a "real person," and the second is to break the ice and relax the audience.

Now, depending on the environment you may be able to skip the, "Hello everyone. My name is John Smith," altogether by creating a pleasant lead-in suitable for welcoming the crowd. Note that a good lead should be delivered in under 30 seconds; 20 is even better. Keeping these couple of fact in brief, concise phrases spares the audience of too much information too soon.

When all the points connect like dots, review the work for any changes with a fresh pair of eyes (or different set if available). True writing is rewriting; scrap the weak items and develop the overly strong ones. The presenter should be comfortable enough with the material by this point that he or she is able to pluck chunks without having to read word for word. Get used to this. A fascinating storyteller is someone who conveys emotion while intuitively queuing up the highlights. Usually, this does not mean looking down to read off note cards.

Remember, a good speech is like a good relationship: you should care about the subject and the audience.

It's All in the Delivery

Okay, even though preparation is key, no amount of research is going to save a speech if the delivery is poor. The presenter does not have to have a great personality to win over an audience – but it is important. Charisma, on the other hand, is a trait that all great orators require; it is also one that even the shyest wallflower can adopt.

Charismatic speakers are the ones who are obliviously enjoying themselves, are confident with their surroundings (external as well as internal), and are able to convey emotion about the subject that is being addressed. They look good; stage presence and polished attire accomplishes this before a word is even spoken. A personable attitude is critical. Channel your confidence so that your audience finds you relatable and in turn they will have the same reaction to your speech.

But how do you capture an audience's attention when the average attention span lasts about 30 seconds? A great presentation hones in on the feelings of the crowd and then hooks them through the persuader's opinion. This authentic and unique delivery skill is one that can be developed over the course of one public speech to the next. Over time, it will become more obvious why statistical information is best kept in small doses or how light-hearted moments bring relief to even the most somber speech.

Nevertheless, speaking before a crowd is a pretty scary situation. It ranks high on the list of Americans' greatest fears – often surpassing death itself. A famous comedian once joked that "at a funeral, the average person would rather be in the casket than giving the eulogy." But even if you are completely overwhelmed with a fear of public speak-ing, it can be overcome. Being prepared makes giving a presentation significantly easier.

Whatever topic is being delivered, it is always better when the speaker adds an element of personality to it. This could be as simple as finding humor in a story or striding casually across the stage and using occasional hand gestures when speaking. These motions reveal a piece of your humanity and make others feel connected to you. Suddenly, you're more than just a talking head to them.

Tools of Presentation

Another method that police use to communicate public information is through multimedia presentations. There are a number of choices. Microsoft's PowerPoint, Apple's Keynote, and Open Office's Impress are some of the more well known. These software presentation tools are great to employ when a more formal speech is needed. The mere structure of a speech meshed with photographs or diagrams provides a powerful impact. However, the purpose of the presentation tools is to aid the presenter; it is not intended to replace the speaker.

There are three basic principles when conducting a slideshow:

- Retain audience focus
- Create brief yet interesting slides
- Maximize delivery

The most effective presentations have simple designs while providing supplemental information. A very common mistake that presenters make is to compose the whole or chunked speech on-screen and read it to the audience verbatim. This is the fastest way to frustrate your audience and make them feel that their time has been wasted. Think about it: the moment someone's attention is lost, the presentation's effectiveness has been lost as well.

Power of Ten

Guy Kawasaki, former Apple Fellow and professional speaking guru, has established a "**Rule of Ten**" method that suggests 10 slides to be ideal for a slideshow presentation. These slides may contain nothing more than a sentence or two along with a supporting image.

The great thing about limiting slides to a select number (such as 10) is that it forces you to deliver your key ideas in a minimum amount of time. There is a higher probability that your audience will retain information when joined with strong images. A pie chart with sectioned "sliccs" is easier to digest than lists of statistics. Photographs are an even better visual aid to ensure a memorable impact.

You should stay focused on your audience and what is in their best interest. They automatically will have the "What's-in-it-for-me?" mind-set, so plan a strategy that will not result in them asking, "Why should I care?" or "Why am I here?" The answers to these questions should be essential to any presentation. Practice the timing so you can give the audience a chance to absorb the information. Pause. Then follow up the text and images with your own amplified comments. This will help make your well-orchestrated slideshow far more appealing.

Resource - Guy Kawasaki gives an excellent speech on presentation rules, which can be found at

http://www.youtube.com/watch?v=liQLdRkOZiw.

Conference Calls

Conference calls are a special form of communication with their own etiquette and guidelines. These calls are a growing form of telecommunication that is more cost-efficient than traveling to meetings, yet they can be as effective as a conference table meeting.

Most people are aware that conference calls are utilized in a business setting, but they are increasingly used in public safety efforts as well. One example would occur when discussing an investigation or the prevention of criminal behavior (see Figure 5.6).

Do your homework before any conference call. To help with this, distribute handouts or emails for participants to look over before the conversation takes place. As the facilitator, it is wise to have a set agenda with time limits and specific goals. Without an agenda or goals, calls tend to lose focus.

Networking is effective in getting the word out to investigators across a state or even the nation quickly. It is helpful in dealing with criminals who cross jurisdictional boundaries during an ongoing criminal enterprise.

FIGURE 5.6: *Law enforcement officers share information using conferencing technology to save time and travel expenses. Photo courtesy of FEMA News Photo*

In October 2008, the Community Oriented Policing Services (COPS) held a conference call with local and federal law enforcement to discuss a continuous problem with mortgage fraud and foreclosure scams. Various representatives offered examples of preventative actions that could be used, so simple networking was invaluable in this case.

Not all police conference calls have to pertain to criminal acts. The notion of using video to conduct anything from meetings to testimonies has slowly been developing with the advancements that technology allows. For example, when the Coos Bay Police Department in Oregon became frustrated by having to commute an hour and a half several times a week to testify in court, they decided to give their court testimony online instead. This process spared them wear and tear on the patrol cars, as well as the officers who operated them.

Whatever the agenda is, it is best to end the conference with summarizing the collected actions for any possible suggestions to be taken later. A follow-up may or may not happen but take the time to verify first. Either way, it is imperative for the participants to walk away feeling assured that all information has been shared. The way a conference call ends usually reflects the current and future relationship of those involved.

Summary

Communication may be a two-way street, but it is not one that is always paved smoothly. Law enforcement is constantly engaged in public relations. It can be as straightforward as a presentation to as complicated as a news conference. Remember that preparation, charisma, and rapport are all qualities that maximize a delivery. And while communicating to a crowd may be stressful, anticipating the common questions – number of casualties/injuries, cost of loss, cause for failure, etc. – is one task that is easy to prep for.

As public figures, it is important for law enforcement to have open communication lines with members of the society while preserving confidential information. It is a balancing act – with the reputation of a police force resting on the public's opinion. A good relationship with the media is the best and fastest way for self-promotion.

Law enforcement agencies should always be on good terms with the local media and have open communication lines. The department should also promote a very strong public relations program so that they do not fall victim to hearsay when problems do arise. The selected representative to address the media, such as the police's Public Information Officer, can help implement a positive social policy and, in turn, the media will see law enforcement agencies less as adversaries and more as partners. A single official should be known to reporters and within the department as the go-to person that conducts a cordial liaison with the media.

While the media does have the strongest influence on the public, not all public relations have to run through news outlets. Simply making the police squad a public figure creates a better public image. The principles of community-oriented policing are an important element for law enforcement agencies; they cannot be public figures if they are not visible to the communities they serve.

Discussion Questions

1. How does a charismatic person who is well prepared for a presentation affect the audience?

2. What are some other ways not mentioned in this module to improve law enforcement public relations?

3. How can the police encourage more neighborhood watch meetings?

4. Think of a situation in which an agency may have an embarrassing public relations failure. How would you handle it? What methods would you use?

Key Terms

Command staff: Position that is responsible for activities at an incident, usually headed by the incident commander.

Community policing: A philosophy that promotes organized strategies that support the partnerships and problem solving techniques between the police and the community.

Conference calls: Calls between more than two people, a teleconference.

Damage control: An effort to minimize or restrict loss.

Defusing meeting: A debriefing type of question-and-answer meeting that privately explains who happened to certain individuals affected by the incident.

Informational briefing: A meeting that is usually given by a select member of the organization that needs to publicly announce some type of information.

Law enforcement public relations: A type of promotion intended to create goodwill for the institution.

Media circus: A news event where the media coverage is suggested to be out of proportion to the event being covered, such as the number of reporters at the scene, the amount of news media published or broadcast, and the level of media hype.

Networking: The act of meeting new people in a business or social context.

Public image: The art or science of creating and promoting a likeable relationship with the public.

Public Information Officer (PIO)**:** Communications spokesperson of select governmental institutions.

Rule of Ten: The key number of slides during a presentation that helps maximize the speech and retain audience focus.

References

Krissah Thompson, "Harvard Professor Arrested At Home," Washington Post, July 21, 2009.

Alex Spillius, "Cambridge police demand apology from Barack Obama over 'stupid' comments," The Telegraph, July 24, 2009.

Larry Jones, "Police and Media Relations: How to Bridge the Gap."

Edward J. Tully, "Mass Media and Law Enforcement – A Time for Reflection," The National Executive Institute Associates Leadership Bulletin, *January 1999*.

Melissa Motschall, "An Analysis of the Public Relations Role of the Police Public Information Officer," Police Quarterly, June 2002.

Louis Ojeda Jr., "Teen makes outcry of sexual abuse during police presentation," KXXV News Channel 25, *July 01, 2010*.

Jane Morse, "Neighborhood Watch Programs Help Build Citizen-Police Trust Communities find fighting residential crime requires cooperation," State Department's Bureau of International Information Programs, March 10, 2009.

"Improvement of *Police Community* Relations," National Crime Prevention Council, 2007-2008.

Linda N. Weller, "Two arrested as police raid house," The Telegraph, December 13, 2010.

Dave Roos, "5 Tips for More Effective PowerPoint Presentations," How Stuff Works.

MODULE 6

Radio Communications

Key module concepts:

- Evolution of technology in broadcasting

- Importance of time when processing instructions
  from officer to dispatcher and vice versa

- Proper guidelines and restrictions the Federal
  Communications Commission has set

- Use of phonetic alphabet

- Purpose for radio codes and why this type of
  communication may be going out of style

- How the tone of a call has a direct correlation
  to its outcome

Introduction

"Dispatch to Lincoln 12, Charlie 12 and Adam 4 X Ray, respond to a 245 in progress at 115 Washington Avenue. Code 3." To the outsider (or even a new recruit), these numbers and codes sound like gibberish, but to public safety officials, this cryptic message speaks volumes. With time of the essence, shortening transmissions to the bare essentials is easier than saying, "Attention Lieutenant and two officers, there is serious and possibly deadly assault occurring right now on Washington Avenue. This is an extremely urgent matter so use lights and sirens and get there as quickly as you can while driving safely as possible."

Radios play an important role in modern law enforcement. The typical radio system in a police car covers multiple frequencies and is often capable of scanning or monitoring radio communications from a variety of sources. However, this has not always been the case. Early **police radio** models were developed from tunable and fixed-**frequency** (channel) radios that would receive channels one at a time, much like a typical commercial car AM radio. As technology advanced in consumer electronics, the police systems soon followed. Simple two-way radio systems evolved into complex computer data terminals with radios, scanners, and information processing systems. For example, between 1990 and 2000, the percentage of local police officers working for an agency that used in-field computers or terminals grew from 73 percent to 92 percent, according to the Bureau of Justice Statistics.

The field radios found in cars are only one component of the communication system. Dispatch centers, which include phone banks, text messaging, email capabilities, and radio broadcast channels, are the backbone of the information and communication sharing systems

In most large cities, it is common to find a number of public safety agencies with overlapping jurisdictions or contiguous geographic boundaries – for example a city may have separate police and fire dispatch centers, or a sheriff, a police chief, and a state trooper may all have jurisdiction on a highway passing through a city. The various dispatching systems need to be able to communicate with each other. This is called **interoperability**. The ability for public safety agencies to communicate when events require a joint response has become a serious concern, particularly since the 9/11 terrorist attacks when some first responders were not able to exchange critical information with each other. In response to this need of interoperability, administrators of networks shared across multiple agencies are designing plans and updating equipment to better suit their needs.

For the most part, operating a radio is not a difficult task, but it takes time and practice to memorize codes, protocols, etiquette, and features. In this module, you will learn the basics about radio operations and procedures.

While this module will touch on different organizations involved in emergency communications, it will emphasize the police role. Also included in this module are simple guidelines for conversing in code and the restrictions set by the **Federal Communications Commission (FCC)**.

Ask Yourself

- When transmitting a call over a scanner, who are the people listening to the information?

- What should I do if I make a mistake about a call or misunderstand the order given?

- How do I summarize what it is I need in an orderly fashion?

History of Public Safety Radios

The use of the police radio dates back to the late 1920s. During this tumultuous time known as the "roaring 20s," gangsters and bank robbers used the lack of communication capabilities of law enforcement and powerful V8 engine-powered automobiles to avoid capture. Police sought out technology to help keep up the pace. The ability to use radios to dispatch units to a crime scene seemed like a great idea, and after many prototypes, one-way radio communication to patrol cars finally became a reality in April, 1928. The era of radio as a crime-fighting tool was officially born. The phrase "You can outrun the patrol car, but you can't outrun a radio" was established. The police used organization, communication, and advance planning to thwart the activities of the gangsters of the roaring 20s, along with a liberal use of heavy firepower.

The way these early radio system worked was very clever for the limited experience with technology the police had at the time. After the switchboard operator directed the call to the police station dispatcher, the dispatcher would then phone an AM broadcaster (see Figure 6.1), and subsequently the private radio station announcer would "interrupt your regularly scheduled programming to bring you this important announcement." Of course, patrol cars would have to keep the radio tuned in for this to work. But when a crime was being committed, police cruisers were given the advantage of being able to arrive on the scene before the criminals got away. The radio revolutionized law enforcement operations. There was only one problem with the system described here – since it was a one-way radio, the officer would have to reply back to headquarters using the following methods:

- Operating poor portable transceivers that resembled telephones, which were bulky and didn't transmit very far

- Utilizing telephone call boxes on the street

- Physically going to the station to notify the desk sergeant

The described system did enable the police station desk sergeant to maintain one-way contact with radio-equipped cruisers, but the system was not particularly reliable. In the mid to late 1930s, two-way radios emerged and a limited number of patrol vehicles and motorcycles were equipped with the two-way system, permitting the officers in the field and the supervisor at the station to communicate. During the Great Depression with the popularity of home radios as the primary source of family entertainment, the public developed an interest in listening to police transmissions. Even though the government provided the police with special frequencies of their own, radio manufacturers produced radios with the police frequencies right on the dial. In fact, a lot of common police radio jargon, such as "Calling all cars" and "That is all" spawned a series of popular catch phrases adopted by the public.

FIGURE 6.1: *Radio broadcaster from the 1930s.*

Resource - As a sergeant for the Los Angeles Police Department in the early 1930s, Jesse Rosenquist was one of the world's first police radio dispatchers. He had no idea, though, that by broadcasting calls over the airwaves he would achieve such recognition. Not only was it the phrases he repeated, but also how he enunciated his last name (ROSE-en-quist) at the end of a transmission.

Later, CBS Radio Network formed "Calling All Cars" with Sergeant Rosenquist providing the voiceovers. No surviving original audio is left of the broadcasts, but copies of the show are still available. To listen to his recordings, go to

http://harrymarnell.net/rosenquist.htm.

By the 1940s, the advances of radio technology had reached the point where most police and fire agencies were using two-way radio systems. The more modern versions of police radio systems were first developed in the 1960s, but general use in the field began during the 1970s. These versions allowed multiple communication channels to be scanned rapidly, and added the capability of being able to switch from channel to channel for two-way transmissions. Officers would insert a quartz crystal for each frequency in order to be tuned to the four or more channels available. Each of the crystals cost $5 to $7, which eventually became very expensive to upkeep. By the end of the decade, this technology was already becoming outdated and crystals were no longer necessary. A keypad was also later installed to enter and save all frequencies.

Public Safety Dispatcher

The **public safety dispatcher (PSD)** serves as first-line communicator who answers all calls of service from the public, establishes the priorities of the call, and follows through with the necessary safety precautions. This information can be processed a number of ways. Sometimes, it involves relaying incidents; other times, it involves maintaining the status of all units. Dispatchers are judged by their communications ability.

Depending on the size of the organization, a dispatcher may have many roles or the task may be divided among several people. Typically, a dispatch center may receive a phone call, a text message, an email, or even a CB radio transmission in which an incident requires police, medical, or fire personnel. In some agencies, there is a call center receiving this information, which is then typed in and transmitted over a computer to a radio dispatcher. In small agencies, one person may take the phone call and dispatch the field units. The dispatcher will collect information from the caller and verbally dispatch or perhaps send the information to the field through a digital text transmission. A dispatcher's responsibility is to rely information to police officers and *not* give commands on where to go or what to do.

So what is a typical distress call like? Normally, the radio dispatcher (see Figure 6.2) scans the **computer assisted dispatch** monitor, commonly referred to as **CAD**, for unassigned calls. When one is found, a link is made between emergency responders. Sounds simple enough, but the dispatcher must be watchful of every transmission. With time for repetition being a luxury that often cannot be afforded, it rests upon the dispatcher to translate a broadcast accurately the first time.

Often, the dispatch center will receive multiple calls from one location. One party may report a petty dispute between two people living together with mild threats involved, for example, the destruction of personal property. The other party may report physical violence perhaps constituting the crime of assault; a neighbor may report the disturbance as a loud party. Good dispatchers must use their instincts and constantly update field units as information is developed. Even though resources are limited and there are constant competing priorities, it is better to send help when it is not needed than not send help when it is actually necessary. The proficiency on the dispatcher's part directly bears upon the welfare of every officer in the field. From handling field units' requests for back-up to coordinating a number of field officers' calls, the dispatcher is a center cog to the law enforcement machine.

FIGURE 6.2: *A dispatcher looks over the CAD system for incoming calls.*

Multitasking Duties

Due to the non-stop action atmosphere of a dispatching operation, it is not uncommon to juggle multiple calls at the same time. In fact, listening while performing various tasks or talking while operating dispatching equipment all at the same time is perfectly normal. A necessary requirement for a successful PSD is having a tolerance for stress. Dispatchers perform under arduous conditions, which include:

- Working under time pressure

- Performing duties with high visibility of crisis situations, tragedies, and emergencies

- Maintaining focus and concentration while being frequently interrupted

- Maintaining composure against extreme pressure without delay

- Memorizing codes for complete accuracy

- Recalling geographical locations and coordinates

Dispatchers must maintain their composure, despite dealing with difficult or sensitive circumstances. For example, imagine sitting in front of a CAD while consulting an abused wife fearing her husband's return, dispatching an ambulance to a different scene, verifying a driver's license information from a traffic stop, all while sitting in one location for eight straight hours and missing a lunch break.

It takes a special type of person to meet the demands of public safety communications, but this job position is growing steadily. In 2008, employment for police, fire, and ambulance dispatchers reached 99,900. The Bureau for Labor Statistics (BLS) predicts that in 2018 that figure will increase to 117,700.

Ⓡ

Resource - Research the Bureau of Labor Statistics for job descriptions and information on Police, Fire, and Ambulance Dispatchers.

http://www.bls.gov/ooh/office-and-administrative-support/police-fire-and-ambulance-dispatchers.htm#tab-1

Maintaining Pleasantries

Since the PSD is essentially the conductor for radio service, he or she sets the tempo and tone for the call. Expressions are mirrored, and a bad attitude can make an emergency situation worse if tempers flare and get out of control. Sometimes, a script will be provided by the police department for routine situations or dispatchers might create their own checklists of what to say or ask in various situations.

Personal names and conversation should not to be a part of radio traffic. Codes, short standard phrases, and even badge numbers should be used instead. Professional transmissions should use a minimum amount of words. If additional or side information is needed, it should be done through a different channel.

Another etiquette tip involves pausing briefly during long transmissions. This break in the conversation allows officers to comprehend the feedback and determine if additional assistance is needed. But, most importantly, a dispatcher who remains calm, speaks clearly, and transmits information concisely will reduce response time for law enforcement.

CASE STUDY

Dispatchers Are the Lifelines to the Street

Often during the dispatcher's shift, an officer will engage in a vehicle pursuit with a suspect. This type of situation becomes very stressful. The officer in the pursuit is busy watching the occupants in the vehicle, avoiding traffic collisions by having intersections cleared by other officers, and giving exact directions over the police radio – which includes knowing the names of each street the suspect is using.

During all this, the dispatcher is listening to the officer. The officer's traffic may be difficult to hear and understand due to the officer's adrenaline and the sirens and traffic in the background. Depending on the speed of the suspect vehicle and the area of familiarity with the officer, the officer may not be able to provide the directions to the dispatcher. The dispatcher is responsible for locating the street names and ensuring that the officer is giving the correct directions. Once the dispatcher confirms the directions, he or she must "parrot back" or repeat the information to the responding officers with a calm and clear tone.

A situation that has occurred on numerous occasions involves officers driving in a pursuit who subsequently become involved in traffic accidents with the suspects, other officers, or citizens. In some cases, officers have been attacked by suspects and require emergency help. Often, the officer involved is consumed with other activities so the officer may provide inaccurate directions to the dispatcher. For this reason, it is imperative for the dispatcher to follow the direction of the pursuit and ensure that the officers are giving accurate directions. If the dispatcher does this during the pursuit, it could result in saving a life.

Although many calls are routine, the safety of the public and the emergency responders is often a function of a skilled dispatcher with a professional, calm, and thoughtful demeanor.

Technology Systems in Communication

There are several different types of radios used in emergency services. Classified as analog/digital, conventional/trunked, repeated systems, and portable/vehicle based all serve different purposes but enhance operations. This section will discuss the function of those radios, as well as their features and benefits.

Analog Versus Digital

Public safety communications and equipment have evolved dramatically over the last 20 years. Radio systems based on analog technologies have been phased out and replaced with digital technology, although some agencies still use a combination of both. The difference lies in signal strength. In regards to analog radio, the signal gradually weakens the farther the user is from the transmitter. Whereas with digital, there is no gradual fade but it instead maintains the strength for longer distances before dropping off suddenly. Even with all the advancements digital has, it is not immune to power failures. Generators offer little power so incident reports are handwritten on cards and then stamped with the current time.

Conventional Versus Trunked

Conventional operating systems are basic analog systems where the user manually selects from a limited number of channels. Trunked systems are more sophisticated and utilize the available channels better. Radio channels are permanently assigned to certain groups. For example, the FCC has licensed 10 public safety radio frequencies to a single town. The system might have one channel for emergency dispatch, two channels for medical, three channels for fire, and four channels for police. The dispatcher has access to all frequencies so when an urgent situation arises, he or she can radio any of the emergency units. While it is possible to have more groups than frequencies (since not all users access the system simultaneously), a disaster plan should cover the additional traffic as needed.

Many who are accustomed to conventional systems find transitioning difficult as they have gotten used to manually selecting from a limited number of channels and checking for channel activity. Others find trunked systems simpler because they perform a number of functions at high speeds, including automatic frequency assignment, verification of calls administered, and regrouping of users. As with all technological advancements, people who know the program would rather not relearn a new system; however, proper and frequent training is a must in this digital age.

Repeater Systems

Most networks need repeater systems to further extend their range of operation. Functioning just as it sounds, a repeater listens to radio traffic and repeats it. The message can travel great distances – to another radio or to another repeater – until it reaches its destination. Modern repeaters are able to receive signals on one frequency and simultaneously retransmit on a second frequency, called **half-duplex operation**. Smaller, mobile repeaters are available, usually mounted inside a vehicle, in areas where range is troublesome. These devices are great for emergency scenarios because units can still be linked to other networks virtually anywhere.

Operating a Field Radio

The standard police radio has a volume, scan, manual, and program feature with other buttons, switches, and knobs to control additional functions designed to receive a range of frequencies. Older radios may have a squelch adjustment knob; however, most modern radios have internal control settings or adaptive squelch so that a squelch adjustment knob is no longer necessary. A public safety radio works by searching programmed frequencies for a transmission. If no transmission is detected, it moves to the next frequency in a constant loop at an average of 100 frequencies or more per second. The radio's squelch setting will stop once a transmission is detected. After a transmission is complete, it resumes scanning again automatically. If they desire, officers have the capability to stop scanning all channels and have their radio on one primary channel for communications. Most modern public safety radios also have a delay function that has the radio pause shortly so as not to miss a reply.

Generally, there are two types of radios used in the field: personal portable (for example, handheld) and vehicle-based models (mounted inside a car or other modes of transportation).

There are a variety of personal portable radios (see Figure 6.3) with varying degrees of power and functionality. The smaller the radio, generally the less power and broadcast range it will have. Typically, radios are worn on a belt. They have a speaker that can be heard in close proximity.

Some models come with a distress button that, when activated, alerts dispatchers to the location of where

FIGURE 6.3: *Responder communicating on a handheld radio.*

the transmission is coming from and sends all units to the officer's location. While seldom used, the red button is vital when an officer is down or has other critical emergencies. The concave feature prevents the user from accidentally pressing it.

Many radios have shoulder microphones, which allow the main section of the radio to remain on the belt and provide the officer with a small shoulder mounted microphone that can be easily used with one hand.

They are usually a preferred means of communication since they keep the officers' hands more free than having to take a large handheld radio off the duty belt, and they provide clearer sound and are easier to access.

Earplugs are used for discreet communications. When responding to calls, officers often have to run a records check on a person who may be wanted for criminal offenses. If using a handheld radio, the dispatcher's transmissions will broadcast through the speaker and provide the suspect with an opportunity to overhear. Soft, clear-colored earpieces offer a private communication between the officer and the dispatcher to prevent the suspect from knowing that an arrest is imminent, as well as keeping the officer's hands free to initiate an arrest if necessary.

Vehicle born radios are much more powerful because they are larger in physical size and their power source comes from the vehicle's electrical system. The antenna is longer and often mounted on the vehicle roof for more range. The sound quality is better since the vehicle can have larger and heavier speakers mounted. Located between the driver and passenger seat, scanners are capable of memorizing the frequencies divided into banks and channels. Channels are memory locations where frequencies are stored. Each is numbered and has the ability to be separated from other channels in case one needs to be excluded. Banks organize these channels into bundles. On some models, there is a feature to have connectors added to record the activity so that nothing is missed.

FIGURE 6.4: *A Police radio mounted on top of a motorcycle.*

Radio equipment will have slight differences from a patrol car to a motorcycle (see Figure 6.4). While the radio device is still located in the "middle" of the vehicle, most drivers nowadays will have a helmet radio transmission, thus greatly improving communication. In the past, patrolmen and women had to utilize a hand-held microphone while driving the bike with the other free hand. The modern systems are not only clearer but also far safer. This technique becomes incredibly useful during a high-speed pursuit when an officer is trying to radio dispatch while weaving through traffic. Other perks typically include a noise-canceling microphone, push-to-talk button on the handlebar, speakers in the headgear, and an interface with the police radio system.

Radio Procedure

The FCC (Federal Communications Commission) is the oversight agency for all airwave-based communications. The FCC determines the licenses, assignments, and rules with radio frequencies. It restricts transmissions to a minimum amount of time, regardless of their nature. Voice and data are monitored to ensure that their practices are being followed.

In general, users should follow these recommendations:

- Keep unnecessary radio traffic off the air; only public safety related information must be shared.

- Speak in a professional tone at all times.

- Refrain from broadcasting any kind of unessential reports or unnecessary information.

- Never use profane, indecent, or obscene language.

In addition to these recommendations, it is important to maintain a calm professional tone and clear diction since communication may be made under disturbing or stressful conditions.

Radio Etiquette

When it comes to "on the air" communication, **radio etiquette** means keeping communications short and simple, yet descriptive enough for the receiver to fully understand the message. Only essential information should be communicated. Officers need to listen to what is being transmitted on the other end and rehearse mentally what they need to say next. This practice lessens the likelihood of miscommunication and those dreaded "um" moments.

Another important etiquette tip: never interrupt! Sure, this may seem obvious, but it happens frequently, due to lack of attention and in some cases because of an emergency. Keep in mind there are always "never say never" situations. Although you do not want to disrupt radio traffic, in cases where an officer needs immediate assistance, an interruption may be necessary. Interruptions can easily be minimized by listening for a beep at the end of the last transmission before speaking. Most radios have this function. Another etiquette rule for keeping messages brief is not to release the microphone button before you are done talking. Doing so cuts off the last syllable or so of your transmission, requiring the person who is receiving the message to ask you to repeat it to verify what you said.

Keeping transmissions brief is a safety rule as well as an etiquette rule. When the transmissions are short, the frequency remains open longer for emergency radio traffic.

Modern radios have very good reception; however, it is normal to have to request a "10-9" (repeat message) from time to time when transmissions are garbled or the information relayed may need clarification.

Even the most experienced radio operators sometimes make a mistake. When either the officer or dispatcher makes an error or breaks a rule of etiquette, do not waste airtime pointing out the mistake. Resist the urge to reply with sarcasm or disrespect. A professional discussion at the station after the shift is more appropriate for correcting errors.

It is reasonable to conduct all radio communications as if someone else were listening. The FCC regulates all activity that is transmitted on licensed frequencies. They decide who in the U.S. is able to use which frequency and for which purpose by administering licenses to specific stations. FCC field supervisors are assigned to monitor radio traffic so that no unprofessional transmissions waste airtime. Be sure that you do not cover an emergency transmission with a joke or prank, and that you do not use language that will result in your agency being visited by an FCC investigator who has the authority to terminate your frequency license.

Another audience to keep in mind when transmitting on your public safety radio will be the everyday civilian. Radio scanners are not illegal to own, but in some states there are guidelines for ownership. For citizens who do not own a scanner, certain websites offer live police feeds made open for public listening. So while police officers and other emergency personnel communicate over these frequencies, just about anyone, including criminals, may tune in to hear any activity that is transmitted.

Resource - For practice, listen to one of the many websites offering free live feeds of police radio and sample what it is like to listen to one. This will offer a sense of pace of a typical radio conversation. Then refer to a handbook to further understand what codes (if any) are being used for what purpose.

CASE STUDY

Scanner Codes

When police agencies began to use radios as a tool, there were problems with interference. Static made the first few seconds of a received call distorted. So in 1937, The **Association of Public-Safety Communications Officials International (APCO)** originally created a set of codes with the prefix "10" cleverly referred as **10-codes**. Most people know that 10-4 means "copy," even if they have never picked up a transmitter.

This code language soon changed how communication was used on the radio. A preliminary code followed by the main code reduced the likelihood of interrupted or misinterpreted messages. This process also accelerated reporting time between the dispatcher and officer. "We literally only have seconds when we're on a scene to make determinations of what resources we need," said Lieutenant David Knowles in an interview from the Bernalillo County Sheriff's Office in Albuquerque.

Police codes usually involve a combination of digits, with numbers starting with a 10- or 11- , and the numbers serve to abbreviate conditions or commands that are familiar to police officers. So if an officer radios back a 10-22 to the dispatcher or another officer, this will be interpreted as the message to be disregarded. Other numbers are used for specific crimes – for example, 187 means homicide or 207 means kidnapping. Then there are radio codes that apply colors or acronyms. Officers commonly use Code Purple to signal gang activity. Another example might occur if a security guard witnessed a suspect shooting a target with a 9mm; this would be referred as ADW, meaning assault with a deadly weapon.

A **phonetic alphabet** is used since certain letters sound alike over the air, such as "B" and "P" or "C" and "Z." Specific words (usually names) that share the same first letter not only help avoid confusion but also can be fun to practice reciting. As a caution, there is no universal police code system, but the following list references common examples.

TYPICAL MILITARY ALPHABET CODE		TYPICAL POLICE ALPHABET CODE	
A	Alpha	A	Adam
B	Bravo	B	Boy
C	Charlie	C	Charles
D	Delta	D	David
E	Echo	E	Edward
F	Foxtrot	F	Frank
G	Gulf	G	George
H	Hotel	H	Henry
I	India	I	Ida
J	Juliet	J	John
K	Kilo	K	King
L	Lima	L	Lincoln
M	Mike	M	Mary
N	November	N	Nora
O	Oscar	O	Ocean
P	Papa	P	Paul
Q	Quebec	Q	Queen
R	Romeo	R	Robert
S	Sierra	S	Sam
T	Tango	T	Tom
U	Uniform	U	Union
V	Victor	V	Victor
W	Whiskey	W	William
X	X-ray	X	X-ray
Y	Yankee	Y	Young
Z	Zulu	Z	Zebra

Remember that the previous table represents only general examples. It is always best to learn and follow your own department's radio codes and policies. Later we will discuss how some radio codes may become outdated and only heard when watching syndicated police television dramas.

If you need to memorize certain lists, the best method is to use flash cards and practice. These learning aides make the process simple and the information easy to retain. Eventually, the codes will become second nature, given enough practice and discipline. You might try stating your name using the police phonetic alphabet, or try the name of a classmate. Practice reading license plates phonetically as you drive down the road. Listening to a police scanner at home is also a good way to immerse yourself in radio etiquette and become comfortable with communicating in code.

Resource - Test your basic police jargon and code knowledge with the TLC quiz available at

http://tlc.discovery.com/games-quizzes/police-women-jargon/
and http://tlc.discovery.com/games-quizzes/decoding-police-code/

CASE STUDY

Securing for Emergency Radio Traffic

The practice of proper radio communication by officers is essential and life saving. Many times an officer will be dispatched to an emergency situation with little or no detailed information on what to expect upon arrival. Depending on the seriousness of the situation, the officer may request to "clear the channel." This message informs the dispatcher as well as other officers that the channel they are using is restricted to communications only relating to this particular situation. Clearing the channel allows the officer to reduce radio traffic so that only critical information is broadcast and any emergency transmission will be heard.

For example, this practice might be used when an officer is dispatched to a suspect with a gun call. When the officer arrives on scene and observes the suspect with a gun, the officer may tell the dispatcher "code 33." The dispatcher will repeat this traffic to other officers. Good radio procedure in this type of situation is critical. The officer must speak clearly so that other officers monitoring the call can understand what is occurring and how to respond.

Using codes allows officers and dispatchers to spend less time on the radio and in the event that the suspect is also listening to a scanner, it's less likely that the suspect will know what the responders are doing.

In an officer hostage situation, when the suspect is holding a gun on an officer, the officer may keep the transmission button on the radio depressed so other officers can monitor the situation, while the rescue teams move to another frequency.

The Push to Plain Language

Over the past decade, there has been a lot of deliberation about whether or not the 10-code system should be done away with and replaced with plain speech. Since there is no universal code system, one concern is that ambiguous language could create confusion for those outside the jurisdiction. The original purpose of 10-codes was to shorten orders and provide safety. However, the argument is that the system that worked in 1937 might not work as well today. Departments that have created a personal code system can sometime create confusion through areas with multiple police agencies.

The notion of plain speech was developed by the **Federal Emergency Management Agency (FEMA)** in order to resolve potential disorder or confusion during large-scale disasters, similar to what occurred during 9/11. Other agencies, such as the Department of Homeland Security's (DHS) **National Incident Management System (NIMS)** and APCO – the creator of the 10-codes – were in agreement with this decision. Due to the after-action reports citing inconsistent, unreliable communication that often resulted in poor performance, a sense of change seemed to be appropriate. So by late 2005, DHS required plain English to be spoken when multi-jurisdictional response teams, especially first responders (see Figure 6.5), arrive at an emergency.

FIGURE 6.5: *An emergency response team member talks on a radio during a disaster.*

Plain Language Debate

In the early stages of radio communication, public safety personnel had a limited number of frequencies that were available to their respective areas. So when technology progressed with numerous frequencies and with the growth of public safety workers, the lack of a universal code hampered the effective use of radio communication. For example, APCO lists the police code 10-37 to mean "run with lights and siren," "your message was delivered," "false alarm, premises were occupied," "contact officer," or "disturbance." It can be confusing, indeed.

In a statement issued by APCO, "...using plain speech is a simple remedy to reduce communication failures. It is essential to functional interoperability across all jurisdictions." The case highlighting how ineffective code use could be occurred after the mass confusion during the World Trade Center attacks. In fact, the various forces that arrived at the Pentagon – including local police departments, Pentagon police, and the FBI – were each communicating in their own individual agency 10-codes.

The confusion hit a tipping point after Hurricane Katrina. Multiple federal, state, and local agencies tried to collaborate, but were unable to speak a common radio language. The need to communicate quickly *and* effectively can mean the difference between life and death. So following federal recommendations, 19 states decided to change their communication to what will be referred to as "plain talk" or "clear text" at the end of 2009. Several large agencies, including the Dallas Police Department, have already made the leap to plain English.

The damage of miscommunication also can happen on local premises. One often-used example was a 2005 case in Missouri. While on a tour of duty, an officer informed a dispatcher of an abandoned state highway patrol car with its door open. Upon examination, he found the patrolman shot eight times with a rifle and left for dead in a ditch. Had the dispatcher radioed a 10-33, which in her department meant "officer down," the Missouri Highway Patrol would have interpreted that as "traffic backup." But since the dispatcher sent a call in plain English, state troopers from miles away responded, and the officer survived.

Currently a Personal Choice

So far, plain talk is only necessary during mutual aid scenarios, although it is strongly encouraged for daily operations as well. Retraining public-safety officials has already begun. Kevin Willett, an instructional coordinator at Public Safety Training Consultants (PSTC), suggests that a one-day class lasting between four and eight hours would be sufficient. A company that has been training first responders for 10 years, PSTC realizes that a "new system" is something that many departments are reluctant to adopt. Although a training class might only last several hours, it could take a couple of years for officer to get the hang of it.

The question remains: Why are codes still largely used despite the pressure to switch? One major reason is the concern for an officer's safety when disclosing sensitive information. Another is simply due to the difficulty that agencies might have in disregarding codes and signals that have been in place for decades. Yet another reason might be that codes solidify the professionalism of police.

"There is still a need for police codes," argued Sergeant Jack Richards spokesman for the Ventura Police Department to its local paper, The Ventura County Star. This is true in the case of highly emotional situations. Verbal communication can easily become distorted, whereas a set of instructions through code alleviates the stress. An alternative suggestion has been to reduce the hundred-plus service call codes to a more moderate number that is uniform for all public safety personals.

The debate remains a hot topic, and it is best (for the time being, at least) for the change be left as an option. Whatever the fate of 10-codes may be, plain, simple language seems to work best during major catastrophes, while code language is best used for daily operations. While some shorthand phrases such as "What's your 20?" meaning "What's your location?" are still regularly used by departments that have done away with the code system, it remains a double-edged sword.

CASE STUDY

Communicating in Code

The 10-codes remain important when it is necessary to communicate with other officers confidentially. Often, an officer is in a situation where there is a need to communicate information with other officers or the dispatch center, and he does not want the general public to under stand the communication.

An example occurred when an officer responded to a vehicle collision where a drunk driver hit two victims, a mother and daughter. The mother was killed instantly upon impact; the daughter suffered severe burns that were eventually fatal. Police shut the streets down to conduct the investigation. The woman's husband was driving by saw his wife's vehicle and realized it had been involved in the collision. He contacted the officers at the perimeter to find out what was going on.

By using the code system, the officers at the scene were able to communicate to the officers dealing with the husband what the situation was without immediately revealing to the husband that his wife was killed and his daughter was severely injured. Had the man found out at the scene, he might have rushed into the middle of the investigation and destroyed evidence. There was also no professional support for dealing with grief available to him at the scene.

Acting on the coded information sent from the investigators, the perimeter officers arranged to take him to the local hospital where he would learn the tragic news. During a critical incident, it is important to keep the public as calm as possible. Imagine the situation at the scene if the father had learned through the police radio that his wife was killed, daughter injured, and the drunk driver who caused the accident was 10 feet away from him.

New Technologies Around the Corner

Technology constantly evolves. Scientists and engineers are creating or improving every piece of technology equipment used by public safety on a routine basis. Often, emerging technologies developed for the military are adapted to civilian use for law enforcement. Global positioning systems (GPS) are now mounted in vehicles so that dispatchers may alert the closest unit to the scene. Some features likely to be available soon could include radio-linked devices that send an alert when an officer remains motionless for too long and voice-activated intercom systems inside automobiles that allow hands-free communication.

In March 2010, a communications software company created an app for BlackBerry (others are in development) smartphones to function as a radio handset. By using the wireless Internet connection and tuning in to supported radio channels, the Mobile Communicator is yet another tool that first responders can use. It works across all cellular carriers and does not require any technological upgrades. Whether the device becomes a game-changer or a major flop, however, is yet to be determined, pending extensive field tests. Often, good ideas are found to be impractical when tested in real-life scenarios.

Summary

The introduction of mobile technology, such as the two-way radio, into law enforcement has aided in improving response time dramatically. New radio technology has evolved, from very simple functionality to store and scan multiple radio frequencies. Early radios were large, expensive contraptions that operated inconsistently with limited range. Thanks to technological advances, systems have become simpler to use, smaller and lighter in size, and they have increased emergency responders' ability to respond quickly.

Radios are regulated to make sure that regulatory guidelines are followed. The Federal Communications Commission states that all radio broadcasts should be restricted to a minimum transmission time. To help with minimum transmissions, sets of codes facilitate communication over police radios, reduce talk-time among personnel, and provide safety for police and dispatchers. However, some codes are being replaced with simple English.

With regard to large-scale disasters, plain English rather than codes does seem to provide better communication for users. With the recent disasters, such as 9/11 and Hurricane Katrina, confusion hindered the performances of different crisis response teams since codes varied from agency to agency. Federal and some local agencies have issued a mandatory "plain talk" order for those communicating over the radio when there is an emergency situation that needs multiple jurisdiction assistance.

Checking on the status of dispatched calls and maintaining radio contact with field units is all in a day's work for a public safety dispatcher. Dispatchers can be summarized in terms of three principal functions: call taking, transmitting information, and utilizing equipment. A dispatcher plays a vital role in the safety of law enforcement and the public.

Discussion Questions

1. What other radio technology advancements could be created given enough time?

2. Cite the pros and cons of police code usage.

3. Besides the police radio, what other types of communication tools and equipment are used by officers and dispatchers?

4. Explain how stress and high-risk situations can hinder your radio communications.

5. Explain the multiple tasks a dispatcher performs while on duty for a law enforcement agency.

6. What is the primary function of the FCC and how does it review radios?

Key Terms

10-Codes: Properly known as 10-signals, these code words are used to represent common phrases in law enforcement.

Association of Public-Safety Communications Officials International: Founded in 1935, it is the world's largest organization dedicated to public safety telecommunications.

AM broadcaster: With regards to radio communication, this was a radio person who helped mediate calls from the police department to patrol officers; this was done before the invention of modern police scanners and digital systems.

Computer Assisted Dispatch (CAD): The machine that dispatchers use to relay field service to emergency service.

Federal Communications Commission (FCC): An independent agency of the United States government that regulates the usage of radios.

Federal Emergency Management Agency (FEMA): An agency that coordinates the response to a disaster that has occurred and overwhelms the resources of local and state authorities.

Frequency: A channel on which a transmission is to be used.

Half-duplex operation: A communication method in which transmissions and receptions can occur in either direction but not at the same time.

Interoperability: Refers to the ability of diverse networks, or in this case frequencies, that work together so that officials may correspond immediately.

National Incident Management System (NIMS): The first-ever federal standardized approach to incident management and response among various federal, state, and local agencies.

Phonetic alphabet: A list of words used to substitute for letters so that when a person is transmitting a message by radio, it helps clarify communications due to letters sounding alike over the air.

Public Safety Dispatcher (PSD): First-line communicator who answers all calls of service from the public, establishes the priorities of the call, and follows through with the necessary safety precautions.

Police scanner: A radio scanner that has been wired to listen to police broadcasts. In essence, they are radio receivers that search for wireless signal transmissions.

Radio etiquette: The ethical and professional way that communication is done through the airwaves.

Trunked radio system: A complex type of computer-controlled radio system with a minimum amount of frequencies. Many people, however, can carry many conversations over only a few distinct frequencies.

Courtroom Documents and Written Communications

Key module concepts:

- Compare and contrast the courtroom players in civil versus criminal courts

- Details that must be included on a forensic report

- How to fill out a form used in the court system

- Basic information needed in a case brief

Introduction

The court system tends to have a language all its own. This module will help define the terminology of the courtroom and some of the types of cases you will encounter.

It's important to always be aware that the written documents you produce in your daily job in the criminal justice world might become legal documents used in the court system (see Figure 7.1). Because of this, there are certain safeguards that must be included on every written document you produce. These written documents include forms you fill out and written reports that contain more blanks to fill in, as well as information written in a narrative form much like telling a story.

FIGURE 7.1: *The agent testifying in this case has a professional appearance and is referencing visual aids in (his/her) testimony*

These documents are often used in court and might be critiqued by attorneys. You will have to explain these reports to jurors who are common laypersons, often several years after you created the documents. There are statements to add to these documents that might help you when you discuss them later in court.

A *briefing* is a common document done for use in the courtroom, and it consists of a simple summary of the case. Briefings, by their very nature, must be simple, brief, and to the point.

Many of your reports and forms will be electronically completed. It's important to use grammar and spell check on these documents. You may also have reports and forms to fill out by hand. You must write legibly and write large enough so that the form will be legible when it is copied.

Ask Yourself

- *Who is the final audience for your reports?*

- *What tactics do attorneys use to discredit your reports?*

- *How can you write a better report?*

Legal Terminology

The court professionals have their own language for use in legal matters and in the courtroom. To make matters even more confusing, the terminology changes for the different courtroom players, depending upon whether the case is civil or criminal. Let's look at the differences between civil and criminal trials.

Remember that as a criminal justice professional, all of your reports are **forensic reports**, meaning your reports are written for use in a court of law.

Many people will read your reports in preparation for a trial. These people include attorneys, police, investigators, and any assistants who help these professionals. The ultimate audiences for your reports are the laypersons of the jury. Reports need to be understood by these laypersons. They need to be written in plain English without using a lot of special jargon. Sometimes, however, special terminology cannot be avoided.

You may choose to explain your terminology in the body of the report. If you don't explain your terms, the attorneys will ask you to explain them when you testify in court, so be prepared to be able to give a simple verbal explanation of your terminology when asked.

Your report is a written description of what you *did* as your role in the specific case. If it is not written down, you did *not* do it, even if you actually did. Recording everything you do is vital in a forensic report. From the attorneys' standpoint, if you did not record that you did something, this means that you did not do it, and you cannot defend yourself when you do not record something you know that you did. A good rule to remember is that if you did not record something in your report, it was not done.

Recording what you did not do, and why you did not do it, is also important. For example, you may have been called to a domestic violence complaint. You were able to interview the husband, and you recorded that information in your report. You did not interview the wife because she was unconscious at the scene, and she was taken to the hospital by paramedics. In your report, you recorded that you did not interview the wife because she was unconscious and was taken to the hospital for medical treatment while unconscious.

This domestic violence case may not go to trial for years. By that time, you will forget the details of this specific case. If there are any problems in your report, the attorneys will try to **discredit** it. This is a tactic where the attorneys try to make you look incompetent in general because of mistakes you made or something you failed to do as documented (or not documented) in your report. The attorneys hope this tactic will make the jury disregard everything you did because other areas you handled may also have been inaccurate or incompetently done. If you fail to include why you did not interview the wife, the attorneys could twist the scenario around to make you look incompetent because you didn't mention her and did not interview her. If your report clearly states why you did not interview her, the attorneys cannot use this information to make you look bad.

Who's Who?

The initial part of preparing written documents and preparing your testimony for court is to understand who is who. There are two major branches of the court system: criminal and civil Those are further divided into jurisdictions, such as federal versus state, and sometimes into various specialty courts. In this module, we will explore the differences between criminal and civil courts because the terminology of who is who is different in these two types of cases. Let's look at criminal cases first. **Criminal cases** are where a crime has been committed that violates a statute of the jurisdiction. For example, if a bad guy, John Doe, breaks a state law, it is a crime against the state, and the case will be named "State v. J. Doe."

Criminal Courtroom Players

You may recall that initially the bad guy in criminal cases is called the suspect. After he is charged, when he is preparing to go to court, he is termed the **defendant**. The term changes because he is now defending himself against the state's (or other criminal jurisdiction's) case against him. Remember, that this is a bit confusing. The state must prove the defendant is guilty, so the responsibility for proving guilt beyond a reasonable doubt rests on the state. The defense team counters the accusations and tries to plant the seed of doubt in the jurors. The defendant is considered to be innocent until proven guilty. In this module, we will call the prosecuting agency "the state," keeping in mind this may actually be a federal, county, or local agency. The defendant's attorneys are the **defense attorneys**. The state's attorneys are the prosecuting attorneys, district attorneys, or **prosecutors**.

Both the defense and prosecution can have designated investigators. This is important because of a rule that prohibits witnesses from watching a trial. Witnesses must be separated from the jury. Witnesses also are not allowed to hear the testimony of other witnesses. The lone exception is the designated investigator who may sit through all the testimony, even though the investigator may be a witness.

Similar to most cases, the trial includes a judge, bailiff, and court reporter. In some cases, there may be a jury if the defendant requests a jury trial.

Civil Courtroom Players

Civil courts are where one party sues another for an alleged wrong-doing or alleged negligence. These cases are generally not crimes, or if they are crimes, the criminal aspect is tried or plea-bargained in the criminal courts first, and then there is a civil lawsuit over the wrong-doing of the crime. For example, the bad guy is tried for murder (the crime) in criminal courts. If the family is upset enough with the bad guy, they can sue him for their loss and suffering in civil court for wrongful death.

FIGURE 7.2: *This is a typical depiction of what a trial in progress will look like. Trials are adversarial with each side trying its best to win the case.*

A civil case may also be a much more minor offense. For example, Jane Doe is walking through the aisle of her local convenience store. Earlier someone broke a bottle of cooking oil in the aisle and the store failed to notice it or clean it up. Doe slips, falls, and breaks her ankle. She may decide to sue the store, alleging they were negligent because they knew or should have known there was a hazard in the aisle.

These civil cases are named according to the names of the persons involved, like "Doe v. Smith." The **plaintiff** is the person who is suing the other party, much like the prosecution side of a criminal case. The party being sued, who is accused of the wrongdoing, is the defendant, just like in a criminal case. The defendant must defend what he did to cause injury or harm to the plaintiff. The defendant's attorneys are **defense attorneys**, and the plaintiff's attorneys are the **plaintiff's attorneys** (see Figure 7.2).

Resource - Terminology used in the courtroom can be confusing. It's a good idea to get familiar with the legal jargon before you might need it. You can find a good comprehensive online dictionary of legal terminology at the Witness Justice organization. They promote victim's rights, and it's a great site to bookmark for future reference.

http://www.witnessjustice.org/justicesystems/terminology.cfm/

The Criminal Trial Process

Criminal trials can be summarized by saying they are an effort by the state to prove a criminal charge beyond a reasonable doubt. To do this, the state must prove a case with evidence and testimony. The process involves calling witnesses to the stand, introducing evidence, and making opening and closing arguments to a judge or jury to make the most compelling case.

A criminal case has many elements that occur before a jury is seated. Some of these include evidentiary hearings, where the defense will try to convince the judge that evidence in the prosecutions case should not be admitted into the trial because it was collected unconstitutionally, and hearings involving the mental condition of the defendant to determine if they are fit to stand trial.

All criminal trials begin with an opening statement from the state and the defense.

The process is structured to hear both sides with the prosecution bringing its case first, facing cross examination by the defense, and then the defense making its case with cross examination by the state.

The process is concluded with closing statements by both sides.

The Civil Trial Process

Often, the criminal court process seems to be overemphasized for criminal justice students, because police officers are more involved with criminal incidents. It is important, however, to have a basic understanding of civil courts as well, because anyone can sue for anything, and a police report may get called into the civil trial process.

For example, you may have been the patrol officer who responded to Jane Doe's 911 call when she fell in the store. Your report is probably simple and to the point, because you had a very small role in the situation. You took Ms. Doe's statement, and possibly Mr. Smith's statement, and the paramedics arrived and took Ms. Doe to the hospital. No crime was committed, so there was not much of a report to write.

Later, you might be called at any part of the litigation process to be interviewed regarding Ms. Doe's fall. In fact, you might end up testifying in civil court about it. You may be confused about the civil courts and why they need you at all.

It is important to understand that a civil case is between two parties who disagree over something. The goal in the civil case is to resolve the disagreement. This resolution may be reached at any point in the **litigation process**, so the case may never get to trial because it was resolved before it got that far. It may also not get resolved at the trial, and may have to go through the appeal process to finally be resolved.

The first step in the civil process occurs when the party who wants to sue visits an attorney with the problem. The attorney investigates the case and makes an attempt to reach a resolution without an actual lawsuit. If there is no resolution at this point and there is a legitimate reason for the suit, the case moves forward.

The civil lawsuit begins when the plaintiff files an official **complaint**. The complaint is a document that explains the situation and why the plaintiff is suing the defendant. The complaint and a summons are served to the defendant to let him know he is being sued. The defendant must respond to the complaint. He has several options as to how to respond, so at this point, he usually gets his own defense attorney who will advise him on how to respond to the initial complaint.

The next step in civil litigation is called **discovery**. This is much like discovery in the criminal process. Reports and evidence regarding the suit are gathered, and persons involved in the situation are interviewed or deposed. A **deposition** is an interview done under oath with both parties' attorneys present. It is a formal interview similar to testifying in court. The person being deposed is sworn in, just like in a courtroom. Court reporters record the deposition, or it may be videotaped. The difference between a deposition and testifying in courts is that there is no judge or jury present at a deposition, and the deposition may be held anywhere; it is not done in the courtroom. The attorneys will question the person in direct cross-examinations just like in a courtroom.

During civil discovery, **interrogatories** may be sent to various persons involved. Interrogatories are simply a set of questions that must be answered in writing and returned to the attorney who sent them.

When the discovery information is complete, there is usually an attempt to reach a **pre-trial settlement**. The pre-trial settlement will keep the case from going to trial. At this point, the attorneys have all the information they will have for the trial, and they can advise their respective clients as to what their chances are of the case being successful or not. If it is in the best interest of the client to settle the case before incurring the expense of a trial, the attorney will recommend a pre-trial settlement, and the case will be finished.

If the civil case is not settled before the trial, it goes to trial. The trial is handled like a criminal trial. The criminal justice professional who is

involved will testify by answering each attorney's questions in the courtroom and explaining his reports when asked. (You'll learn more about testifying in the next module.)

FIGURE 7.3: *Ms. Doe states her case.*

If the trial is over and the parties involved are not satisfied with the verdict, the case may be appealed and go through appellate courts until the case is resolved.

There are different ways that a civil case can be resolved. **Legal remedies** are financial awards given to the plaintiff, otherwise known as being awarded "damages." **Compensatory damages** are moneys paid to compensate for an injury, which may include paying for damages, such as the medical costs incurred by the injured party, plus some agreed-upon sum paid to compensate for pain and suffering.

Before damages are awarded, both parties have a responsibility to **mitigate the damages**. This means that the person who was injured must take steps to minimize the damages. For example, let's say Ms. Doe refused to go to physical therapy after she got her cast off from her broken ankle so that she would have more of a disability, hoping to get more money from the store (see Figure 7.3). Assuming her refusal to cooperate with medical advice comes out during discovery, she could not be compensated for damages incurred from her refusal to mitigate the damage. The fact that she now has a frozen ankle that will not move is her responsibility, and the store is only liable or responsible for the original broken ankle from spilled oil on the floor.

- **Punitive damages** are damages the defendant must pay as a punishment. These damages do not reflect any pain and suffering the plaintiff might have had, but rather they are a punishment of the defendant for his wrongdoing. Punitive damages may also be called *exemplary damages*.

- **Nominal damages** are simply a token amount given to the plaintiff when no harm was done, or no harm can be proven. This amount may be as little as one dollar.

- **Equitable remedies** are non-financial remedies that may not be granted by juries. Only judges can grant equitable remedies. There are two major types of equitable remedies.

  - **Specific performance** is an equitable remedy where the defendant is ordered to do something to correct the situation. For example, the store may be required to have regular inspections of the aisles scheduled.

  - **Injunctions** are another type of equitable remedy where the defendant is ordered to stop doing something. There are different types of injunctions. For example, let's say the store owner is really angry with Ms. Doe for suing him, so he has been calling her and threatening her, and yelling at her when he sees her. He may receive a permanent injunction that forces him to stop his harassment forever.

CASE STUDY

A Valid Lawsuit or Not?

Mr. Christian McGuire lived in a town that required homeowners to remove snow from their public sidewalks within 24 hours of a snowfall. A snowstorm came through, and Mr. McGuire shoveled his sidewalk. Freezing rain occurred after the sidewalk was shoveled. There were no requirements for homeowners regarding ice.

Mrs. Mary Sheehan, an 84-year-old female, was walking on the ice in front of Mr. McGuire's house. She fell and broke her hip. She had an extensive medical history that included osteoporosis (thin bones that break easily). Because of this, Mrs. Sheehan had been instructed by her physician not to walk outdoors unassisted.

Mrs. Sheehan had her hip replaced in the hospital. The pathology report on the removed broken hip described it as being very thin with "extreme osteoporosis." Mrs. Sheehan was recovering well, and was in physical therapy when she became short of breath, collapsed, and died. The autopsy showed she died of a large blood clot in the arteries of her lungs that is a known complication of a hip replacement. The medical examiner stated the cause of death was "Complications of hip fracture due to a fall" with the manner of death stated as an "accident."

Mrs. Sheehan's children were upset by her death and blamed Mr. McGuire for it because he did not remove the ice from his sidewalk. They sued Mr. McGuire for negligence in not removing the ice.

The civil case was not resolved during any of the pre-trial attempts at resolution. The plaintiff's attorney advised Mrs. Sheehan's children that the case would likely not go in their favor, but they insisted on moving forward. At the trial, Mr. McGuire explained how he had shoveled his snow as required, and that there were no requirements regarding how to handle ice on the sidewalk. He showed a receipt dated the day of the fall for salt, which he put on the ice after Mrs. Sheehan's fall to make the sidewalk safe for others.

Mrs. Sheehan's doctor testified, and he showed the jury the medical record that indicated she had severe osteoporosis and doctor's instructions not to go out without someone to help her. He also stated that many patients with this degree of disease could break their hip simply from walking and then fall due to a broken bone. He testified that Mrs. Sheehan was outside in the ice against medical advice, and that it was entirely possible that the hip broke first, and the fall occurred because of the break, and likely had nothing to do with the ice.

The jury did not deliberate for very long. They had Mr. McGuire pay a nominal damage of one dollar to Mrs. Sheehan's children, because there was no proof that Mr. McGuire caused any harm.

Court Forms and Reports

Different courts may have different forms that need to be filled out prior to the court date of the suspect, now the defendant. These forms will vary depending upon the jurisdiction and level of the court. The agency supervisor and attorneys involved will help the police officer with the forms that need to be filled out prior to a trial.

There are some pitfalls to avoid when filling out forms for the court system.

First, any reports you write as a criminal justice professional are considered to be forensic reports or reports written for use in a court of law. The content of the report will depend upon the type of criminal justice job you have and the type of report and case you are reporting. As with forms, there are certain rules to follow to make your report better for the court system, allowing it to stand up to the scrutiny of attorneys.

Rules for Writing Reports

You should create your report in plain English, keeping in mind that the jury of laypersons is the ultimate audience for the report (see Figure 7.4). This is not always possible to do, depending upon your report type. Be prepared to explain the terminology to the jury when the attorneys ask you what the terms mean when you testify in court.

The most basic form that is used in court is the report regarding the incident. This may be a police report or other forensic report about the complaint to police, the injuries, or the parties involved. "Forensic" simply means a report prepared for use in a court of law – civil or criminal. The most important rule to remember about these reports is to make them understandable to anyone reading them, if possible. Police, attorneys, and investigators may read these reports. Whatever your role is in the criminal justice system, you must remember that the end audience who needs to understand your report is the jury. Jury members are laypersons, so all reports must be written in plain English so they can understand them. If you use abbreviations, explain each one the first time you use it, or have a key within the report that lists each abbreviation you used and what it means. Do not use your professional jargon unless you explain it. If it is not appropriate to explain it within the report, the attorneys will have you explain it during your testimony.

Try to paint a picture with words of visual aspects of the incident. Use simple units of measure if you are reporting the size of something. For example, do not measure things in centimeters or meters. Laypersons understand inches and simple increments of inches, like 3/4 of an inch. They may not understand how large 9/16 or 3/32 of an inch is.

For example, consider these two reports excepts regarding a suspected abused child:

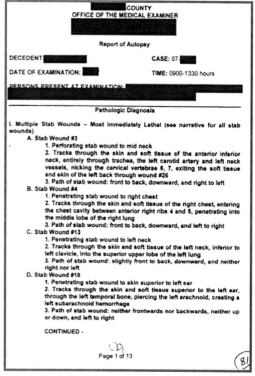

Report #1

There is a 1 cm. round second-degree burn on the anterior chest, 2 mm. right of the anterior midline and 22 cm. below the cranium. There is a red abrasion, 2 x 2 cm. on the posterior right arm, 18 cm. below the acromion process, and two round purple contusions on the medial and lateral arm, respectively, each 12 mm. in diameter, 4 cm. below the acromion process. X-ray demonstrates an acute fracture of the medial epicondyle of the right humerus.

FIGURE 7.4: *Here you will see a report from an autopsy that includes a lot of medical terminology. The investigator must be knowledgeable about these terms if called to testify about observations made during an autopsy.*

Report #2

There is a ½ inch round, blistering burn on the chest, consistent with a cigarette burn, located 1/4 inch right of the anterior midline, 10 inches below the top of the head. There is a red scrape on the back of the forearm, 1 x 1 inch, located 8 inches below the top of the shoulder. There are two round purple bruises on the medial and lateral upper arm, consistent with finger marks, 3/4 x 3/4 inches each, located 2 inches below the shoulder. X-ray shows a broken right arm at the medial elbow of the upper arm bone, the humerus.

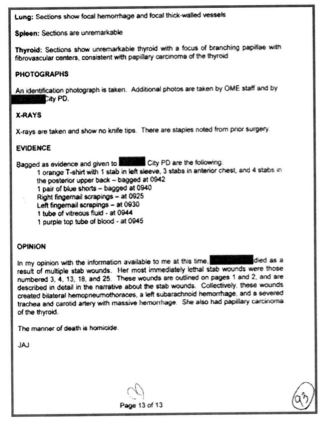

Lung: Sections show focal hemorrhage and focal thick-walled vessels

Spleen: Sections are unremarkable

Thyroid: Sections show unremarkable thyroid with a focus of branching papillae with fibrovascular centers, consistent with papillary carcinoma of the thyroid

PHOTOGRAPHS

An identification photograph is taken. Additional photos are taken by OME staff and by ▇▇▇ City PD.

X-RAYS

X-rays are taken and show no knife tips. There are staples noted from prior surgery.

EVIDENCE

Bagged as evidence and given to ▇▇▇ City PD are the following:
1 orange T-shirt with 1 stab in left sleeve, 3 stabs in anterior chest, and 4 stabs in the posterior upper back – bagged at 0942
1 pair of blue shorts – bagged at 0940
Right fingernail scrapings – at 0925
Left fingernail scrapings – at 0930
1 tube of vitreous fluid - at 0944
1 purple top tube of blood - at 0945

OPINION

In my opinion with the information available to me at this time, ▇▇▇ died as a result of multiple stab wounds. Her most immediately lethal stab wounds were those numbered 3, 4, 13, 18, and 25. These wounds are outlined on pages 1 and 2, and are described in detail in the narrative about the stab wounds. Collectively, these wounds created bilateral hemopneumothoraces, a left subarachnoid hemorrhage, and a severed trachea and carotid artery with massive hemorrhage. She also had papillary carcinoma of the thyroid.

The manner of death is homicide.

JAJ

Page 13 of 13

FIGURE 7.4: *Here you will see a report from an autopsy that includes a lot of medical terminology. The investigator must be knowledgeable about these terms if called to testify about observations made during an autopsy.*

Which report excerpt do you think could be better understood by the jury? While the injuries may be more accurately described in metric measurements, or calculated to tiny increments of inches, the jury is more likely to understand a report written in more common language. Also notice the injuries that appeared to be a cigarette burn and finger marks from grabbing the child. The report states the injuries are "consistent with" these mechanisms, as the examiner did not actually see what caused the injuries (see Figure 7.5).

The injuries look like other injuries the examiner has seen that were known to be cigarette burns and grab marks. Describing them as consistent with these mechanisms does not exclude that something else caused them, but gives the reader a mental picture of what they looked like. The defense team will have to come up with an explanation of what caused the injuries, or the defendant will have to state what happened. The child may have run into someone holding a burning cigarette and then fallen down the stairs to get the arm injuries.

FIGURE 7.5: *The officer has to report the facts that he sees in terms that anyone can understand.*

Resource - The Crime Scene Investigator Network is a website with many useful articles regarding how investigators should handle various aspects of the crime scene. This article, "Written Documentation at a Crime Scene," provides some additional tips on how to write up a crime scene. You may want to bookmark this website for future reference.

http://www.crime-scene-investigator.net/document.html

Notes Versus Quotes in the Report

The rule of using common English applies to all reports that you write, as much as possible. One exception is if you are interviewing a suspect or witness and you quote what they told you. They may be an expert in something and use unfamiliar language. Put this language in quotation marks and record exactly what you were told. You may ask the person what this means, and then state their explanation in your report, either paraphrased in your words or stated in the person's exact words in quotes.

You may take notes and then use them to write your report. Write your notes legibly. The final disposition of these notes will depend upon the policies of your jurisdiction. Some jurisdictions have notes shredded, while others keep them in the case file. If they are kept, they are obtainable for use in the trial, so they need to be legible. Do not write anything unprofessional in your notes. For example, you may have witness names and statements and make notes to remind yourself who is who. It is fine to write "blonde mustache" or "tall, thin with glasses." Never write anything you would not want to see in court like "fat" or "jerk," as these are opinions, not facts.

Depending upon your agency, you will likely have standard report forms to fill out. You will be trained by your agency on how to fill out the reports, and you need to fill them out in the way you are trained; however, it is advantageous to look at reports and forms in general from an attorney's standpoint.

Looking at Forms from an Attorney's Perspective

All forms regarding a criminal justice or forensic case are considered legal documents, so there are rules that must be followed regarding them. The first rule to follow is that if the form has a blank to fill in, you must insert something in it, and *never* leave it blank. The form may have instructions for what to place in a blank that does not apply or when the information is unknown. If not, insert "N/A, not applicable" in the first blank that does not apply. After that, you may just document "N/A" if the question is not applicable. If the information is unknown, you may write the entire word, or write "UNK, unknown," and then you may use "UNK" after your initial entry.

If you are filling in the form by hand, make sure that your writing is legible. Write large enough so that the writing is legible on any copies that might be made of the form. Where the date is asked, always include the year. It may be obvious to you that you are filling out the form this year, but the case may not go to trial for several years. You may have difficulty in recalling what year you filled out this particular form. It is also helpful for you when you go to court to state the day such as Mon. 11-15-10. You are often asked what day it was when you go to court several years down the road. This saves you from looking up the day later. The form may or may not have a space to list the time. It is always a good idea to insert the time, even if not asked to do so. List the time after the date. Give times in military times, using the 24-hour clock. In this way, if you forget to write a.m. or p.m., or it is not legible, there is no question of a.m. or p.m. using military times. Examples of military times are 0800 = 8 a.m., 1300 = 1 p.m., 1600 = 4 p.m., 2000 = 8 p.m., and 2400 = midnight. One minute after midnight is 0001.

If the form has several blank lines to insert narrative, and you do not use all of the lines, place one line through the extra lines, diagonally. This indicates that you did not use them, and it prevents someone from entering other information you did not intend to have added. If someone else needs to add something, he must use his own new form.

Forms filled in by hand should be written in ink. This should preferably be black ink, because it copies better. The exception to black ink may be with the signature. Because copies look so good now, some agencies have you sign your signature in colored ink that will appear black on the copies. The original form or report will be obvious because of the different colored ink on the signature.

If you make a mistake on a form you are filling out, there are specific ways to handle these mistakes. You should be using ink, as discussed earlier. Never try to erase your mistake. *Never* use whiteout or correction tape that covers the mistake. Never scribble out the error. Defense attorneys will say you changed something and are covering it up. Do not write over the mistake, such as converting a 0 to an 8, or fixing a misspelled word. The mistake must be crossed out with a single line through it that allows the mistake to be legible to attorneys, but clearly is an error and not a part of the report. Place your initials near the crossed out line to indicate that you crossed out the error, but your initials must be in a location that allows the attorneys to read through the mistake to make sure you are not covering up anything, and you are simply fixing an honest mistake.

Sign all forms. This indicates that you filled them out, and is your "okay" that the forms are correct. You may have a multi-page form with a signature line on either the first or the final page. Sign on that signature line, and if there is no line to print your name, print it beneath your signature, and include your badge number if you have one. Date and time all signatures. Go back to all the pages of the form, and either sign or initial each page to indicate it is the form you filled out. If there are no page numbers on the form, write them in. Legal forms and reports are typically listed as "Page X of Y" with the Y equaling the total number of pages of this particular report or form. For example, you fill out a six-page form that has no page numbers on the pages. You hand write on each page, "Page 1 of 6," "Page 2 of 6," etc. Following this procedure ensures that when the forms or reports are faxed, scanned, emailed, or copied, all pages of the report are being sent out. Figure 7.6 shows an example of a form that was properly written.

It is always good to add a simple disclaimer to all forensic reports and forms. You may add it to reports and print it before the signature line on forms. It simply states, "This information is true and correct with all the information available to me at the present time." This line shows the attorneys that this is all you knew at the time, and if more information comes out later in the investigation and you were not a part of that, the attorneys cannot discredit you. Remember that discrediting you basically means that the attorneys are trying to make you look incompetent to the jury so they will not believe anything you said. In this way, you state what you knew at the time, and the attorneys cannot discredit you for what the investigation turned up later. If you are the investigator who acquires new information that may contradict your original report or form, you write and issue an **addendum report**, or fill out a second form and label it "Addendum." You explain the new information and how it was obtained, list the same disclaimer in case even more information is uncovered, and sign, date, and time the addendum.

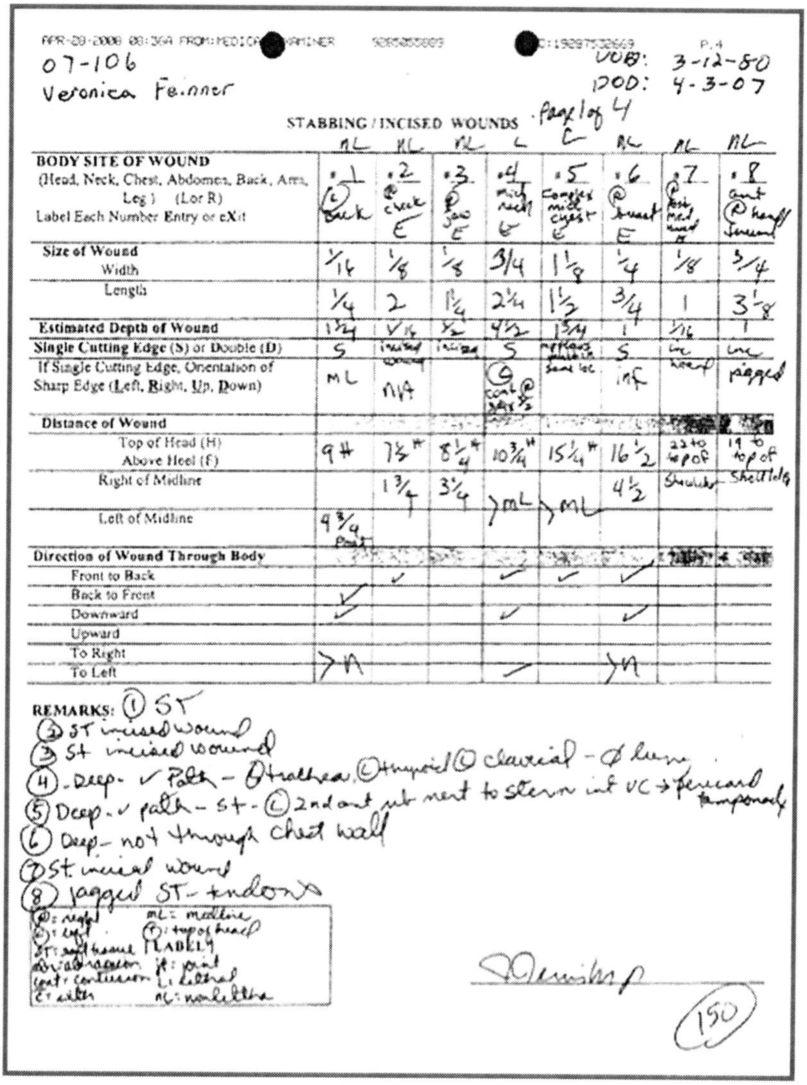
07-106
Veronica Feinner
DOB: 3-12-80
DOD: 4-3-07

STABBING / INCISED WOUNDS Page 1 of 4

BODY SITE OF WOUND (Head, Neck, Chest, Abdomen, Back, Arm, Leg) (L or R) Label Each Number Entry or eXit	#1 back	#2 cheek E	#3 jaw E	#4 mid neck E	#5 complex mid chest E	#6 breast E	#7	#8
Size of Wound Width	1/16	1/8	1/8	3/4	1 1/8	1/4	1/8	3/4
Length	1/4	2	1 1/4	2 1/4	1 1/2	3/4	1	3 1/8
Estimated Depth of Wound	1 1/4	1/16	1/2	4 1/2	1 3/4	1	1/16	1
Single Cutting Edge (S) or Double (D)	S			S		S		
If Single Cutting Edge, Orientation of Sharp Edge (Left, Right, Up, Down)	ML	n/a				inf		jagged
Distance of Wound Top of Head (H) Above Heel (F)	9"	7 1/2"	8 1/4"	10 3/4"	15 1/4"	16 1/2		
Right of Midline		1 3/4	3 1/4	ML	ML	4 1/2		
Left of Midline	9 3/4							
Direction of Wound Through Body								
Front to Back		✓		✓	✓	✓		
Back to Front	✓							
Downward	✓			✓		✓		
Upward								
To Right								
To Left								

REMARKS: (1) ST
(2) ST incised wound
(3) St incised wound
(4) Deep - path - trachea, thyroid, clavical - lung
(5) Deep - path - St - 2nd ant rib next to stern int VC → pericard tamponade
(6) Deep - not through chest wall
(7) St. incisal wound
(8) jagged ST - tendons

ML = midline
LABEL

(150)

FIGURE 7.6: *Here is a forensic form that follows the basic rules of writing forms.*

CASE STUDY

The Value of Original Reports

Many years ago, there was a high profile stabbing murder of a local politician's wife. The politician became a suspect after a long investigation, and he was eventually arrested.

The trial was a big news event for the community. The medical examiner was called to explain the stab wounds. He took the stand and the preliminary questions were asked regarding his background so he could be called an "expert witness." He was asked to describe how many stab wounds were present, which he did. He was asked which one caused the death, and he stated "Stab wound #4."

The attorney asked the medical examiner to describe stab wound #4, using the report the attorney was projecting in the courtroom using the **elmo**, a projection device to enlarge reports and photos in the courtroom. The medical examiner had the attorney advance through the pages, and there was no page with the description of stab wound #4. All pages ended at the end of a paragraph. There was a page that ended with the description of stab wound #3, and then the next page began with stab wound #5. The attorney began to try to discredit the medical examiner, accusing him of mislabeling the stab wounds, which meant there was no lethal stab wound inflicted.

The medical examiner was initially ruffled, and then asked to refer to his copy of the report, which he had made from the original report that morning and brought with him to court. He was allowed to look at it, and he had the missing page with the description of stab wound #4, so he was not discredited and the trial went on.

This case was back in the days before page numbers were placed on each page. This was before fax machines, when copies were made of reports, and then picked up by personnel from each attorney's office. Supposedly, the report was copied with two pages stuck together, and because the pages all ended and began with a new paragraph, the mistake was not apparent to the attorneys. The defense attorneys hoped to discredit the medical examiner and win their case, but the report brought by the medical examiner proved that he was not the incompetent physician they'd hoped to portray.

This case is used in teaching about reports. It is told in training as if it really happened, but no one ever produces the real case. Whether or not it actually happened is irrelevant. It does have two good teaching points. First, numbering the pages as "page X of Y" prohibits this problem from happening, even if the final pages are missed in copying or faxing. The second good point to remember is to always keep the original reports in the case file. Make a new copy of them and take them with you to court. Ask to refer to them, if needed. These copies are the best for you to have, and if pages are missing or if someone has altered anything on a report that makes it into court, you have a copy of your original and can avoid being discredited.

Writing a Case Brief

Case briefs are simply a summary of a case (see Figure 7.7). There may be situations where an investigator for the prosecution or defense may have to write a brief. This practice allows an attorney with a large case-load to review a number of cases quickly, particularly in jurisdictions with heavy caseloads. In many police reports, the synopsis of the case that will be the beginning of the report narrative will look very much like a case brief.

It may be a summary of a case that is going to court. It may be a summary of a case that has been tried already and is going to appellate court. Sometimes, attorneys need briefs of cases that have been settled in appellate court, because there are similarities in a new case to the settled appellate case, and based upon case law, the attorney expects to use the outcome of the earlier case to argue the present case.

The case brief has the same title as the original case or the current case, if you are summarizing a current case. The title will generally look like this: "Doe v. Smith" or "State v. Doe."

The facts of the case are discussed first. This is a one or two paragraph description of the crime or offense and the basic surrounding facts. If this is an appellate case, the court's original decision and reasons behind that decision are included in the facts.

FIGURE 7.7: *Here a criminal justice professional is conducting research in a law library in preparation for a case filing.*

The next discussion is the legal issue or issues at stake in the case. For example, the legal issue may be whether or not an officer used excessive force in arresting someone. The jurisdiction's policy on use of force may be included in this section.

If the case has already been decided, the next section discusses the court's decision in the case and how the decision was reached.

The following section is where you include the court's reasoning on why they reached the decision they did.

The final section for a case brief in a case that has been appealed is the disposition section. This is simply what the result was in the final appellate court decision.

CASE STUDY

Writing an Opinion

You are called to be an outside expert for a criminal case regarding an officer-involved shooting that has not yet gone to trial. You were not involved in the case originally. The case involved a different police jurisdiction. The officer is being tried for manslaughter for shooting a man that was unarmed, yet was using his finger in his pocket as though he had a gun. Your job is to go through all the case information and offer an opinion regarding the behavior of the officer.

You write a brief on the case. The facts are discussed first. The crime and facts surrounding it are discussed next. Then the legal issues are discussed. You include the police department's policy on use of force and when an officer may shoot someone. You read through all the discovery material regarding the incident. You write up your opinion regarding the shooting. You may refer to some of the witness statements in your opinion. You may look up other cases that have been tried and reference the case and its resolution in your opinion. You may look up literature articles and reference them in your opinion. In this example, you will include a bibliography or references cited page. You submit your brief with your opinion, listing all the records you were given to review, for example, "Interview with Officer Dunn," "Interview with Agnes Jones," "Ballistics Report," etc. You might add the statement that with the information available to you at this time, it is your opinion that...(whatever opinion you formed). The attorneys will probably interview you prior to the trial, and if the case is not settled before the trial, you will be sworn in as an expert witness and asked to testify about your opinion.

Summary

Producing written documents for use in court will be a part of your daily job as a criminal justice professional. Using all the basics discussed in this module will prevent attorneys from discrediting you on some of the basic mistakes typically made on reports.

The most important thing is to document everything you do. A general rule to follow: If you do not document it, you did not do it. Make sure that you also document everything you did *not* do, and the reason you did not do it. Use legible handwriting, good spelling, and proper grammar. Leave nothing blank on a form. Place the date, including day and year, and the time in military time on all forms and reports. Put page numbers on all pages with "Page X of Y" with Y being the total number of pages. Cross out all errors with a single line through the error with your initials, so it is clear that it is an error, but the error is still legible to the attorneys.

If you must write a case brief, keep it brief and include only pertinent facts. It is not an all-inclusive report describing everything about the case. If you follow these practices and procedures, you stand a better chance of having a successful court outcome.

Discussion Questions

1. Diocuss the similarities and differences in civil cases versus criminal cases.

2. Explain how to make a report or a form stand without question in court.

3. Describe everything that must go into a case brief of a case that was resolved in appellate court.

4. Discuss the types of equitable remedies.

5. Create a sample report that describes arm and leg injuries on a child who suffered minor injuries from being hit by a hit-and-run driver of a small car.

Key Terms

Forensic reports: Reports created for use in a court of law – civil or criminal.

Discredit: A tactic where the attorneys try to make the witness look incompetent by highlighting one error in the report so the jury will not believe any of the testimony of that witness; it is a way to create mistrust for a witness in the eyes of the jurors.

Criminal case: A crime has been committed that violates a statute of the jurisdiction; the subsequent trial is a criminal case

Prosecutors: The prosecuting attorneys for the jurisdiction where a crime was committed; they represent the jurisdiction's case in a criminal trial

Civil courts or civil case: The court where trials are held when one party sues another for an alleged wrongdoing or alleged negligence.

Defendant: The person accused of a crime in a criminal case, and also the person being sued in a civil case (same term for both).

Defense attorneys: The attorneys who represent the defendant in either a civil or a criminal case (same term for both).

Plaintiff: The person who is suing the other party civilly for alleged wrongdoing or negligence.

Plaintiff's attorneys: The attorneys representing the plaintiff in a civil trial; the person who sues someone else.

Litigation process: The time from the onset of a civil suit until its resolution.

Complaint: A document that explains a civil lawsuit and why the plaintiff is suing the defendant; it is served along with a summons to go to court to the defendant being sued in a civil case.

Discovery: The time when reports and evidence regarding a civil lawsuit or a criminal trial are gathered, and persons involved in the situation are interviewed or deposed.

Deposition: An interview done under oath with both parties' attorneys present, with court reporters present, but without a judge present; the witness undergoes direct and cross-examinations.

Interrogatories: A set of questions sent by an attorney for a civil case that must be answered in writing and returned to the attorney who sent them.

Pre-trial settlement: An agreement reached by the parties involved in a civil lawsuit that is reached prior to a formal trial so that no trial is needed.

Legal remedies (also called "damages"): Financial awards given to the plaintiff at the resolution of a civil lawsuit.

Compensatory damages: A type of legal remedy where moneys are paid by the defendant to compensate for an injury, which may include pain and suffering.

Mitigate the damages: The responsibility of both parties in a civil lawsuit, meaning that each party must take steps to minimize the damages.

Punitive damages: A type of legal remedy where the defendant in a civil case must pay moneys as a punishment for his wrongdoing.

Nominal damages: A type of legal remedy where the defendant gives a token amount to the plaintiff in a civil case when no harm was done, or no harm can be proven.

Equitable remedies: Non-financial remedies to resolve a civil case that may not be granted by juries; a judge is the only one who may grant them.

Specific performance: A type of equitable remedy where the defendant is ordered to do something to correct the situation to resolve a civil case.

Injunction: A type of equitable remedy where the defendant in a civil case is ordered to stop doing something.

Addendum report: A supplemental report written at a later time after the original report, and it adds new information discovered about the incident described in the original report

Elmo: A projection device to enlarge reports and photos in the courtroom.

Case brief: A summary of a case the includes the pertinent facts, legal issues, and current status of the case.

MODULE 8

Courtroom Testimony

Key Module Concepts:

- Proper attire for the courtroom

- The swearing-in process in court

- Various attorney tactics used to discredit or impeach an officer's testimony

- Alternatives to appearing in court in person

- The use of evidence and exhibits in the courtroom

- Compare and contrast the types of questions used in the court system: voir dire, direct examination, and cross-examination

- Techniques to give effective testimony in the courtroom

- What to take with you to court, including how and when to use these materials

Introduction

Going to court may be an intimidating experience for the new criminal justice professional. It is a formal event in a strange room with many strangers present. You may be wearing clothes you don't normally wear. You swear to tell the truth. You must speak into a microphone and may be videotaped by news media. You are the unwilling star of the show for a time. Attorneys may yell at you, treat you with contempt or anger, or try to make you look incompetent in front of everyone. Or the attorneys may do *all* of these things to you!

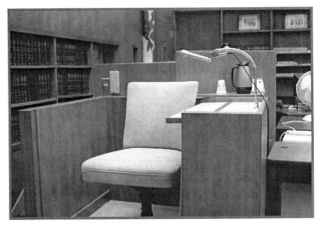

This is not at all what you went to school to do. You are normally confident and are the criminal justice professional in control. You are now in the court-room, and you are nervous and not at all in control of anything. The attorneys try to control and manipulate you. You may swear that if you get out of this courtroom alive, you will go back to flipping burgers and never look back.

Going to court is part of most jobs in the criminal justice world. It is not as bad or intimidating as you may think at first, but simply a matter of understanding the process. Once you understand things, you will be more comfortable with courtroom testimony.

Attorneys do use some tactics that may surprise you. Yes, they are trying to manipulate you. They may want to make you get angry. They may want to make you look incompetent. Usually, if the attorneys use these tactics on you, it is because you did a good job on the case, and you are a threat to their case. Upsetting you or making you look stupid may be the only way they have to get around the fact that your information and report condemns their client or their case. You must learn not to take these tactics personally. They are actually a compliment to you, and are an attempt to remove you as a threat.

We will examine this process of courtroom testimony in this module. You will gain an understanding of common attorney tactics so that you know how to respond to these tactics.

Ask Yourself

- *What should you wear to court?*
- *What should you take to court with you?*
- *What will you be asked?*
- *What kinds of things are you expected to say?*
- *How will the attorneys treat you?*
- *What can you expect?*
- *Is it possible to get out of going to court?*

In the Courtroom

Criminal justice professionals frequently have to testify in courtroom trials. Most of these are criminal trials, but some will be civil trials. Your role will generally be the same, regardless of the type of case.

At first, you might think of going to court as playing ball in someone else's ball diamond. You are like the visiting team. The room is unfamiliar, you don't always know the other players, and even the rules seem to be different.

Gaining an understanding of what is expected in court will help you become more at ease in the courtroom. A few tips and a knowledge of attorneys' courtroom tactics will help you be more comfortable in court.

Most trials are public. It will help you if you can go sit in on a public courtroom trial where you have no involvement in the case. You can go for the entire trial, which may last anywhere from hours to days or weeks, or you can spend the day at the courthouse, watching parts of several trials to see the different attorneys' tactics. Watch the witnesses. See what they wear. Watch how the jury responds to different witnesses. Watch how the witnesses respond to the attorneys, and how the jurors seem to view these responses. Observe the various courtroom procedures like swearing in, objections, and overall courtroom behavior.

Knowledge, understanding, and experience are the things that will help you become more comfortable in the courtroom. You will begin to feel more at ease in court, and may learn to even enjoy your courtroom appearances.

The Preliminaries and Swearing In

You will be notified in advance of an upcoming trial in which you must testify. You may be working with an attorney on the case, and he will simply tell you about it. You may get a phone call from the attorney's office. You will get an official court order for your court appearance, called a **subpoena** (see Figure 8.1). The subpoena actually might be your first notice notification of the upcoming trial.

Attorneys from both sides of the case will contact and interview you during the evidence gathering part of the case, called **discovery**. Discovery usually occurs early in the process of the case and long before the trial. The discovery interview is less formal than going to court. This interview is usually audio taped by the attorneys, and it is not held in a courtroom. The attorneys are simply gathering information, and it is generally a cordial interview where they ask you about the case, your role in it, and your reports and photographs of the case. You are not officially sworn in to tell the truth; however, it is vital to tell the truth in all encounters with attorneys. If they feel you are changing your story when you testify at the trial, they may read back the transcription of what you said during your discovery interview to try to **discredit** you.

The subpoena and trial usually happen much later. The court system is very busy. It depends upon how busy your jurisdiction is, but the trial may even be years later. There are different types of hearings you may be requested to attend. The most common is the jury trial where the defendant is determined to be guilty or not guilty of the accused wrong-doing. Sometimes, this trial is a **bench trial**, where the attorneys have agreed to allow the judge to determine guilt, and there is no jury, but this is less common. There are grand jury hearings, preliminary hearings, sentencing hearings, post conviction release hearings, and many others. The general rules are the same, although in some hearings and jurisdictions, the juries can ask you questions. In some cases with no jury present, the judge can ask you questions. Because the rules vary slightly depending upon the jurisdiction and type of hearing, they will be explained to you before you testify.

Some attorneys will have you meet with them before you testify so that they can go over your testimony with you and tell you what they expect the other side will do. Other attorneys will not speak with you beforehand. The situation depends upon how busy they are, and whether or not this is a high stakes or high profile case. If you have any questions regarding your testimony, call the attorney who issued your subpoena.

FIGURE 8.1: *The subpoena is the legal document that is used to bring someone or something before the court*

The subpoena will always be served to you, regardless of how you are originally informed about the trial. It is an official court order for you to testify in court. It will inform you of the case and the defendant, and will tell you which side, the prosecution or the defense, is calling you to appear. Even if you are a police officer who usually is subpoenaed by the prosecution, sometimes the defense will subpoena you if your information supports the defendant's story. Rarely will both sides subpoena you, depending upon the rules about this in your jurisdiction, but it could happen.

The subpoena will tell you where you must appear. It will list a date and time for your appearance. It will give you a phone number to call to confirm the court information.

It is imperative to call and check on the trial. Some subpoenas list the actual date and time you are expected to testify. Other subpoenas will list the date and time the trial begins, so you may not be needed until several days later. Many cases are continued, meaning the attorneys have gotten permission to reschedule the trial for a later date. You will be sent a subpoena for the next trial date. Each trial may have several **continuances**, so even if a particular case has had one continuance, the second trial date may still be continued several more times.

The defendant can always plead guilty or **plea-bargain**, admitting guilt for a slightly lesser crime to avoid the trial. The attorneys will tell you when you call them to check on the trial if the defendant has pled out, or admitted guilt, and there will no longer be a trial to determine guilt. Sometimes, when a defendant pleads out, you will still get a subpoena for the sentencing hearing, depending on the case and your jurisdiction.

The subpoena is a court order, and a warrant will be issued for your arrest if you do not appear. If the case is plead out or continued for a later date, you must still ensure that no warrant was issued for your arrest.

When the case does go to trial, you will usually have to sit in the hall outside the courtroom until you are needed. While most trials are public, when you testify, you are not usually allowed to listen to the testimony of other witnesses in that particular trial. There are exceptions to this in some jurisdictions. There may be news media people and video cameras in the courtroom. Whether or not the news media can videotape a trial is left to the judge's discretion, so do not let the presence of film crews upset you.

It is never certain how long each witness will testify, and it is up to the judge to grant **recesses**, or breaks, in the trial. You may have to wait for a while to testify, and sometimes you have to come back the next day. Be sure to bring reading material or something to do while you wait. Also, make a fresh copy of your report and any materials you need for court. Bring it in a plain file or large envelope with no trial name on the outside. Beware of looking at your trial materials while you wait. Do not talk about the trial to anyone while waiting to testify. You do not know who may be watching you or listening to you. Do not let anyone talk to you about the trial while you wait. You cannot allow anyone to influence your testimony or have allegations that someone has influenced you.

At the trial, before you testify, you must swear to tell the truth. This is the **swearing in**. You must be sworn in before you take your seat at the witness stand. You will be instructed where to stand to be sworn in. You will have to raise your right hand. You extend your right arm in front and to the right of your body with 90-degree bend at the elbow, and hold your hand toward the official, with the palm facing him or her with your fingers extended. The court official who swears you in is either a court clerk or a bailiff. The clerk will also raise his or her right hand toward you. This official will ask you if you swear the testimony you are about to give is true under penalty of **perjury**. Perjury is lying under oath, and it is a felony. In some jurisdictions, you may still have to place your left hand on a Bible, and the court official will ask you if you swear to tell the truth "so help you God." Generally, most references to God and swearing in on the Bible have been removed out of respect for non-Christian religions. The standard response to the swearing in statement that you say is "I do" or "I will," depending on the wording of the swearing-in statement.

The court official will lower his or her hand, and you may take your seat at the witness stand. It is usually up several stairs. Use caution with the chair in the witness stand. It may be on rollers, be a standard chair, or it may swivel but be attached to the floor. There is usually a podium type enclosure in front of you with a microphone on it. Adjust the microphone and place your closed folder or envelope with your court materials on the top of the podium. There is usually a glass and pitcher of water for you to drink on the podium. You may be speaking for a while, and the water is for you to keep your throat moist. You may place your purse and any other personal items on the floor to the side of your chair on the side opposite the stairs or entrance to the witness stand.

Ⓡ **Resource** - PoliceOne offers tips for officers going to testify in court. This is a good, concise resource to read before a courtroom appearance.

http://www.policeone.com/corrections/tips/2006247-6-tips-for-more-effective-courtroom-appearances/

Demeanor and Dress

You will be nervous the first few times you go to court. Remember to have good posture. You must maintain a professional demeanor. Review the nonverbal communication module before going to court. You want your nonverbal communication to be that of confidence and relaxation. Review the nonverbal cues of dishonesty and anxiety, and make sure that you do not use any of them. Keep your hands open and on the podium. Do not clench your fists or cross your arms. Do not fidget in your chair. Make eye contact with each juror throughout your testimony, so that you have made eye contact with all jurors at some point during your testimony. Make eye contact with the attorney who questions you, and then make eye contact with several jurors each time you answer. Make eye contact with the judge when he or she speaks to you, and then look back to the jurors.

Making eye contact with the jurors does several things. It encourages the jurors to trust you. It makes each juror feel important. The jurors are, after all, the most important people in the courtroom because they make the ultimate decision of guilty or not guilty. Making eye contact with the jurors individually makes each one feel you are speaking directly to them as a person. It encourages them to maintain interest and pay attention to what you are saying.

The jurors want to get to know you. Be yourself when you testify. If you have a sense of humor normally, it is okay to use it in limited appropriate situations in court. Do not appear phony or stiff. The jurors like to see your personality. If you normally make hand gestures when you speak, go ahead and do that. The jurors have to sit through a lot of witnesses. They do not want you to be boring, monotonous, or pompous. They want you to be a real person with information and education that helps them make an educated decision about the facts of the case.

Do not chew gum or have anything in your mouth when you testify. Do not manipulate any small objects in your hands. The attorneys may make you step down and point at photos, evidence, or exhibits during your testimony, so keep your belongings out of the way of the exit from the witness stand. Wear clothing and shoes that allow you to get up and down easily if you have to get up to point at something.

Attorneys have studied jurors carefully. These studies have shown what clothing witnesses should wear to best earn the jurors' trust. Oddly enough, jurors have been shown to look closely at your shoes. Your shoes should be clean and polished. They should be in good repair and con-servative in type. They should match your outfit. Studies show that jurors feel you do not respect them or the court system if you wear dirty or unpolished shoes.

Clothing is also important. If you normally wear a uniform on the job, and have to testify during your normal workday, you may feel you need to wear your uniform, but consult with the attorney who subpoenaed you before you do. If you wear your uniform, make sure it is clean and pressed. If you are not working on the day you testify, speak to the attorney who sub-poenaed you. Some attorneys ask that you wear your uniform to portray the image of your job in the criminal justice world. For example, if you work in the crime lab, the attorney may ask you to wear a lab coat to show that you are a criminal laboratory professional. If you do not normally wear any type of uniform, or the attorney does not want you to wear it, there are guidelines for what witnesses should wear to court, based upon jury studies. If the attorney does not want you to wear a uniform and you are working, keep some clothes to wear to court avail-able. This is a good idea anyway, for the rare case when you get called in to testify at an unexpected time with little advance notice, for example, if the witness scheduled before you gets sick or has an accident and your testimony is moved up unexpectedly. This is especially important if you are to testify in a case soon in which the attorney has specified that you should not wear your uniform.

Men

Studies show that the clothing witnesses wear is important to the jurors (see Figure 8.2). Men should wear standard business or professional attire. This usually means a suit, although this is regional in nature. If you live in a very casual region, for example in many areas of the West, a nice shirt and tie may be appropriate. The suit or slacks should be dark blue or gray. The jurors may have to look at you for long periods of time, so it is recommended that you avoid plaids and prints, because they are harder to look at for long. The shirt should be clean and pressed, and fully buttoned.

Studies have shown that jurors do not like beige shirts because they consider them boring. If you do not wear a suit coat, the shirt should be conservative with no prints or wild stripes. The tie should match and not have any kind of wild pattern. Studies have shown that jurors do not like bow ties. Wear long dark socks so that your legs are never exposed in the event that the witness stand podium does not extend clear to the floor. Choose fabrics that do not wrinkle easily in case you are sitting around waiting for a long time to testify, or if you are asked to get up and down from the witness stand to

FIGURE 8.2: *Appropriate male attire in court creates instant credibility and projects a professional appearance.*

point out objects. Wear conservative jewelry if you wear any at all. Make sure that your hair and facial hair is neat, clean, and trimmed.

Women

Studies have shown that women witnesses have greater respect from
the jurors if they wear a dress or skirt, so you should never wear slacks
to court, unless you are asked to wear your uniform and it consists of
pants with no option to wear a uniform skirt. If you wear professional
clothing and choose a skirt, wear a nice blouse or sweater with it.
A jacket is optional. Make sure that your clothing is neat, clean,
and pressed.

Jurors are more relaxed about colors for women. Women may wear any
color as long as it is not exceptionally bright. Small prints and plaids
are acceptable for women as long as the prints are not extremely large
or bright. Studies show that jurors prefer a feminine look. Do not wear

extremely short skirts, and do not show
cleavage. Wear hosiery and pumps. Do
not wear stiletto heels. Make sure that
you can walk and climb stairs gracefully
in your shoes. Keep jewelry tasteful and
not gaudy. Wear clothing that does not
wrinkle easily for the same reason as
men. Any hairstyle is acceptable, as
long as it is neat and clean; however,
keep in mind that you may need to look
down at your report or have to get up
and down to point at objects. Flipping
your hair around or out of your eyes is
distracting to the jury, so try to choose
a hairstyle where you will not have to
touch or flip your hair.

FIGURE 8.2: *Appropriate female attire
in court creates instant credibility
and projects a professional
appearance.*

CASE STUDY

Wardrobe Failures and the Court

A female expert witness was scheduled to testify in an important trial.

It was a long trial, and she had a prolonged wait in the hallway before she was called into the courtroom to testify.

She read a book in the hallway for hours. She did not speak to anyone, and she did not look at her courtroom documents in the hall.

She was called in to testify toward the end of the day. She was rushed by the person who called her in, because the judge wanted to finish her testimony before the end of the day.

She rushed into the courtroom and was told to stand in front of the court clerk to be sworn in. When she stood where she was told, there was a horrified gasp from the jury box. She was standing with her back to the jurors. She had worn a cotton dress that was rather short. It had wrinkled, accordion style, in the back. It was bunched up, showing things best not shown in court!

In a different court, another female witness was called to testify and was sworn in without incident. She was wearing stiletto heels with a professional, conservative gray skirt business suit. She had three steps to go up to enter the witness stand. She stopped suddenly on the second step. Her heel was caught in a wooden safety strip secured to the leading edge of the step. She could step out of her shoe, but it was stuck tight in the step. The court had to take a recess for maintenance to come and remove the strip and free the shoe.

In addition to these style failures, there is always the case of the male witness approaching the bench after forgetting to zip his trousers. It happens more often than one would like to think. The stress of court appearances can cause witnesses to be less focused on their appearance than they would normally be.

The Questioning

You are well dressed for court, have been sworn in, and have taken the witness stand. What happens now? Let's look at your testimony and review tactics that attorneys may use in court. We will also discuss the materials you take with you to court, as well as the exhibits and evidence used in court.

The Witnesses

Before you go to court, you should know what kind of witness you are. There are many types of witnesses. A **fact witness** has direct personal knowledge of facts important to the case, for example, a witness who actually saw a robbery in progress. Fact witnesses may only answer the questions asked of them with facts. They may not give opinions.

Expert witnesses have special knowledge, experience, and credentials in a particular area. Their credentials are reviewed in court to have them admitted as an expert, as shown in Figure 8.3. If they have testified in court as an expert witness many times, the attorneys may stipulate to the fact that the witness is an expert. This means the expert is allowed to testify as an expert without going through all the reasons why he or she should be admitted as an expert. When asked, an expert witness may give opinions. A witness may be both a fact witness and an expert witness, for example, in the case of a physician who treated a patient in an abuse case. The doctor may answer questions about the facts of the injuries, and then be asked an opinion question. An example of an opinion question for an expert witness might go something like this: "So, doctor, with reasonable medical certainty, what is your opinion regarding the cause of Natalie Johnson's injuries?"

Witnesses are also further categorized as official, friendly, or hostile. **Official witnesses** are involved in the case because of their official capacities. These official witnesses are police officers, municipal, state, or federal employees, corporate officers, or association or interest group members. **Friendly witnesses** are usually friends, relatives, or business associates of the defendant. **Hostile witnesses** are against the defendant. They may not have hostile behavior, but may have hostile opinions toward the defendant or his actions. Attorneys must often balance friendly and hostile witnesses to provide a clear picture of what happened in the case in order for the jurors to hear both sides of the case.

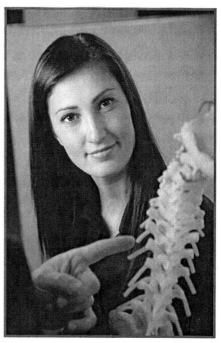

FIGURE 8.3: *In this case, a medical examiner demonstrates a point using a plastic skeleton. Sometimes demonstrations are the most effective way of communicating to a jury.*

Initially, you will most likely be a fact witness who is also an official witness. As you gain more experience and credentials, you may also become an expert witness.

Your Testimony

When you are in the witness stand, make it a habit to wait a few seconds before you answer every question, beginning with the first question, which is usually, "State your name." There are two reasons for waiting a few seconds to answer. First, it gives the opposing attorneys time to object to the question asked by the attorney. **Objections** from the opposing attorneys mean you do not answer the question because something is wrong with it. If you have started speaking when the objection is raised, stop speaking immediately and do not finish your sentence or thought. The judge will tell you if the objection is **overruled** and you may answer the question anyway. If the objection is **sustained**, the attorney must ask you a different question. The second reason for the pause is to allow you to collect and organize your thoughts before you speak.

The reason you begin the pause with the very first question on the witness stand, is to get in the habit of always pausing when answering all questions while on the witness stand. This pause is different from answering questions in a normal conversation, so you must continually remind yourself to pause.

The attorneys who subpoenaed you to court ask the initial questions. These questions are usually about your background, including education, experience, and employment. The opposing attorney does not usually object to these questions, but it is still a good idea to get used to pausing after all questions. In the very beginning of your testimony, it is good to state your name and then look at the jury and ask them if everyone can hear you. Adjust the microphone if there are problems.

The attorney will get to the case after all the background questions. The case questions usually begin with a question like, "On Wednesday, June 10, 2009, did you encounter Mr. Joe Smith?" You usually will not remember this for sure, so at this point ask the attorneys if you may refer to your report. They will usually say yes, and you can get out your report, take a look at it, and then answer the question.

Only answer the question asked, and do not elaborate on your answer. If it is a yes or no answer, answer only yes or no. Do not answer, "Yes, but he was ....." If you don't know the answer to a question, simply state you don't know. If you are asked about an area that is outside your area of expertise, state that this is outside your expertise and suggest the question be asked of the expert in this area, for example, "That question is outside my area of expertise. I suggest you ask the ballistics experts."

Answer all questions truthfully. If you are asked to get up and look at a piece of evidence and state whether or not it is the evidence you gathered, get up and look at it if it is too large to give to you in the witness stand. Then answer your question and go back and sit down. If you are asked to get up and demonstrate something, like "Where on this mannequin did you see a gunshot wound?" get up and point this out, and go back and sit down in the witness stand.

Try to speak in plain English when testifying. Avoid professional jargon that the jurors may not know. If you use a word the jury does not know, the attorney will probably ask you about it. For example, there was a murder trial about a man who was stabbed and bled to death. The witness discussed the case about the man bleeding to death, and at the end of the testimony, slipped up and mentioned something about the man exsanguinating. "Exsanguinating! But you said the man bled to death." The witness then had to explain that exsanguination is the medical term for bleeding to death.

In some cases, you may have to refer to literature articles or textbooks. This is uncommon, but if this applies to a case, bring copies of the appropriate literature in your court folder or envelope. When asked about the literature, if you need to refer to it, ask permission from the attorney, and when granted, get out the materials and refer to them.

The attorney will ask questions until finished, and then the opposing attorney has a turn. Remember that the attorney who subpoenaed you does the **direct examination** questions. These are questions that require you to supply the answer. The opposing attorney asks the **cross-examination** questions, which may consist of leading questions. Leading questions are ones in which the attorney gives the details in the question, and you can only confirm or deny the statement without elaboration. After the opposing attorney finishes, the original attorney can ask more. The questioning can go back and forth several times with re-direct and re-cross. Answer the questions until the attorneys finish asking them. In some jurisdictions, jurors are allowed to ask clarifying questions. Answer them if asked. If the judge calls a recess during your testimony, take a break and return early, before the time the judge says the trial will resume. When your testimony is finished, you will be told you are finished and you can leave.

Tactics of Attorneys

Attorneys have many tactics to confuse you, discredit you, or **impeach** you. These tactics are all done to make the jury doubt the things you say. It is usually the opposing attorney who will use these tactics. One simple tactic to confuse you is a long, convoluted question or multiple questions run together into one question. You only have to answer one question at a time, and you must understand the question, so you have the right to say, "Can you rephrase the question?" The attorney has to restate the question in simpler terms.

If you have a criminal justice job with any advocacy center, for example, a domestic violence or sexual assault advocacy center, you may be asked if you are an advocate for these victims. Never admit to being an advocate. State you are an advocate only for the truth. If you admit to being an advocate, the opposing attorney will begin to call you "Advocate Lopez," rather than "Officer Lopez," because the attorney wants the jurors to remember you have said you were an advocate. This tactic basically impeaches your testimony so that none of it is believed, because being an advocate for a certain type of victim implies bias, and the attorney is implying you are not an impartial witness.

You know the entire story and so do the attorneys. Sometimes, only a part of your story supports the opposing attorney's side. This attorney may ask you questions about a few of the facts – the facts that support his client. You may want to elaborate on the facts that oppose his client's story, but you may not elaborate on your answers. The attorney who subpoenaed you will have another turn, and will ask you the questions that will clarify all the true facts in the case, so do not get frustrated by this tactic.

Attorneys may also ask you many questions about the same event, but phrased differently or separated by other questions. These are multiple questions about the same thing. The goal of this tactic is to confuse you and make you appear to change your story. If you fall for this tactic, the attorney may say, "Earlier, you said the man was wearing a black ski mask, and you just said he had black hair. Which was it?" This tactic is designed to make the jurors mistrust what you say.

Attorneys will often ask questions that are outside your area of expertise or ask something they know you don't know, for example, by asking you how the toxicology was performed to show the defendant was using cocaine. They are trying to trap you into making something up, or saying something that will later be contradicted by the expert involved. You simply say, "I don't know." In the question about the toxicology, you may say, "I don't know how that testing is done. That is a better question for the toxicologists."

Another tactic is to pick out a weak or missing point in your report. The attorney will dwell on this problem with several questions about it, designed to make you look incompetent. The attorney may even say,

"Wouldn't you say, sir, that anyone who leaves out a fact this important is an idiot?" You answer yes. "Then, sir, are you admitting you are an idiot?"

The attorney may even resort to yelling at you, pointing at you, or belittling you (see Figure 8.4). These tactics are designed to make you lose your temper and yell back. Do not do this! Remain calm and state all answers in a normal voice without yelling back or saying something sarcastic. Even if you are frustrated, do not show it.

Why do the opposing attorneys use these tactics? The usual answer is because you have done your job well, and you are a threat to their case. Your facts and report may be solid, and the only way they can make the jury doubt you is to try these tactics. Consider that the use of these tactics to try to upset you or discredit you is actually a compliment. The better you have done your job, the worse the opposing attorneys will treat you in court.

Remember, the jurors have watched all these attorneys with all the witnesses. Certain attorneys have their favorite tactics they use frequently. The attorney who subpoenaed you may know this and may have warned you about it. The jurors have watched the attorneys yell or try to confuse all the witnesses. They know this is a game, and they have watched the other witnesses' responses to these tactics. You will impress the jurors with your calm and professional response to these tactics when you fail to get trapped by them.

FIGURE 8.4: *An attorney gets aggressive with a witness in an attempt to rattle his testimony.*

Voir Dire

The jurors probably have sympathy with you, the witness. They have also been put through a questioning process to be selected to be jurors for this particular trial.

Jurors are randomly selected from a large pool of people, such as those with driver's licenses or those registered to vote. They are summoned for jury duty. They appear for jury duty and wait to be selected for a case. A large group of potential jurors are selected for a particular case – many more than are needed. This large group of potential jurors is called the **venire**, or jury panel.

The members of the venire go through **voir dire**, which is French for "to speak the truth." Voir dire is handled differently in different jurisdictions. Potential jurors may have to fill out a questionnaire about themselves, their experience, beliefs, and values. Voir dire is the actual verbal questioning of the potential jurors by attorneys from both sides and the judge. The answers to these verbal questions are compared to the answers on the questionnaire, if it is used. Voir dire may be done as a group or individually.

Questions asked during voir dire vary greatly. They may include education and occupation. They may include prior court experience as a defendant or when other loved ones were the defendant in a case. They may include memberships in organizations and what newspapers, websites, and magazines are routinely read. They may include opinion questions, such as asking about the individual's opinion regarding the death penalty. The reason for all the questions is to select those individuals who are the most impartial toward the type of case being tried.

Sometimes special jury consultants assist with the jury selection. They are expensive, and are usually only used in high profile cases. These consultants help to "read" the potential juror to predict how they will respond to the facts of the case. Whether or not consultants are used, the attorneys and judge select the final jury. These are the jurors who must sit through the entire trial and then deliberate to determine whether the defendant is guilty or not guilty. There are one or more extra persons selected to be on the jury. These are the **alternates**. The alternates do not know who they are. These alternates are used if another member of the jury must be excused from the case for any reason, such as illness or injury. If no one has to be excused from the jury, after the closing arguments in the case when the jury is to deliberate, the alternates are told who they are. The alternates are then excused, and are not allowed to participate in the deliberations.

(R) **Resource** - This is an interesting compilation of trial attorney tactics, compiled for a high school course. You will probably want to bookmark it for future reference.

http://mr_sedivy.tripod.com/usgov_8.html

Exhibits and Evidence

The point of a trial is to present all the facts to the jurors in a way that they will understand so they can make a decision about whether or not the defendant is guilty. You spell out the facts as well as you can in words in a report. You may take lots of photos of a crime scene or of the injuries on a murder victim. You answer questions with plain English in detail on the witness stand. However, you may still need other props, or **exhibits**, to make the jurors fully understand the case.

For example, there are guidelines on how to take crime scene photos in a room or of wounds on a body. Photos that are admitted into court are called *exhibits*. If any of these photos are bloody or graphic, they may not be admitted into court because the violence they depict may upset and prejudice the jurors. They may project their emotions onto the defendant and decide he is a monster, and then decide he is guilty without really listening to all the facts.

Photos must all be admitted to court in their original form without alterations. Some cases have details that are complex enough that if the photos are allowed, they need to be labeled using computer graphics so the jury can understand them. Copies are made of the photos used for alteration so that the originals remain unaltered. These altered photos become additional exhibits, and you must have the originals to show that you did not alter anything except to label something in the photo.

The jurors may not be able to look at a series of photos of a room and be able to mentally put them together to decide what the room looked like in three dimensions in the proper scale. For example, the distance across the room may be the key to the bullet's **trajectory**, or path, but if the jurors cannot really tell how large the room was, they may not understand your point about the trajectory.

Exhibits help the jurors understand these details (see Figure 8.5). Exhibits should be simple enough for the jurors to understand. You can use drawings or mannequins. You can use computer graphic art printed out in a large poster, for example, of a scale drawing of the layout of the crime scene room or house. Ask what technology is available in the courtroom. Computer animated reenactments of crimes or crashes are sometimes used when there is a computer and a large screen available.

While bloody crime scene photos and horrible wound photos may not be admitted into court, drawings or artwork depicting these things usually are admitted. Drawings of bloody violence do not evoke the emotional response that actual photos do, so that is why they are usually admitted. The jurors may need these depictions to fully understand the case.

Mannequins may be labeled with the locations of wounds. Styrofoam wig stands with trajectory rods in them are used to show how bullets go through the head in murder cases. If you have an idea for an exhibit that will help your testimony, work with the attorney who subpoenaed you to work out who will create the exhibit and label it correctly. The attorney may have more access to artists, architects, and computer graphic professionals than you do. These professionals may create the artwork, and then you may have to label it. The attorney may have access to a mannequin, and then have you place stickers on it to show where the wounds were. An artist may print out a large map of city streets, and you will have to show him where to insert skid marks and cars involved in a crash. You can plan the details of the exhibits with the attorney who will then work to get the exhibit admitted into court.

You can collect a variety of types of evidence at crime scenes. This evidence is usually admitted into court. The evidence may speak for itself, or you may be asked about it in your testimony. The evidence comes to court in evidence bags. You may be asked to confirm the fact it is your initials on the evidence bags and be asked to describe how it was collected. You may have to show the photos of the evidence before it was collected or be asked to explain the significance of the evidence. You may have to explain the chain of custody of the evidence or explain the photos regarding the case. Sometimes, you may be asked to remove the evidence from the evidence bags to show and explain it to the jurors.

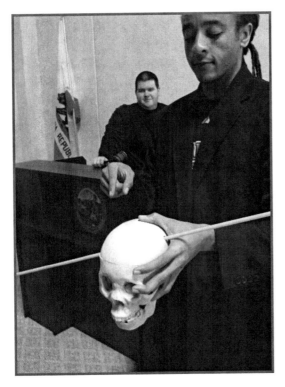

FIGURE 8.5: *A demonstration of bullet trajectory is accomplished through the use of props.*

CASE STUDY

Getting Photos Admitted to Trial

Getting real injury photos admitted into evidence as exhibits is always a challenge, because while they are very important for the jurors to see, the problem of the possibility of adversely prejudicing the jury always comes up. Certain judges have particular problems with photos, and when the attorneys will be working with certain judges, they know this will be a particularly challenging problem.

One judge, known to dislike wound photos, was assigned a death penalty homicide to try in her courtroom. Certain wound photos were admitted with great reluctance. The medical examiner was testifying, and was showing and explaining an entrance gunshot wound. The juror box was near where the medical examiner, a physician, was standing. One juror gasped in the middle of the explanation, and said, "I think she's sick."

The medical examiner saw the juror with the problem. It was a young woman having a seizure. The jurors' chairs were bolted to the floor, and the sick juror was wedged in her chair in such a way that her neck was bent, her airway was blocked due to her position, and she was turning dark blue.

The jurors' box was surrounded by a decorative wooden fence/railing. The medical examiner, in an above knee-length skirt, leaped over the fence to assist the sick juror. The attorneys and the judge just stared. The sick juror was wedged in tightly. The medical examiner shouted to the attorneys, "Come and help me move her!"

The attorneys looked at the judge who shouted at them to go ahead. The judge told the bailiff to call 911. The attorneys ran in and helped the medical examiner carry the woman to the middle of the courtroom floor. The medical examiner held her head to keep her airway open as the seizure subsided. The judge dismissed the jury, and they left the courtroom.

Paramedics arrived and took the sick juror to the hospital. Court was dismissed for the rest of the day, and was set to resume the next day. The sick juror was excused, and one of the alternates took her place.

The prosecutor discussed the situation with the medical examiner after the paramedics left. He told her the attorneys couldn't enter the jury box without the judge's permission. If they do, the judge can declare a mistrial or an end to the trial, requiring it to be started over. This is why the attorneys looked to the judge for permission, even in the face of a true emergency. The prosecutor was also concerned about the status of the photographs. Follow-up on the now hospitalized juror revealed a true disease process, so the photograph had nothing to do with provoking the problem.

The trial resumed the next day. The photos were shown. The medical examiner was embarrassed about her gymnastics in the courtroom, but her testimony went well. The prosecution won the case.

Distance Court Appearances

When you are a criminal justice professional, you have the potential to be subpoenaed into court at any time. The trials are not scheduled around your vacations or other trips. You may take a different job and move away, but may still be subpoenaed to testify in cases in your old jurisdictions. You deserve to have a life outside of the criminal justice world, so there are many ways to be involved in a trial that is far away from where you are located at the particular time the trial is being held.

How this situation is handled varies greatly. It depends on the type of case, the type of hearing, the jurisdiction, your role in the case, and the technology and financial resources that are available for the case.

If you are considered important to the trial, the attorneys will make

FIGURE 8.6: *Sometimes you have to travel to testify.*

travel arrangements and hotel accommodations for you (see Figure 8.6). You will have to take a break in your travel plans or travel from your new home, but will be returned as quickly as possible. The travel may be on public transportation, such as a commercial train or plane, or you may be transported to the trial using a private transportation mode that is available to the trial jurisdiction, such as a private jet.

In some trials, a substitute person may be allowed to testify for you, using your report. This substitute should have essentially the same credentials you do, and should have an understanding of the case. For example, if a forensic pathologist moves away for another job, a forensic pathologist still employed in the jurisdiction may testify for the original one, because they have similar credentials, see similar cases, and prepare similar reports and each one has expert training in cause and manner of death. In rare situations, a person who has knowledge of the particular case but who has different credentials may be allowed to testify in your place.

Depositions

A **deposition** is much like trial testimony, and may be used if you cannot attend the trial (see Figure 8.7). In a deposition, you are sworn in, and questioned by both side's attorneys. There is a court reporter present to take down the proceedings, but there is no judge present. You must still pause before answering because the opposing attorneys can make objections. There is no judge present to rule on the objections, so after they are voiced, you answer the question. If the judge later sustains certain objections, your answers to those questions are stricken from the record. The deposition may be videotaped. If it is not video-taped, you will be instructed that you must answer "yes" or "no." Because the court reporter cannot document nodding or shaking of your head, and may record, "Uh huh," but without audible voice intonations, it is difficult to determine if you mean yes or no when the transcription is read. The attorneys may travel to your location to take your deposition. Depositions are used for other aspects of a trial, and are not used only for a witness who must be absent from the trial.

FIGURE 8.7: *The deposition is an official record and will take place outside the confines of the court.*

If the deposition is not videotaped, and is only transcribed by the court reporter, you have the right to read over the transcription and make corrections. You usually receive a form to fill out and sign that contains the corrections. You return the form with the corrections, either to the attorneys or the court reporter. This is something you must do. It is surprising how many words are taken down incorrectly and are transcribed as a similar-sounding word. These incorrect words may completely change the meaning of what you actually said. In other cases, the court reporter did not hear you, and the record will just state "inaudible." You must correct all of the mistakes and inaudible transcriptions. Clearly, you must make these corrections as soon as you receive the transcription so you remember what you actually said.

The videotape or final transcription of the deposition is shared with the jurors at the trial. The jurors use the information provided in the deposition to consider the facts when it is time for deliberations.

Distance Testimony

Testifying long distance is possible, and is dependent upon the technology available, the type of case, and the attorneys and the judge. The witness may testify over the phone after being sworn in, or the witness may testify after being sworn in by using videoconferencing software. Using this software, the jurors can actually see the witness on the screen, and all questions are answered in real time, just as though the witness is present. The witness must still pause and respect all objections to questions.

Sometimes, videotaped interviews are played for the jurors without questions being asked of the witness by the attorneys. This most frequently is used when a child is the witness. The child is interviewed by a specially trained child forensic interviewer, and the interview is videotaped. The videotape is played for the jurors to show that the child was not asked any leading questions. This procedure is done to spare the child the trauma of going to court. Children may forget details when they go to court, especially if the trial is delayed. These videotapes are often used in cases of child sexual abuse, so the child does not have to face the defendant in court. Often, the child interviewer is there to testify in the trial regarding the details of the child forensic interview.

CASE STUDY

When Witnesses Are Out of the Jurisdiction

A family was murdered, and the suspect was in custody. The suspect, a male, was charged with the murders. The prosecutor decided he would not accept a plea-bargain, and was seeking the death penalty. The case had multiple continuances over the course of two years. The prosecutor was an older gentleman, who retired before the case went to trial.

The new prosecutor on the case was not as set on pursuing the death penalty. He eventually allowed the defendant to plead guilty on all counts, thus avoiding the death penalty.

The judge and attorneys wanted to have a sentencing hearing to determine sentencing. The judge wanted to have a full understanding of the pain and suffering of the victims, so he asked to have the photographs of the wounds explained to him at the sentencing hearing.

The medical examiner prepared all the photographs and worked with the prosecution on the case regarding her testimony about the injuries. The medical examiner was unexpectedly called out of the country to assist in a public crisis and emergency after a large earthquake. The infrastructure of the country was disrupted, and communication to the United States was virtually nonexistent.

The judge did not want to postpone the sentencing hearing, so he granted permission for the medical examiner's death investigator to explain the injuries in the medical examiner's absence. The death investigator was not a physician like the medical examiner, but the death investigator had been present at the crime scene and at the autopsies, so she was deemed to have enough information and experience with the case to explain the injuries.

The death investigator had moved to another city, but remained in the same state as the hearing. It was far cheaper to fly her to the hearing than to fly the medical examiner back from overseas, since any kind of telephonic or videoconferencing were out of the question, given the lack of available communication after the earthquake.

The death investigator attended the hearing. She was able to explain all the photographs and answer all of the judge's questions, so the perpetrator was successfully sentenced in the absence of the testimony of the medical examiner.

Summary

Going to testify in court should no longer be an intimidating experience. You now understand your role in the courtroom when you testify. You will be professional and well dressed. You know what to bring with you to court, and you know to ask permission before you refer to any of your materials.

You are now versed in the courtroom tactics of attorneys, and you have gained an understanding of why these tactics are used. If you go to court to testify, and the attorneys are particularly hard on you, you know you can be proud that you did your original job well and were a threat to the opposing team of attorneys. You will not take the treatment personally. You will not be angry, and you will not feel incompetent.

Each time you testify, you will learn more about the entire process, and you will experience different attorney's tactics. You will learn that testifying can be rewarding and fun, and you will no longer be intimidated when you are served with a subpoena to testify in court.

Discussion Questions

1. What questions might an attorney ask in an attempt to anger, discredit, or impeach a witness? Give examples.

2. Discuss examples of clothing a female witness should wear in court. Discuss examples of clothing a male witness should wear in court? Why are juries more relaxed about the acceptable colors for female clothing? Why do you think jurors care about shoes?

3. Discuss all the reasons you must contact the courts before you appear in response to a subpoena?

4. Explain all the alternatives to appearing personally in court to testify and their pros and cons.

5. Discuss Constitutional legal issues with videoconferencing in a witness for a trial. (From Resources pop-up: "Champion Magazine" article for the National Association of Criminal Defense Lawyers.) Discuss student opinions about these issues.

Key Terms

Alternates: Extra persons on the jury who sit through the entire trial whose function it is to replace a juror who must be excused; they do not know who they are and are excused at the end of the trial if not needed and are not allowed to participate in deliberations.

Bench trial: The attorneys have agreed to allow the judge to determine guilt, and there is no jury present at the trial.

Continuance: The attorneys involved in a trial get permission to continue it on a later date rather than when it was supposed to happen.

Cross-examination: Questions asked by the opposing attorney, which may consist of leading questions; questions in which the attorney gives the details in the question, and the witness can only confirm or deny the statement without elaboration.

Deposition: An interview done under oath with both parties' attorneys present, with court reporters present, but without a judge present; the witness undergoes direct and cross-examinations.

Direct examination: Questions asked by the attorney that subpoenaed the witness that require the witness to supply the answer.

Discovery: The time when reports and evidence regarding a civil lawsuit or a criminal trial are gathered, and persons involved in the situation are interviewed or deposed.

Discredit: A tactic where the attorneys try to make the witness look incompetent for one error so the jury will not believe any of the testimony of that witness: a way to create mistrust for a witness in the eyes of the jurors.

Exhibits: Documents, photos, evidence, or other props to help the jury understand the facts in a trial that must be agreed upon by the attorneys and judge, or admitted, before use in a trial.

Expert witness: A person with special knowledge, experience, and credentials in a particular area who is asked to testify in a case and determined to be an expert at the trial; he or she may state facts and opinions.

Fact witness: A person who has direct personal knowledge of facts important to a case and is asked to testify; the person can only state facts and not opinions.

Friendly witness: Witnesses asked to testify in a trial that are friends, relatives, or business associates of the defendant.

Hostile witness: A person asked to testify at a trial who is against the defendant or his actions.

Impeach: An attempt to make the jury believe that everything a particular witness has testified about is false; done using special tactics by attorneys while questioning the witness.

Mistrial: An end to a trial before its natural conclusion, requiring it to be started over.

Objection: The opposing attorneys find something wrong with a question asked by the other team of attorneys; the judge determines whether or not the witness may answer the question.

Official witness: A person involved in a trial who is asked to testify because of his or her official capacities, such as a police officer.

Overruled: A ruling by the judge regarding an objection that means the question is fair and must be answered by the witness.

Perjury: Lying under oath during testimony, which is a felony.

Plea-bargain: Admitting guilt for a slightly lesser crime to avoid a trial.

Recess: Small breaks in a trial granted by the judge, for example, for lunch or other short breaks.

Subpoena: An official court order that orders a person to appear in court to testify.

Sustained: A ruling by the judge regarding an objection that means the question is inappropriate and cannot be answered by the witness; a different question must be asked.

Swearing in: The oath a witness takes before testifying to swear they will tell the truth on the witness stand.

Trajectory: The path something takes.

Venire: Also known as the jury panel; a large group of potential jurors that must be narrowed down to those persons to serve on the actual jury.

Voir dire: French for "to speak the truth": a series of verbal questions asked of the venire by the judge and the attorneys in a case for trial to determine the most impartial persons who should be selected to serve on the jury.

Technology-Based Communication Tools

Photo courtesy of FEMA News Photo

Key Module Concepts:

- History and development of the Internet

- Basic Internet technologies

- Principles of Internet etiquette

- Growth and usage of Internet social networks

- Information security risks and basic countermeasures

- Privacy risks and protective measures

Introduction

Advances in communication technology frequently have dramatic, even revolutionary, impacts on human society. Martin Luther probably did not set out to launch the Protestant Reformation, but the Gutenberg system of moveable type (ca. 1439) brought Luther's 95 Theses out of academia and onto the street. Typesetting also fanned the flames of the Renaissance and the Scientific Revolution.

Other advances in communications – telegraph, telephone, radio, television, and computer technology – have wrought their own changes on the economy, politics, and society. The **Internet** stands on and

extends all of those previous accomplishments, bringing truly unprecedented opportunities, challenges, risks, and rewards to mankind.

Ask Yourself

- *How has the Internet changed the way we communicate?*
- *How do I manage the risks of being on the Internet?*
- *What are the expectations of privacy on the Internet*

Internet History

On October 4, 1957, the Soviet Union launched the first artificial satellite into space. The success of Sputnik 1, in those early days of the Cold War, came as a rude shock to American policy makers and military planners. In an effort to regain the technological lead, the Department of Defense created the Advanced Research Projects Agency (ARPA).

An early concern of the Defense Department was the ability of military communications to survive in the event of a nuclear strike. Extensive research determined that **packet switching** provided the most robust and survivable technology. Work began in earnest in 1965. On October 29, 1969, the first two nodes of the ARPANET (University of California at Los Angeles and Stanford University) went live. By the end of 1971, 15 sites were connected to the ARPANET.

In 1975, Bolt, Beranek, and Newman (BBN), the private contractors for ARPANET, launched the first public packet switching network, called Telenet (not to be confused with the **Telnet** remote session protocol). BBN installed free public dial-up access points in cities throughout the United States.

ARPANET originally ran on the Network Control Program (NCP). In 1974, the Transmission Control Program (TCP) specification was published. This coined the term "Internet" to describe a single, global TCP network. On January 1, 1983, all **hosts** on the ARPANET were switched over to the new TCP/IP protocol. TCP/IP remains the standard Internet protocol to this day.

The 1980s saw increased use of personal computers as costs dropped, computing power increased (Moore's Law), and affordable productivity applications and popular games hit the market. Online bulletin board services (BBS) such as Compuserve, Prodigy, and AOL provided connectivity to their respective subscribers. The Internet, however, remained the province of scientists, academics, and the military. By the late 1980s, subscription Internet services appeared for professionals and enthusiasts who wanted direct access to the Net and who were versed in the UNIX shell commands necessary to do so. Communications remained text-based, due to software and hardware limitations and the slow speeds available on dial-up connections.

Who is Gordon Moore?

Gordon Moore, co-founder of Intel, predicted in 1965 that the number of transistors on a circuit would double every two years for the foreseeable future. This has since been redefined as the density of data doubling every 18 months. Over the years, it has consistently held true, although Moore himself now states that the law can't go on forever.

In 1991, the European Organization for Nuclear Research (CERN) published the **World Wide Web** project, an invention of British scientist Tim Berners-Lee. Early Web browsers were text-based, but as Moore's Law continued to hold true, cheaper and more powerful hardware, easier to use graphical user interfaces (Macintosh and Windows) and the proliferation of relatively inexpensive broadband connections brought more computers into the home and workplace. Demand increased for online graphics and real-time information sharing technologies such as Internet telephony, streaming media, and teleconferencing. As these demands were met, and more users were drawn to the Internet, creating explosive growth. Internet usage grew at a rate of 100% per year during the 1990s, with an even greater spike in the years 1996 - 1997.

As of June 30, 2010, there were an estimated two billion users on the Internet. The greatest avenues for future growth are expected to be in Brazil, Russia, China, India, and Indonesia. The next few years also will see the transition to Internet Protocol version 6 (IPv6) as the supply of IPv4 addresses is nearly exhausted. The proliferation of mobile network-enabled devices, such as smartphones, ebook readers, netbooks, and tablet computers, and the concomitant proliferation of public Wi-Fi hotspots, is another growing trend.

Email

Email is one of the oldest applications on the Internet (see Figure 9.1). Messages are delivered to a user's email address in much the same way that postal mail has been delivered for centuries. Email, like all other Internet applications, originally was plain text-based. As hard drive space has become cheaper, computers more powerful, and Internet connections speedier, the trend has been to the use of Hypertext Markup Language (HTML) – the language that powers the World Wide Web – in emails. There also has been an increasing use of email to send file attachments, such as photographs, contracts, video clips, and music.

Law enforcement uses email as a tool for communication just like any other business: to send documents, to touch base with staff, or to communicate with citizens.

In today's fast moving and global world, law enforcement has been taking advantage of the pace by creating email notifications to reach out to citizens. CrimeWeb.Net is the oldest and most advanced alerting system of its kind. Since 1997, countless notices have been sent to Americans informing them of a crime with a description of the suspect(s). Recipients are then encouraged to contact police with any information, similar to *America's Most Wanted TV* show with John Walsh. As with AMW, this spin-off version is used as another effort to partner with the community, although it is not limited to just CrimeWeb.Net, as police departments all over the nation are setting up the same type of inbox notification.

FIGURE 9.1: *Computers, which were rare in police agencies in the early 1990s, have become an indispensable tool*

Photo courtesy of FEMA News Photo

Chat

Chat is another early application that has evolved considerably with technology. Internet forums, chat rooms, and the older bulletin board services (Compuserve) typically arc organized along a many-to-many basis, in which someone posts a comment or query and awaits a response if necessary or desired. Instant messaging operates more like a telephone call, in which users bandy back-and-forth in real time on a one-to-one basis. Internet Relay Chat (IRC), AOL Instant Messenger (AIM), Google Chat, Yahoo!, and other networks are also popular. An early limitation of these networks was that the anyone wanting to chat had to be on the same network as the person with whom they were chatting. Multi-protocol clients quickly developed to address this shortcoming. Video chat is now available to anyone with an inexpensive webcam and a microphone; video chat applications and services, a number of them free, are available from Apple, Google, Skype, and other vendors.

Departments are creating police blotter blogs that are capable of displaying messages in real-time. A variety of news – sometimes more detailed than a regular police report – that the public needs to know is readily available for all to see. Sometimes journalists write their stories from the stream of data straight from the source without having to attend a press conference.

Videos chats work as a great and inexpensive aid to conduct meetings with magistrates, but they are especially useful for departments in rural areas. Officers from the Vinton Police Department in Virginia and their suspects can now sit in front of a screen and talk to a judge far away, cutting down on hundreds of driving hours. Before this capability was available, officers would have to make the 16-mile drive, sometimes with the suspect, if the magistrate decided not to detain the person.

Social Networks

A **social network** is defined as a social structure made up of individuals or organizations, called "nodes," which are connected by one or more specific types of interdependency, such as clan or kinship, financial exchange, social status, and sexual relationships. Most studies of human society, from anthropology to social psychology, now employ some degree of social network theory.

Social network services are Internet sites and platforms that build on and reflect these types of social networks. Unlike Internet chat rooms and forums, which tend to be group-oriented, social network services are individual-oriented. Users define the size and scope of their personal networks according to their own interests, feelings, beliefs, and degrees of trust. Facebook, MySpace, LinkedIn, Flickr, and Twitter are examples of social networks.

Facebook

Facebook is a social network service and website launched in February 2004. As of the end of 2013, Facebook has 1.23 billion active users and is the second most accessed site on the Internet after Google.

Facebook users may create a personal profile, add other users as friends and exchange messages, including automatic notifications when they update their profile. Additionally, users may join common interest user groups, organized by workplace, school, political affiliation, religion, or other characteristics.

A "facebook" (aka froshbook or freshman yearbook) is a book given to university students at the start of the academic year to help them get to know each other better. Interestingly, for our discussion of security, Facebook began when co-founder Mark Zuckerberg, then a sophomore at Harvard University, hacked into the University's computer system, obtained students' private dormitory ID photos, and created a website around them. Although Zuckerberg initially faced expulsion, the University dropped academic charges against him. The rest, as they say, is history.

As you will see later, Facebook users (and other social networking users) should exercise caution in their online privacy settings. Profile information generally is publicly visible if not restricted by the user.

Around the nation, police departments have begun to incorporate Facebook into their policing efforts to serve a variety of needs. Posts from missing people to school closures to press releases have all proven successful – not to mention the success rate of catching criminals, which has increased from tipsters. When it comes to leaving info about criminal activities, more people feel comfortable posting on the Facebook Wall rather than talking on the phone.

While setting up the Massillon Police Department's page, officer and page administrator Brian Muntean found that the public checked Facebook more often than the newspaper. Ohio's "finest" figured it was the perfect spot to share mug shots and other information, but never did they expect that people with outstanding warrants would turn themselves in. Currently, three people have done just that, including a mother who coaxed her son to turn himself in after seeing his warrant on Facebook.

Twitter

Twitter combines social networking with **microblogging**. Based on the 140-character limit of **SMS** text messages, Twitter derived its name, according to co-founder Jack Dorsey, from two dictionary definitions: "a short burst of inconsequential information" and "chirps from birds." These messages are called tweets; they are visible to the public, but users may restrict them to members of their network. Users may subscribe to other users' posts; this is called "following," and members of the user's network are called "followers." By using hashtags (e.g., #police), users may group and search tweets by subject matter.

In response to a sharp spike in auto theft, the Seattle Police initiated a program in which stolen car information was tweeted to the public. This creative approach to use social networking tools to fight crime may put additional sets of eyes on the street watching for a stolen car within minutes of the police receiving the report. Seattle PD has over 1,037 followers.

"One of the important messages from all of this is as technology continues to grow and expand, we are growing and expanding," said Lieutenant Mike Edwards of SPD Investigation Procedures.

LinkedIn

LinkedIn is a business-oriented professional networking site that works much like other social media sites. There are an estimated 250 million members, with about one third of them being in the United States. LinkedIn members reside in over 200 countries and territories. The fastest growing demographic is college students and recent graduates. LinkedIn users specifically focus on professional development and networking.

Law enforcement officers can use LinkedIn for the same reasons as other users. They can create and participate in LinkedIn groups focused on particular issues, geographic areas, expertise, and so on; leverage shared expertise to solve business problems; and build personal networks for career development. Chief David Molloy of the Novi, Michigan Police Department is a big fan of LinkedIn and the ability to reach out both within and outside the law enforcement community: "Others can see my organization is on the cutting edge. My contacts are CFOs and COOs who comment that the police agency is not afraid to take risks, and we're willing to share what we're doing. We're not cloak and dagger as law enforcement is known for."

For law enforcement, it is important to recognize how new and old technologies and approaches can be combined to achieve important synergies (see Figure 9.2). In 2010, Maryland police made a number of sweeps involving drugs, prostitution, and human trafficking. Investigators used a combination of Internet searches, education of and tips from hotel staff, and physical surveillance.

FIGURE 9.2: *The way people gather information is rapidly evolving from newspapers and TV networks to social media and other Web-based communication tools.*

Internet Etiquette

Internet etiquette (otherwise known as *netiquette*), like conventional etiquette, is a set of social conventions devised to provide a universal set of rules for polite, Web-based human interaction. In this case, the interaction takes place in Usenet newsgroups, Web forums, email, chat, social networks, and so on. The "rules" are spelled out in IETF RFC 1855.

Concerns about netiquette began in the early days of the Internet. Users quickly realized the need for an established set of social mores governing the use of email, Telnet, Usenet, and other early protocols. The term *netiquette* has been in use since at least 1983.

Like much else on the Internet and in real life, netiquette exists in a state of flux and varies from community to community. A lively debate in one venue may be unimportant in another area. A few general rules seem generally agreed upon:

Help new users. No one was born to the Net. Some are young people getting on for the first time; some are senior citizens getting on for the first time; some are citizens or expatriates of developing countries getting on for the first time. Everyone was new once, so be considerate.

Research before asking. Search engines, including the Search functions of various newsgroups, bulletin boards, and so on, contain a wealth of information. Many questions have been asked before, and some have been asked enough to be codified into FAQs (Frequently Asked Questions). Try not to waste others people's time and bandwidth with questions that have been asked and answered numerous times before.

Remember emotion. The Internet does a poor job of conveying subtlety or wry humor. It is easy to be misunderstood, even to the point of appearing insulting. Make your point plainly; emoticons can help, but their use in business correspondence is controversial.

People aren't organizations. Email sent from an individual's work account should not be deemed to be speaking for the organization itself. If you send email from your work account, and are not speaking for the organization, consider adding a disclaimer at the end.

Assume that everything you write or forward is public. This is possibly the most important thing to remember.

Too often, anonymity leads people to behave in ways they shouldn't; riots and road rage are well-known examples of this phenomenon. On the Internet, this frequently takes the form of boorish conduct such as trolling, flaming, and thread-jacking.

Three Common Boorish Behaviors on the Web

Flaming involves verbal abuse of other users, either individually or as a group. This frequently includes the use of abusive and profane language.

Behaviors on the Web

Thread hijacking involves taking over a conversational thread on a message board or forum by taking part of the original topic and twisting it in a direction that may reasonably be said to be off-topic.

Trolling is the act of purposefully antagonizing another person on the Internet. It is deliberate conduct, calculated to provoke an emotional response from others. The best practice is simply to ignore it. On moderated forums, trolling usually results in banning.

Inadvertent breaches of netiquette usually can be avoided by thinking before you post. Do not say or do things on the Internet that you would not do if you were face-to-face with a particular person or group of people.

When sending email, forum and newsgroup postings, and chat, keep messages clear, concise, and relevant. Don't use all-capital letters or grossly exaggerated fonts; these have the effect of yelling. Don't forward things you haven't read. Use discretion in forwarding items, as they may have been intended for your eyes only, not for everyone in your address book. If people ask to be removed from your email list, or that you refrain from sending certain types of email to them (e.g., jokes), honor their request.

Law enforcement officers should be aware of and adhere to the rules, both with respect to the Internet generally and department policy specifically. Most agencies have rules in place for computer usage: departmental computers should never be used for inappropriate purposes or in an inappropriate manner, even seemingly innocuous ones. Personal postings, in email or in public forums, should not bring disrepute to an officer or his/her department; such postings could be used to impeach the officer's credibility in a court of law.

CASE STUDY

The Power of Social Networking

While Internet social networks may have begun for personal pursuits, such as finding dates and keeping in touch with friends, they have expanded to fill a role in broader areas of social order, political movements, and international relations.

During the street protests and government crackdowns that followed Iran's June, 2009 elections, the Iranian government blocked cell phone text messaging. Opposition candidate Mir Hossein Mousavi and his followers turned to Twitter as a means of taking their message to the outside world. Since tweets are broadcasts, and go out over both the Internet and SMS, they reach a broader audience than other forms of Internet communication or social networking; this makes Twitter a tool well-suited (though not ideal) to use by a mass movement.

Coincidentally, Twitter had scheduled a network upgrade during this time. Downtime was expected to be brief, and was scheduled for the middle of the night to minimize its impact on American users. The problem, from the dissidents' perspective, was that the middle of the night in America is middle of the day in Iran. The dissidents feared loss of communication at a critical time. U.S. State Department official Jared Cohen called his friend, Twitter co-founder Jack Dorsey, and convinced him to postpone the upgrade until 2 p.m. Pacific Time, (1:30 a.m. Tehran time).

Concerns with Twitter arose because of the very anonymity and accessibility that made it attractive. How reliable was the information being put out? Who were the people tweeting? Were expatriate sympathizers tweeting, potentially discrediting the very cause they thought to support? Were Iranian agents provocateurs tweeting, in an effort to blunt or discredit the movement? Was the government using Twitter to track and monitor dissidents?

Twitter is a mass communications medium, subject to many of the strengths and weaknesses of other media. The Iranian regime wasn't toppled by tweets; the street demonstrations were suppressed the old-fashioned way, with clubs, rifle butts, gas, and bullets. Still, the new medium did demonstrate its ability to maintain open lines of communication when the regime shut down others. In the end, people interested in the free exchange of ideas will always find a way around government controls; it is an endeavor to which the Internet is particularly well suited.

Internet Security

While ARPANET was designed to be robust and survivable, little attention was given to issues of security and privacy. ARPANET began as a trusted network: access was limited and expensive; nodes were few; users were responsible adults with serious work to do and all pretty much "knew" each other, either personally or by reputation. In such an environment, it made little sense do divert scarce development resources to combat nonexistent threats. Applications like Telnet (remote login) and File Transfer Protocol (FTP) transmitted user names, passwords, and data in the clear.

Today, security on the Internet is a much greater concern. Ease of access has given rise to a new world of crime (cyber crime), from petty acts of vandalism (e.g., spam) to large-scale acts of identity theft and Internet disruption. Security experts look for ways to secure their networks against outside attacks; programmers develop secure equivalents of older, insecure applications; anti-**malware** companies compete for consumers' dollars; law enforcement and national security agencies scour the Net for terrorists, child pornographers, and identity thieves; privacy advocates and civil libertarians worry about unwarranted surveillance; national governments mount attacks on the networks of rival countries; repressive regimes seek to monitor, censor, and control the Internet, while those who chafe under those regimes use the Internet to maintain contact with supporters abroad and to get their message to a global audience.

The Internet Crime Complaint Center (IC3) is a partnership of the FBI, the National White Collar Crime Center (NW3C) and the Bureau of Justice Assistance (BJA). According to their mission statement: "IC3's mission is to serve as a vehicle to receive, develop, and refer criminal complaints regarding the rapidly expanding arena of cyber crime. The IC3 gives the victims of cyber crime a convenient and easy-to-use reporting mechanism that alerts authorities of suspected criminal or civil violations. For law enforcement and regulatory agencies at the federal, state, local, and international level, IC3 provides a central referral mechanism for complaints involving Internet related crimes."

In 2009, there were 336,655 complaints filed with IC3, up 22.3% from 2008. Dollar losses reported to law enforcement reached an all-time high of $559.7 million. And 146,663 cases were referred to law enforcement, more than twice the 2008 figure.

The purpose of Internet security is to secure information. Information security is concerned with three main areas:

Confidentiality: Information is available only to those who rightfully have access to it.

Integrity: Information can be modified only by those who are authorized to do so.

Availability: Information is accessible to those who need it, when they need it.

These principles apply to home computers as well as to business and government systems. Failure to adhere to good information security practices can lead to identity theft, financial losses, damage to reputation, and loss of data of sentimental value (family photos and videos). For example, consider the following cases:

In 1999, an unknown attacker planted child pornography on the work computer of a legal scholar at Lund University in Sweden. System administrators found 3,500 photographs on the researcher's computer and notified the school's administration, which assumed the researcher downloaded them knowingly. He lost his job, fled the country after his name was made public, and suffered severe health problems due to stress. In 2004, he was acquitted of all charges after it was learned that his computer had been controlled remotely via NetBus (Swedish for "Net Prank").

In 2000, Canadian teenager Michael Calce (aka MafiaBoy) launched a series of **Denial-of-Service** (DoS) attacks against high-profile corporations, including Yahoo!, Dell, eBay, and CNN. Financial losses worldwide from Calce's week-long rampage were estimated to be as high as $1.2 billion USD.

In 2009, an 18-year-old hacker used a **dictionary attack** to gain access to a Twitter administrator's account; he reset the passwords of 33 high-profile accounts, including Barack Obama, Britney Spears, and Fox News, and freely distributed the new credentials to other intruders.

FIGURE 9.4: *Physical damage to computers and smartphones can be caused by intention or by accident. Defenses against this type of attack are different than the defenses against cyber attacks.*

In addition to protecting against malicious intruders, information security should protect the user from loss of data due to natural or man-made disasters, such as fires, earthquakes, and power outages, as shown in Figure 9.4.

Network Threats

Computer **viruses** have infected the Internet from its very early years.

Viruses, worms, trojans, rootkits, and other malware go back to the early days of Internet mainframe computers and stand-alone personal computers. The first major malware attacks were typically distributed on infected physical media, such as floppy disks and CDs. These "Sneakernet" viruses predate Internet viruses.

As the system and the network have become one, the most common means of infection now is through the Internet. The hacking threat has morphed from immature pranksters seeking self-validation to sophisticated criminal gangs out for big money and real damage. At any moment, there are thousands of hackers and compromised systems scanning the Internet, searching for systems with unpatched security holes, negligently open ports, and unnecessary and insecure services running.

In September, 2010, more than 60 people were charged in international schemes that used Internet viruses to steal almost $4 million from bank accounts in America. U.S. Attorney Preet Bharara summed up the issue quit succinctly: "The modern, high-tech bank heist does not require a gun, a mask, a note, or a getaway car. It requires only the Internet and ingenuity. And it can be accomplished in the blink of an eye, with just a click of the mouse."

Many of the programs thought of as malware actually have legitimate uses as diagnostic and development tools. Under the right circumstances, law enforcement can make use of them to bring criminals to justice. In 1999, pursuant to a search warrant, the FBI used a **rootkit** to install a **keylogger** on the computer of mobster Nicky. The keylogger allowed the FBI to capture Scarfo's PGP encryption password and decrypt his data, thus obtaining evidence needed to convict him on illegal gambling and loan sharking charges.

In 1988, the first worm, written and promulgated by a Computer Science graduate student at Cornell University, crashed most of the Internet then in existence. The incident sparked ARPA to create the United States Computer Emergency Readiness Team (US-CERT) to track and provide information on Internet security threats. US-CERT's mission is to provide defense for the Federal executive branch against cyber attack, and to share information with state and local governments and private sector partners.

Resource -

United States v. Scarfo "http://epic.org/crypto/scarfo.html", *Electronic Privacy Information Center (EPIC)*

http://epic.org/crypto/scarfo.html

Network Defense

The proliferation of always-on broadband Internet connections, as well as the increasing use of mobile devices such as laptops and smartphones, means there no longer is a sharp distinction between "system" and "network." The growing use of **botnets**, particularly, means that the

FIGURE 9.5: *Network and computer systems are subject to both physical attacks and software attacks.*

network must be secured down to the individual computer. As always, a layered approach to security, properly implemented, will yield superior results (see Figure 9.5).

Corporate and government users generally have little to no say over the computers they use at work, so it is incumbent upon the organization's IT department to select the best mix of security features consistent with the organization's goals and objectives.

Anti-virus software need not be an expensive proposition as there are several excellent, free tools available. Antivirus software should be kept up-to-date with the vendor's latest patches and definition updates. Many of these products can be configured for real-time scanning. When running a scheduled or manual scan, it is important to fetch any program and definition updates first.

Regardless of technical measures, the ever-fallible human user remains the weak link in the security chain. Bremerton, California Police Officer John Rivera advises: "Even with the proliferation of effective antivirus solutions, there is one very important carbon-based (human) fix you can use every day: be wary of forwarded emails from friends, family, or familiar-looking addresses."

FIGURE 9.6: *Having a backup created can protect users against expensive loss of data.*

There is another important but frequently overlooked step – back up your data (see Figure 9.6). This is not optional and should be automated. A good backup plan will protect data from malicious attacks, hard-drive failures, electrical disruption, and other catastrophes. Off-site backup protect against catastrophic failure of the computer's physical location due to fire, flood, and soon. Inexpensive online backup and storage is available and should be used in conjunction with a local backup. Be sure to back up data only; applications can be backed up from their original sources (CD/DVD or download).

CASE STUDY

Malicious Attacks on Social Network Sites

In August, 2009, concerted attacks disrupted Twitter, Facebook, LiveJournal, and some Google sites for two days. Twitter and LiveJournal were shut down entirely for a time.

The target of the attacks was a **blogger**, Cyxymu (real name unknown), who identified himself as a professor at Sukhumi State University. Cyxymu said he was a refugee from Abkhazia, a disputed region between Russia and Georgia. The attacks apparently were intended to shut down his blog posts, where he had begun revisiting the events of the brief territorial war over South Ossetia between Russia and Georgia in 2008. Cyxymu's blog and social media pages were created, he said, to allow fellow refugees to exchange memories of their homeland. "Cyxymu" is a Latin transliteration of the Cyrillic name of the capital of Abkhazia, Sukhumi.

The attacks took place in two parts. First, the attackers sent out a wave of spam under the name Cyxymu. This technique (a "joe job") is designed to discredit an Internet user by making him appear to be a spammer. The emails contained links to several of Cyxymu's accounts, including his Twitter account.

Next, the attackers launched a Distributed Denial-of-Service (DDoS) against Cyxymu's pages on LiveJournal, Facebook, Twitter, and YouTube, in an effort to disable them. The attackers used a botnet, a network of thousands of malware-infested computers controlled from a single source. The flood of messages overwhelmed the services' servers, slowing Facebook and YouTube to a crawl and knocking out Twitter and LiveJournal entirely. Mikko Hypponen, chief technology officer at F-Secure, described the attacks as, "the equivalent of bombing a television station because you don't like one of the newscasters."

Cyxymu believes that the FSB (formerly KGB) were behind the attacks. The Russian government denied responsibility for the attacks, claiming they were the work of hyper-nationalistic Russian hackers. Moscow also has denied responsibility for the massive DDoS attacks against Georgia's communications infrastructure a few days after the start of the South Ossetia War and, as we have seen, neither a spam flood nor a DDoS requires the resources of a government to succeed.

Whatever the source of the attacks, the incident, like the post-election events in Iran, demonstrated the degree to which the Internet has become a global forum for political discussion, and how vulnerable the system is to disruption.

Internet Privacy

"The house of every one is to him as his castle and fortress, as well for his defence against injury and violence as for his repose."
    – Sir Edward Coke, *Semayne's Case* (1604)

"The right of the people to be secure in their persons, houses, papers, and effects, against unreasonable searches and seizures, shall not be violated, and no Warrants shall issue, but upon probable cause, supported by Oath or affirmation, and particularly describing the place to be searched, and the persons or things to be seized."
    – The Fourth Amendment to the United States Constitution

The Internet can be a very private communication tool and a powerful world-wide communications forum. How much privacy should one expect when using the Internet? Should governments monitor net activity to watch for crime much as a patrol officer works a neighborhood beat, or are governments intrusive and in violation of our expectation of privacy? Should the government have the power to shut down the Internet in an emergency?

These questions are dynamic in nature. We want violent terrorists and criminals monitored, but we don't want our personal emails read by government agents. Privacy issues have led the private sector to create new industries in encryption software and the courts to address legal implications of privacy on the Web.

Attacks on Privacy

Threats to privacy come from many sources. In the Internet Era, people may want to snoop through the emails of personal, professional, or political enemies. Likewise, identity thieves may try to obtain personal information to loot bank accounts or to conduct fraudulent transactions in another person's name. And governments may dislike the unfettered, widespread, and inexpensive flow of information.

The Internet, as mentioned previously, was not designed with a heavy emphasis on security or privacy: some things that should be secure, such as email, are not; other things, like social networks, never were intended to be private.

Tweets Gone Bad

In November, 2010, Chinese activist Cheng Jianping (Twitter name: wangyi09) was arrested on her wedding day and sentenced by the police to one year of "re-education through labor" for "disturbing the social order" by re-tweeting a post from her fiancé. Twitter is banned in China but is widely accessed through proxy servers that circumvent "The Great Firewall of China".

A week before Cheng's arrest, UK Tweeter Paul Chambers lost his appeal of his conviction for tweeting a joke about blowing up Robin Hood Airport due to their inefficiency.

Egyptian blogger and former law student Kareem Amer was released from prison on November 15, 2010. In February, 2007, he was sentenced to three years in prison for insulting Islam and inciting sedition and one year in prison for insulting Egyptian president Hosni Mubarak.
http://www.freekareem.org/

Almost everything we do on the Internet involves providing our personal information along the way. When you open an Internet account, you provide personal information to the ISP; this may include your Social Security number, bank account, and employment information. When you pay your bill, you provide financial information to the ISP.

Email is an insecure application. Messages are passed across the Internet in the clear, leaving them vulnerable to snooping. Emails are easily copied, forwarded, and hacked. Deleted emails are not gone, but merely moved to another folder; even emails that actually have been deleted may be recovered by commonplace file recovery techniques. Also, either party to an email exchange may legally disclose its contents.

Private Conversations on the Web Don't Always Stay Private

In 2001, the CEO of Cerner Corporation (NASDQ: CERN) sent an email flame to the managers of the company's Kansas City, Missouri plant, denouncing the employees for laziness and the managers for incompetence or indifference. The email quickly got around the company. The day the email was posted to Yahoo!, CERN's stock price fell by more than 20%.

Private Conversations on the Web

From June 18 to June 24, 2009, South Carolina governor Mark Sanford disappeared. He allegedly told his staff that he was going to hike the Appalachian Trail. He was reported as missing to the South Carolina Law Enforcement Division (SLED) after failing to return 15 phone calls from his staff and not calling his family on Father's Day. On June 24, a reporter, acting on, "a hunch," intercepted Sanford at an airport in a neighboring state as he disembarked from a plane returning from Argentina. Sanford quickly called a press conference to confess that he had been engaged in an extramarital affair with an Argentine woman. On June 25, South Carolina newspaper The State published a selection of emails from Sanford to his mistress.

On October 18, 2010, David Bartholomew, chairman of the Virginia Beach (VA) Republican Party, resigned after allegedly forwarding a racist email that ended up on the Internet.

Web surfing leaves tracks, a bit like Figure 9.7, although not quite so obvious. Websites can track and log your surfing on their site by IP address, operating system information, browser type, and other identifying information. Search engines log IP addresses, system names, and search terms, building up, over time, an individual user profile. Often, companiescross-reference data to create a user profile for advertising and marketing purposes.

FIGURE 9.7: *Web Surfers often leave tracks just like a truck tire on a muddy road.*

Website and ISP logs can be useful to the law enforcement investigator. Access to such information almost certainly will require a search warrant.

As always, users themselves pose the greatest threat to their own privacy. We tend to assume that the same laws and mores that govern our lives in the real world apply to our digital lives as well. We don't consider that we are doing things online that we wouldn't do in real life, or that we are doing them in ways that we wouldn't in real life. This is particularly true in the era of social networking: users fail to check the security settings of their accounts and "friend" total strangers.

**Government Monitoring
of Social Media**

In October, 2010, in response to a Freedom of Information Act (FOIA) lawsuit relating to federal surveillance of social networks, the Electronic Frontier Foundation (EFF) learned the U.S. Citizenship and Immigration Service, "is specifically instructing its agents to attempt to 'friend' citizenship petitioners and their beneficiaries on social networks in the hope that these users will (perhaps inadvertently) allow agents to monitor their activities for evidence of suspected fraud, including evidence that their relationships might not live up to the USCIS' standard of a legitimate marriage...".

Also in response to the FOIA lawsuit, EFF learned that, in the run-up to the 2009 inauguration of President Barack Obama, the Department of Homeland Security established a Social Network Monitoring Center (SNMC) to log "items of interest" on social networks, news, and political commentary sites.

Geotagging is a popular way of linking photos to locations. Researchers at UC Berkeley looked into photos and videos at popular social media sites and determined that 1.3% to 4.3% are tagged with location data. Smartphone cameras implement geotagging, frequently by default.

Adam Savage, host of the popular Mythbusters television program, recently was surprised to learn that a photo he tweeted of his car parked in his driveway was geotagged with the latitude and longitude of his home. Savage knew about the geotagging feature in the iPhone, but overlooked the fact that it is activated by default and must be turned off manually.

Many celebrities have unknowingly disclosed their whereabouts, in real time, with photo uploads from their smartphones Researchers at the International Computer Science Institute in Berkeley, California, used simple tools available online to find the home addresses of a Playboy Playmate and a number of TV personalities. Massachusetts-based computer security experts Ben Jackson and Larry Pesce found William Shatner, M.C. Hammer, Arnold Schwarzenegger, and others.

Since a number of popular sites, including Facebook, Twitter, and Flickr, provide APIs for developers to enhance and extend their sites' functionality, it would be a trivial matter to program a systematic geotag search.

Resource -

Applying for Citizenship? U.S. Citizenship and Immigration Wants to Be Your "Friend," *Electronic Frontier Foundation.*

http://www.eff.org/deeplinks/2010/10/applying-citizenship-u-s-citizenship-and

Cybercasing the Joint: On the Privacy Implications of Geo-Tagging, *International Computer Science Institute.*

http://www.icsi.berkeley.edu/cgi-bin/pubs/publication.pl?ID=002875

Protecting Your Privacy

Security and privacy are interrelated concepts, so adherence to the security features listed previously will go a long way toward protecting your privacy. We will list some suggestions specifically tailored to protecting your privacy online.

First and foremost: Be skeptical! Ask yourself how much information you truly want to put out to the public. Do you really need a million "friends" you've never met? Is the person making a friend request really who he says he is? Do you really want your photograph in your profile, particularly if you're posting anonymously, via proxy server, from within a repressive regime? Are your security settings really as locked down as they should be? Who is that pop-up, telling you that your computer has a virus and "Click Here" to clean it, really from? Is the email from your bank really from them? Are you really on the bank's website, or are you on a **phishing** or **pharming** site? Do you need to send this email to your entire address book, or is it aimed at one person? Do you truly understand that your emails, instant messages, and chat sessions are not truly private?

In a controversial but growing trend, police departments are beginning to require that recruits allow background investigators to view their social network pages and to provide confidential information such as usernames, passwords, and text message logs. A 2010 survey of over 700 agencies by the International Association of Chiefs of Police revealed that one-third of agencies already were doing so, with many others in the policy-development stage. "As more and more people join these networks, their activities on these sites become an intrinsic part of any background check we do," said Laurel, Maryland Chief David Crawford.

CASE STUDY

Political Attacks by Hacking Emails

During the 2008 presidential campaign, a hacker accessed the personal email account of then Alaska governor and Republican vice presidential candidate Sarah Palin. The case provides a classic example of what not to do, from the perspectives of both the victim and the attacker.

Palin used Yahoo! email. When signing up for an account, Yahoo! asks for several pieces of personally identifying information, "known only to you," to verify your identity. One of the uses of this information is to verify the user's identity in case she needs to reset her password.

Unfortunately, as a public figure, Palin had put much of this biographical information on the Web. Her attacker submitted a password reset request, "verified" himself as Palin with her personal information, reset her password, and read her emails – "All of them."

Palin's attacker, "Rubico," then went to the Web to boast of his mighty feat. He admitted that he had found, "... nothing that would derail her campaign as I had hoped, all I saw was some personal stuff, some clerical stuff from when she was governor... and pictures of her family...".

Unfortunately for Rubico, he failed to consider how much identifying information he was posting about himself. He routed his attack through only one proxy server. He posted screenshots of Palin's Yahoo! Mail account, including the URL of the public proxy server through which he routed his attack. The proxy service kept logs, which the FBI was able to use to determine Rubico's actual IP address.

Even that elementary bit of cyber-forensics was unnecessary, though. Rubico's screen name was linked to his own Yahoo! Mail account. A few searches of Google and YouTube linked this account to David Kernell, a student at the University of Tennessee at Knoxville and the son of a Democratic state representative. Kernell was quickly arrested, tried, and convicted.

On November 12, 2010, David "Rubico" Kernell was sentenced to incarceration for a year and a day (the judge recommended a halfway house instead of prison), three years probation, and psychological counseling.

Summary

Gutenberg's press lowered information costs by eliminating the need to laboriously copy documents by hand. The telegraph, telephone, and radio did the same by reducing the need to carry physical documents from sender to recipient, and by moving communications at nearly the speed of light. The Internet Revolution has effected similar changes, the repercussions of which have yet to be fully felt.

People around the world are now able to connect with each other cheaply and instantaneously, opening new avenues for the exchange of information, goods, and services. In less than 15 years, eBay has grown from a personal website to a multi-billion dollar corporation with localized operations in 30 countries and is a component of the Standard & Poors 500. Internet telephony dramatically lowers the cost of long-distance and international telephone calls. Video conferencing reduces the need to physically move people, and streaming media eliminates the expense of duplicating and shipping physical media.

Distance learning lowers the cost of education and makes that education available on flexible schedules that suit the needs of working adults. Entrepreneur Salman Khan has launched his Khan Academy to fulfill his vision of a "free classroom for the World." Online degrees up to graduate level are now available from reputable educational institutions. Even brick-and-mortar schools are transforming: the Stanford University School of Medicine, for example, has begun issuing iPads to incoming students to improve their learning experience.

Along with these changes come new challenges. How will society adapt to economic, political, and social changes sparked by the Internet? How will people protect their privacy in an increasingly open world?

Law enforcement faces its own unique challenges and opportunities. Falling information costs increase the opportunities to cooperate across jurisdictions, even transnational ones. Unfortunately, as has been seen in several recent fraud, human trafficking, and child pornography cases, the same holds true for criminals. Law enforcement and other public safety can reach out to the citizenry as never before, including the use of SMS text alerts of incidents or imminent danger, but scam artists and sexual predators can farm for thousands of potential victims with one press of a button. Issues of fact give rise to issues of law; law enforcement, the courts, the legislatures, and the people alike will confront Constitutional challenges arising from the broadening acceptance of the new media.

Discussion Questions

1. Does the Internet lower information costs? What are the implications for society, commerce, education, etc.?

2. How do users filter good information from bad on the Internet?

3. Do you use mobile devices? If so, have they changed the way in which you use or experience the Internet? Is mobile computing effecting its own paradigm shift in the evolution of Internet communications? Discuss.

4. The right of privacy has been deeply ingrained over the centuries. Does the widespread availability of publicly searchable databases render these protections moot? Does the conduct of users in voluntarily posting large amounts of personal data for public view create a lower expectation of privacy in cyberspace? Is the Fourth Amendment a dead letter? Discuss.

5. What is the role of law enforcement in cyberspace? What new challenges and opportunities are available in the public safety sphere?

Key Terms

Blog: A website or part of a website. Blogs are used for everything from online diaries to newsletters, marketing, and educational tools. Blogs typically are regularly updated (daily or several times daily) and frequently contain embedded video and audio, and links to other blogs and websites. Unlike static websites, blogs usually are interactive, allowing viewers to comment and, if the site allows, privately message each other. Blog also is used as a verb, meaning to create, write for, or post to a blog.

Botnet: A collection of software agents (robots) that run autonomously and automatically. They are used legitimately in distributed computing applications, but are also the normal means of carrying out *Distributed Denial of Service* attacks.

Chat: One-on-one conversations or text-based group conversations (formally called *synchronous conferencing*) that take place on the Internet via tools such as instant messengers, IRC chat tools, and multi-user dungeons (MUDs – used primarily for online role-playing games).

Cookie (Web cookie, browser cookie, HTTPS cookie)**:** A piece of text stored by a user's Web browser. Cookies are useful for authentication, online shopping, session management, and so on. They are not viruses, since they are not executable, but can be used as *spyware* or hijacked in order to provide access to a user's session on the originating server.

Denial of Service (DoS) Attack: An attempt to make a computer resource unavailable to its intended users. A Distributed Denial of Service (DDoS) Attack accomplishes this through a distributed network of computers, usually a *botnet*.

Dictionary attack: A means of searching for cracking weak passwords by use of a program that moves recursively through a dictionary until it finds a password set to a common word.

Domain Naming System (DNS): The "phone book" of the Internet. Its most important function is to translate human-friendly domain names into IP addresses.

Email: "Electronic mail," a method of exchanging electronic messages across the Internet or other computer network. With increases in computing power, disk space, and network bandwidth, email is increasingly used to transfer file attachments, such as pictures, video, and audio.

Geotagging: The process of adding geographical metadata to various media, such as photos, video, and SMS text messages.

Host file: A computer file used in an operating system to map hostnames to IP addresses. Usually named *hosts*, it is a plain text file and vulnerable to attack.

Hypertext Transfer Protocol (HTTP): A networking protocol for distributed, collaborative hypermedia documents. HTTP is the foundation for data communication over the World Wide Web. Sensitive information should always be transmitted over the secure version, HTTPS.

Internet: A global collection of interconnected computer networks that use the standard Internet Protocol Suite (TCP/IP) to communicate with one another.

Keylogger: A computer program that records a user's keystrokes; used as a means of monitoring activity and of obtaining passwords and other user-input data.

Malware: A portmanteau of *malicious software,* used generically to describe software installed on users' computers without their informed consent for reasons hostile to the users' interests.

Microblogging: A broadcast medium in the form of a Web log (blog). Microblogging differs from traditional blogging in that its content is generally smaller, both in actual size and aggregate file size. Twitter presently is the best known microblogging service.

Packet sniffer (network analyzer, packet analyzer, Ethernet sniffer, Wireless sniffer, etc.)**:** A hardware device or software used to intercept and log packets passing across a network. Can be used for legitimate purposes of network management and security, or as a means of hacking into a computer or network.

Packet switching: The fundamental technology underlying the Internet. Data is broken into smaller units, called *packets*, and encapsulated with information about the IP addresses of the sender and the recipient, the packet sequence number, error checking code, etc. Packets are sent to their destination by the best route available to each packet, and then they reassembled in the proper order at the recipient's computer.

Pharming: An attempt to redirect a website's traffic to another, fraudulent website (usually a *phishing* site). Pharming usually is accomplished by altering the *host's file* on the victim's computer or by exploiting a vulnerability in DNS server software.

Phishing: The criminally fraudulent process of attempting to acquire sensitive information, such as user names, passwords, and financial information, by masquerading as a trustworthy entity in an electronic communication (usually email or instant message).

Proxy server: A computer or software application that acts as an intermediary for clients seeking resources from other servers. Proxies have numerous, legitimate uses such as security, load balancing, and Web caching. They also can be used to enhance privacy, circumvent restrictions on Internet access, or to mask illegal activity.

Rootkit: Software that enables continued privileged (root) access to a computer while actively hiding its presence from administrators by subverting standard operating system functionality or other applications. Rootkits are not inherently malicious, but frequently are used for malicious purposes.

Router: A specialized computer that intercepts data packets moving across a network and directs them along the best routes to their destinations. Routers on an interconnected network "talk" to each other to learn and store the best paths to other networks. In simplistic terms, the Internet can be thought of as a vast collection of routers.

Script kiddies: Unsophisticated hackers who download and use, with little or no modification, readily available scripts from the Internet. Even in the absence of sheer malice, script kiddies can be the cyber-equivalent of children playing with matches, dangerous because of their lack of knowledge.

SMS (Short Message Service): A form of text messaging used by mobile phones. Twitter broadcasts by both the Web and SMS.

Social network: Internet sites and platforms that build on and reflect a user's relationships with others based on mutual interests, school and work affiliations, family ties, or other criteria and degrees of trust as defined by the individual user.

Spyware: A type of malware that can be installed on a computer and used to collect bits of information without the user's knowledge. Sometimes used legitimately in the corporate environment, as a security measure, to monitor a user's use of work computers.

Telnet: A network protocol used to establish bidirectional communication via virtual terminal to a remote host. Because usernames, passwords, and session data are transmitted in the clear, Telnet use has waned in favor of Secure Shell (SSH).

Uniform Resource Locator (URL): A means of determining a resource's location on the Internet and the means of retrieving it. A website address is a form of URL. Hovering the mouse cursor over a link in an email or website will reveal that link's URL and can provide protection against pharming and phishing attempts.

Uninterruptible Power Supply (UPS): A device that provides battery power to electronic devices in the event of a power failure. A UPS also contains a line conditioning circuit to protect equipment from damage due to voltage sags and surges. A UPS designed for computer use usually is sold with software that performs an orderly shutdown of the computer before the UPS's battery is drained, in order to protect against data loss.

Virus: A malicious computer program that can copy itself and infect a computer. Viruses usually are used to corrupt or modify files on the victim's computer.

World Wide Web (WWW): A system of interlinked hypertext documents accessed via the Internet. Naïve users frequently think the World Wide Web is the Internet. WWW documents may contain text, graphics, audio, and video.

Worm: A self-replicating malware program that exploits security vulnerabilities to send itself out to other computers on a network. Unlike viruses, worms do not need to attach themselves to other programs; worms frequently are used to carry viruses, though.

Zero-Day Exploit: A vulnerability previously unknown or undisclosed to the software developer

References

Electronic Privacy Information Center
http://epic.org

Schneier on Security (includes links to books by Bruce Schneier).
http://www.schneier.com

United States Computer Emergency Readiness Team
http://www.us-cert.gov/

The Art of Deception: Controlling the Human Element of Security by Kevin Mitnick: Wiley, 1st edition (October 17, 2003).

Hacking Exposed: Network Security Secrets and Solutions by Stuart McClure, Joel Scambray, George Kurtz: McGraw-Hill Osborne Media, 6th edition (January 5, 2009).

Secrets and Lies: Digital Security in a Networked World by Bruce Schneier: Wiley, 1st edition (January 30, 2004).

Steal This Computer Book 4.0: What They Won't Tell You About the Internet by Wallace Wang: No Starch Press, 4th edition (April 14, 2006).

Ty Swenson, "UPDATE: Seattle police to use Twitter "Get Your Car Back" account to combat auto theft," West Seattle Herald, December 1, 2010.

Sara Inés Calderón, "Police Use Facebook to Fight Crime, Talk to Residents," inside Facebook, February 19, 2010.

Lauri Stevens, "Three reasons why every cop should be on LinkedIn," ConnectedCops.net, October 25, 2009.

Heather Rawlyk, "Police sweeps net 35 arrests, $542K in seized drugs," HometownAnnapolis.com, December 9, 2010.

Jim McKay, "Vinton Police Discover Video Conferencing," Government Technology, August 27, 2002.

John Rivera, "P1 Tech Help: Beating computer viruses," PoliceOne, November 25, 2008.

Kevin Johnson, "Police recruits screened for digital dirt on Facebook, etc.," USA Today, November 12, 2010.

Applied Technology for Criminal Justice Communications

Key Module Concepts:

- Uses of home detention and electronic monitoring

- Strengths and weaknesses of GPS monitoring technologies

- Expansion of community corrections and new approaches to supervising offenders on probation or parole

- New technologies and approaches to reporting and investigating crimes

- New developments and future trends in alarm communications

- Uses of cable television and YouTube in criminal investigations and community outreach

Introduction

Like the rest of society, law enforcement has been profoundly impacted by advances in communications technology. The telegraph, telephone, radio, and the Internet have improved the ability of law enforcers to prevent, detect, and solve crimes.

In an unfortunate shift, though, as communications improved, police came to be more isolated from the communities they served. The cop walking the beat and interacting with people in the neighborhood, gave way to the patrol officer isolated from the public by his patrol car. Officers no longer exclusively lived where they worked. The image of the police as an anonymous outsider, with the citizenry cast as mere "civilians," became dominant for several decades, to the detriment of police-community relations.

Society itself, particularly in the urban areas, became more fragmented and transient. Fewer people knew their neighbors and became less likely to get involved in reporting crime.

Incarceration rates increased as new crimes and stiffer penalties for existing ones were created. Government budgets experienced fiscal strain associated with large-scale incarceration, prison overcrowding, new prison construction, and personnel costs.

Eventually, the pendulum began its return swing. The concept of "community-oriented policing" was adopted by agencies seeking to return to a partnership between police and citizenry. At about the same time, serious thought began as to how to use new advances in technology to improve interagency cooperation, community relations, and widespread public outreach. In the corrections field, technology came to be seen as a potential tool to reduce jail and prison overcrowding and improve supervision of probationers and parolees.

Offender Surveillance

According to the U.S. Bureau of Justice Statistics, at the end of 2009, a total of 7,225,800 people were either in prison, on probation, or on parole in America.

In 2008, federal, state, and local governments spent nearly $75 billion on corrections, the bulk of which was spent on incarceration. The number of incarcerated persons has increased by more than 350% since 1980, while the population has grown by only 33%. Interestingly, 60% of the people who are incarcerated are nonviolent offenders.

Incarceration presently costs an average of $26,000 per inmate per year, just in salaries for guards and electricity costs. That same inmate, working at the current federal minimum wage of $7.25 per hour, would earn $15,080 per year, substantially less than the cost of locking him up.

Cash-strapped jurisdictions have been motivated to find alternatives to incarceration. But "**community corrections**" – parole and probation – are not costless and also are subject to overloading. Furthermore, a 1994 Justice Department survey of 15 states revealed that two-thirds of parolees are rearrested and over half of them returned to prison within three years of their initial release.

We will examine some ways that technology can help reduce prison overcrowding and improve supervision of parolees to achieve better outcomes. We also will discuss the weaknesses of the present systems of monitoring and supervision.

House Arrest

House arrest is a measure by which persons may be legally confined to their homes. As an alternative to incarceration, it may be used both for unsentenced defendants and for convicted offenders.

House Arrest

Interesting People Who Have Been Under House Arrest

House arrest in general is not a new idea as you can see from the following list of notable people who were under house arrest at one time:

- *Galileo Galilei (1633), Scientist: Convicted of heresy by the Roman Inquisition, for defending the Copernican theory that the Earth revolves around the Sun (heliocentrism). Lived under house arrest until his death in 1642.*

- *Liliuokalani (1895), Queen of Hawaii (deposed, 1893): Convicted of treason by the Hawaiian Provisional Government, for concealing arms for the failed 1895 Counter-Revolution. Pardoned, 1896.*

- *Mohammed Mossadegh (1953), Politician, Premier of Iran, Time Magazine, Person of the Year, 1951: Deposed by Anglo-American coup, 1953. Lived under house arrest until death, 1967.*

- *William Calley (1971), U.S. Army officer (dishonorably discharged): Convicted of murder in the killing of civilians at My Lai, Republic of Vietnam, 1968. Pardoned, 1974.*

- *Martha Stewart (1995), Businesswoman, TV personality: Five months of home confinement following her release from prison on federal conspiracy and obstruction of justice charges.*

- *Michael Vick (2009), Professional athlete: Convicted of federal charges of running an illegal dog-fighting ring. Served two months in home confinement after 21-month term at Leavenworth Federal Penitentiary.*

- *Bernard Madoff (2008-2009), Stockbroker, investment adviser: Home confinement pending adjudication of federal fraud charges for running the largest Ponzi scheme in U.S. history, with losses to clients totaling $65 billion. Pleaded guilty, sentenced to maximum term of 150 years in prison.*

Electronic Monitoring

Persons under house arrest in the United States are rarely confined strictly to their homes. House arrest in addition to reducing prison crowding, helps the rehabilitation process by allowing those who would otherwise be confined in a jail to be released into the community to seek or continue employment, to maintain ties with their families, to pursue education, and to attend rehabilitative programs. Persons under house arrest generally are required to pay the costs associated with monitoring them.

The very oldest systems of house arrest relied on the community having knowledge of the offender and having everyone participate in watching that person. In later years, an offender might be required to answer a telephone call placed at a random time. Beginning around 1964, in both the United States and the United Kingdom, proposals for using "electronic tagging" to monitor offenders were launched. In 1983, the first sentence of house arrest with an electronic ankle bracelet was handed down by Judge Jack Love of Albuquerque, New Mexico.

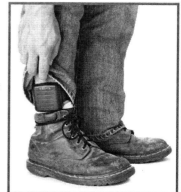

Electronic ankle bracelets utilize a transmitter worn by the offender. A signal is emitted from this transmitter and received, usually via phone signal, by a computer to report the offender's location or status. The electronic ankle bracelet (or sometimes wrist bracelet) is a transmitter that communicates with a receiver in the subject's home. If the distance between the bracelet and the receiver exceeds established bounds, an alarm goes off in a monitoring

FIGURE 10.1: *SCRAM monitors can report alcohol use to the monitoring station.* Photo courtesy of AMS.

station. Agencies normally outsource these monitoring activities to private firms; if an alarm goes off, the operator calls the responsible offi-cial, usually a parole or probation officer. The bracelets also are alarmed to make them tamper-resistant. The SCRAM™ bracelet, such as the one famously worn by actress Lindsey Lohan, is capable of measuring blood alcohol content (BAC) through the skin (see Figure 10.1).

GPS Monitoring

The **Global Positioning System (GPS)** uses artificial satellites to provide reliable location, navigation, and time services anywhere in the world, in any weather, as long as the receiver has an uninterrupted line-of-sight view of at least four satellites (see Figure 10.2).

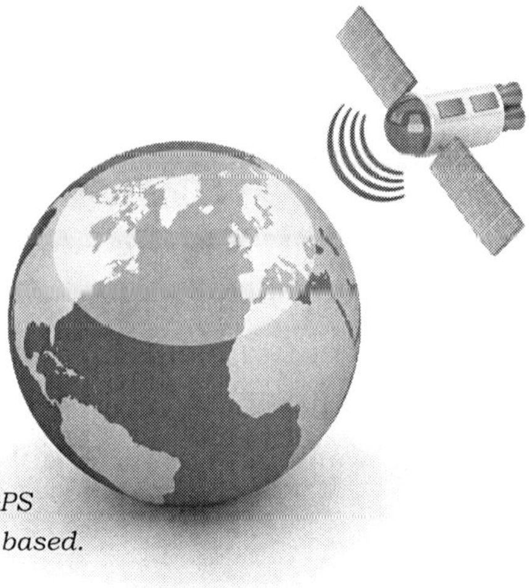

FIGURE 10.2: *The GPS system is satellite based.*

GPS is a project of the United States Department of Defense. GPS has its history based in radio navigation systems developed during the Second World War. Although originally created for military navigation systems, GPS is freely available throughout the world.

As with most technology, the size, weight, and cost of GPS receivers has gone down while quality has gone up. Cars now sport in-dash GPS systems as options, while weight-conscious backpackers carry small, handheld units. Cell phones get their time signals from GPS, and many of the current generation of smartphones are GPS navigation-enabled.

These changes make remote monitoring of persons under house arrest more convenient, affordable, and effective, both for the subject and for the people charged with the surveillance. Lighter weight, more compact units mean that a monitored subject may go about his or her daily business with an easily concealed monitor. Lower costs expand the number of potential participants.

Electronic monitoring may use real-time (active) or after-the-fact (passive) data collection. Low-risk offenders may only have their data uploaded to the central computer once per day, to ensure compliance with court orders. High-risk offenders may be continuously monitored, for example, to ensure that a domestic violence offender is not stalking a victim, or that child molesters are not detouring through schoolyards between home and work.

Unfortunately, a tendency persists to see technology as the solution to all problems and these devices are often too heavily relied on to do the job of probation and parole departments. Overuse of the system burdens parole and probation officers with low-risk offenders who do not truly require monitoring. On the other hand, misclassification of offenders leads to high-risk clients being classified as low-risk and not supervised closely enough. Technical failures occur due to weather, topology, and the nature of cellular communication. Since the monitoring bracelets are tamper-resistant, not tamper-proof, the door is open for attempts to defeat the technology.

- A 2007 study by the Arizona legislature found more than 34,000 false alerts by 140 GPS-monitored offenders.

- In California, Jessica's Law requires GPS monitoring of all paroled sex offenders. Since the law was passed in 2006, the number of homeless parolees has increased by 900%. Lacking a permanent residence, homeless parolees fall into noncompliance as they take up residence in places where cellular reception may be poor, such as public hospitals, or in areas lacking electrical facilities with which to recharge the batteries in their monitors, such as park benches, bus shelters, under bridges, and in homeless encampments.

CASE STUDY

Systems Do Fall

GPS monitoring combines GPS technology with cellular technology, frequently magnifying the weaknesses of both. In Connecticut, David Pollitt was paroled in September of 2007 after serving 24 years in prison for a series of rapes. Pollitt was placed on GPS monitoring and confined to his sister's property.

In September of 2008, Pollitt was rearrested after GPS placed him in the next block from his sister's home; Pollitt's family testified that he was in the backyard at the time. Investigation determined that Pollitt's transmitter could not find a cell tower on his block and "bounced" the signal to the tower in the next block. Pollitt's monitor had, in fact, generated more than 40 false alarms in the year after his release; his family had resorted to putting the house phone in his room because of frequent, middle-of-the-night calls from his parole officer, responding to false alarms. The company contracted to track GPS-monitored offenders testified that they couldn't say with any certainty that Pollitt had left the property. Charges against Pollitt eventually were dropped.

On the other side of the coin, knowing where a parolee is and knowing what he is actually doing are two different things. On August 26, 1988, Phillip Craig Garrido was released on federal parole after serving 12 years in federal and Nevada state prisons for kidnapping a woman in South Lake Tahoe, California and transporting her to Reno, Nevada, where he raped her. In 1999, Garrido was released from federal parole and returned to the Nevada jurisdiction. Nevada released him from prison on lifetime parole. Because Garrido lived in California, responsibility for his parole supervision was transferred to the California Department of Corrections and Rehabilitation. Under the terms of his parole, Garrido was required to wear a GPS ankle bracelet, and regularly was visited by parole agents and police.

On June 10, 1991, Garrido and his wife, Nancy, kidnapped 11-year old Jaycee Dugard from a street in South Lake Tahoe, in broad daylight and in full view of her horrified stepfather and classmates. In spite of Garrido's high-risk potential (he had been charged in 1972 with kidnapping and sexually assaulting a 14-year-old girl, but charges were dropped when the victim refused to testify); the co-location of the crime with the site of Garrido's previous crime; the close match of the suspect vehicle with Garrido's car; and frequent contacts with police and parole agents (who accepted his explanation of the young girl at his house as his "niece"); and even a brief return to federal prison in 1993 for parole violation; Garrido held Dugard captive for 18 years, repeatedly raping her and fathering two children with her.

Dugard's captivity ended in August, 2009, after an alert special events manager at University of California at Berkeley tipped an equally alert UC Berkeley police officer to the suspicious man who had come to campus with two strangely behaved girls (his daughters by Dugard, ages 15 and 11 at the time) to request permission to hold a revival meeting. The officer ran Garrido's name, learned he was a paroled rapist, and notified his parole agent. Parole agents went to Garrido's house, began investigating in earnest, and learned the truth before they left. Phillip and Nancy Garrido were arrested and, at this writing, have pleaded "Not Guilty" to all charges and are awaiting trial.

Kiosk Technology

Although jail and prison overcrowding are a problem, there also has been a rise in persons assigned to community corrections programs. These, too, place stress on a system with too little money and too few parole/probation officers required to "supervise" hundreds of clients. Many jurisdictions have sought ways to leverage technology to free up parole and probation officers' time to focus on their higher-risk clients.

A technology in use in a number of jurisdictions is the **probation kiosk**. Low-risk probationers, on their first meeting with their probation officer, are trained in the use of kiosks placed in the lobby of the probation office. Probationers use the kiosk to report in, answering tailor-made questions about their housing, employment, child support, new arrests, and so on. Kiosks also are able to take court-ordered payments for program fees, child support, restitution, and so on. If no red flags are raised, for example, there has been no new arrest, the probationer is issued a receipt and is free to go. The process, on average, takes approximately four minutes to complete.

In some cases, the probation officer may have put a note in the client's profile requiring a face-to-face meeting, or such alerts may be triggered by a report of a new arrest, an out-of-area address change, or a random drug screen. A kiosk attendant may be stationed in the lobby to ensure that these requirements are met before the probationer is allowed to leave the building.

Probation Tracking

Parole and probation officers frequently have caseloads that defy any effective span of supervision. In addition to heavy caseloads, problems arise in sharing data between general law enforcement and community corrections. Effective data sharing can be instrumental both in both managing probationers and preventing future crimes.

In the 1970s and 1980s, Washington State found itself bedeviled by serial killers (Ted Bundy, Gary Ridgway). In response, the Washington State Attorney General's Office created the Homicide Investigative Tracking System (HITS) unit in the Office's Criminal Division. The concept was a success from the beginning, and in 1991 the state legislature mandated that it track all violent crimes, including sex offenses.

Supervision Management And Recidivist Tracking (SMART) Partnerships began in 1992 as a collaboration between the Redmond, Washington Police Department and the Washington State Department of Corrections. There are two components to the SMART Partnerships concept. In the first component, Redmond police officers are assigned one or two parolees to monitor directly. Officers make random visits to the parolees' homes during their hours of curfew. If the parolee is not at home or if the officers detect other violations, they document the violations and report them to the parole officer responsible for the offender's case; if the police officers detect criminal activity, they respond as they normally would. This home visit component allows beat officers to become personally acquainted with the parolees living in their areas and builds working relationships between the police officers and the parole officers. Some offenders also have reported better re-integration into the community as a result of the home visits.

The second component of the SMART Partnerships concept aims to improve communication about a parolee's activities. When beat officers have a random enforcement contact with a parolee, for example, traffic violation, domestic disturbance not resulting in arrest, suspicious circumstances, etc., the officer completes a standard Field Interview (FI) Card. This FI card is then routed to the Department of Corrections Community Corrections (Parole) Division and forwarded to the relevant parole officer.

CASE STUDY

The Probation Dashboard

In early 2008, the state of North Carolina was rocked by two senseless murders in its academic community.

In January, Abhijit Mahato, a 29-year-old Ph.D. student at Duke University, was found shot to death in his apartment, the victim of an apparent robbery. In March, 22-year-old Eve Carson, student body president at University of North Carolina at Chapel Hill, was kidnapped from her home, driven to a bank where her ATM card was used to extract money from her account, and then taken to a residential area where she was shot dead.

A minor, 17-year-old Lawrence Lovette, was arrested and charged with both murders. According to police, Lovette and accomplice Stephen Oates carried out the robbery and murder of Abhijit Mahato. Lovette and a different accomplice, 21-year-old Demario Atwater, were alleged to have kidnapped, robbed, and murdered Eve Carson. Lovette's face was captured on an ATM security camera as he used Carson's card to withdraw money from her account.

The families and friends of the victims, and the community at large, had one more blow delivered to them in the aftermath of the arrests: both Lovette and Atwater were on probation at the time of the killings. Lovette's probation officer had over 125 cases assigned to him, even though he had not yet completed basic training. Atwater's case had been shuffled through 10 different probation officers, none of whom had ever met with him.

Faced with public outcry over these revelations, the state legislature appropriated $140,000 to develop a computerized probation tracking system. The system, called the *Probation Dashboard*, was operational in six months. Initial development work involved a painstaking, manual process of matching and disambiguating court records with Department of Corrections records. The Dashboard gives the probation officer a single page view of his cases. It flags offenders who are due for drug testing, home or work visits, or who have failed to check-in as required. Like the Washington State HITS/SMART system, it automatically alerts the probation officer to contacts his clients have had with law enforcement; in many cases, this information has been used to track down and retake offenders who have violated their probation.

Would the Probation Dashboard have prevented the murders of Abhijit Mahato and Eve Carson? That is impossible to know. We do know that, without effective supervision of high-risk offenders, there was very little hope of preventing these crimes and others like them.

At this writing, Lawrence Lovette and Stephen Oates are awaiting trial for the murder of Abhijit Mahato. Lovette also is awaiting trial for the murder of Eve Carson; Demario Atwater pleaded guilty to both state and federal charges, in separate plea-bargains, for life without parole in lieu of the death penalty in both jurisdictions.

Crime Reporting in the Digital Age

The digital age brings new opportunities, as well as new challenges, to crime reporting (see Figure 10.3).

Crime reporting addresses both the means by which crimes are brought to the attention of the authorities and how the authorities process and share information about crimes. As we have seen in the impetus behind the Washington State HITS/SMART, the effective use of data breaks down when separate, poorly communicating parties hold separate pieces of the puzzle.

FIGURE 10.3: *Officers wear a surveillance camera capable of streaming live images to a control center. Photo courtesy of Hunter Systems Group*

Technologies used for reporting also are changing. Police agencies are becoming more bandwidth-hungry; petty crime reporting is being relegated to departmental websites; and agencies are leveraging multimedia technology for evidentiary and documentary purposes:

• A growing number of law enforcement agencies have adopted or are testing wearable cameras, capable of recording audio and video, for use by individual officers.

• The city of Memphis, Tennessee has received $11 million in Homeland Security grants since 1993. Most of that money has been used to fight crime, including installing surveillance cameras to monitor residents of high-crime housing projects and problematic street corners.

• Motorola recently demonstrated over-the-air Long Term Evolution (LTE), including features such as multi-agency communications, dynamic reallocation of bandwidth (for example, first responders in a disaster scenario would have priority until the situation was stabilized), and increased speeds to accommodate streaming video from an officer's camera.

Alarm Communications

Alarm company systems have evolved from noisy bells that go off when a door is forced open to complex systems that detect motion, record video, report fires, and dispatch responders to panic alarms. Most residential and commercial alarms these days are not alarms at all, but communication devices. When activated, they dial into a monitoring station, either a commercial entity or the local law enforcement dispatch. With the growth of the Internet and mobile technology, some homeowners have chosen to become their own alarm monitors.

- A Brazilian businessman traveling in Germany received an alert on his cell phone from the security system in his beach house in Brazil. He logged on to his laptop and via the Internet saw live images of the burglar at work. He then phoned his wife, who was not at the house but called the local police. The police arrested the burglar while he was still in the house, stuffing bags with the victims' belongings.

- A Boynton Beach, Florida woman installed a Web camera system in her home. One day, while at work, she watched two men in the act of burglarizing her home and dialed 911. Police arrested the burglars in the home, as well as two accomplices waiting in a pickup truck outside.

Although live streaming presents the best opportunity to catch an intruder in the act, motion-sensitive Web cameras and software can email photos of suspects to burglary victims, allowing later identification by police.

FIGURE 10.4: *Officers can monitor multiple locations at the same time in control centers. Photo courtesy of cbp.gov*

Regardless of the technology in use or the means of monitoring, alarms have one essential function: to protect life and property (see Figure 10.4). The increased use of Internet-based communications, multimedia technology, and mobile communications hold the potential to reduce expensive false alarms, improve law enforcement response times, provide better information to responding officers and protect their safety, and increase apprehension and conviction rates.

Reporting and Information Sharing

Many police departments are having difficulty keeping up with demands for service. "Routine" calls and petty crimes are being handled over the phone, as resources are focused on serious offenses.

- San Jose Police Department allows crime reporting and posts crime statistics online.

- tip411 allows citizens to send anonymous SMS text tips to participating law enforcement agencies.

- Many communities allow their residents to subscribe to SMS text messages for emergency notifications, Amber Alerts, etc.

There are over 18,000 federal, state, local, and tribal law enforcement agencies in the United States engaged in the business of preventing crime and tracking down criminals when crimes occur. When criminals do cross jurisdictional boundaries, it becomes especially difficult for investigators to connect the dots linking a crime in one jurisdiction with similar crimes in another:

The need to effectively share information, led to the creation of the Law Enforcement National Data Exchange (**N-DEx**).

The FBI's Criminal Justice Information Services (CJIS) Division is the sponsor, developer, and host of N-DEx, which began in 2005. N-DEx rolled out in prototype form to selected agencies in 2008, and it became fully operational in 2010.

The key design criteria for N-DEx are the following:

- N-DEx is built to support law enforcement investigations, and is built on a foundation of local law enforcement data.

- N-DEx is not a statistical reporting tool.

- N-DEx is not an intelligence gathering system.

- Data entered into N-DEx is owned by the agency entering it.

- Local records collection practices are not affected.

FIGURE 10.5: *Computerized government database.* Photo courtesy of FEMA News Photo

N-DEx offers a number of valuable tools to first responders (see Figure 10.5). These tools include the ability to send and receive notifications quickly and efficiently by a variety of means, including mobile data terminals and SMS text messaging; analysis of crime patterns and modus operandi, to identify potential targets of criminals and possible avenues of escape; and a shared knowledge base, providing officers with access to more information in order to establish reasonable cause for an arrest or issuance of a warrant.

CASE STUDY

A Killer Eludes Authorities

Angel Maturino Resendiz, aka Rafael Resendez Ramirez, aka The Railway Killer, murdered 30 people across the United States between 1986 and 1999. According to FBI Agent John Douglas, "The manhunt for the accused killer (had) been hampered by the lack of a coordinated computer system that would allow law enforcement officials to compare notes instantly and determine patterns."

Resendiz was a known illegal alien with a long history of crimes, deportations, and illegal returns. Police had identified Resendiz as a suspect in the December, 1998 murder of Dr. Claudia Benton, a pediatric neurologist at the Baylor College of Medicine, at her home in West University Place, Texas. In May of 1999, Resendiz was linked to three more murders in Texas and Kentucky. The FBI organized a multi-agency task force and added Resendiz to their "Ten Most Wanted" list. Both local police and Border Patrol Intelligence attempted, unsuccessfully, to enter warrants for Resendiz in the Border Patrol and Customs Service computer systems.

On June 1, 1999, Resendiz was stopped by Border Patrol agents while attempting to illegally enter the United States near Santa Teresa, New Mexico. Because there was no outstanding warrant for Resendiz in the Border Patrol's computer system, he was allowed to return voluntarily to Mexico. Less than 48 hours later, he murdered two women in separate attacks near Houston; he claimed his last victims, a father and daughter in Illinois, less than two weeks after the Houston killings.

On July 13, 1999, following negotiations with American law enforcement and pressure from his family, Resendiz crossed the border from Ciudad Juarez, Mexico and surrendered at the Border Patrol station near El Paso, Texas.

Public outrage over the fact that, with state and federal warrants for his arrest outstanding on multiple murder charges, Resendiz had been arrested and released, sparked Congressional hearings and an investigation by the Justice Department's Office of the Inspector General (OIG). The OIG's report cited widespread confusion among Immigration and Naturalization Service (INS, now Immigration and Customs Enforcement) employees about the INS's IDENT fingerprint system; deficiencies in the design and implementation of IDENT; and "ineffective or non-existent" training on IDENT. The report also noted that, although the FBI's Integrated Automatic Fingerprint Identification System (IAFIS) was not operational at the time, the Resendiz case illustrated a need to ensure that IDENT was properly integrated with FBI and INS databases.

Angel Maturino Resendiz was tried and convicted of the robbery, rape, and murder of Dr. Claudia Benton. He was executed by the State of Texas on June 27, 2006.

Mass Media

Mass media has a role in the technological response to crime. Mass media has the capability of reaching millions, instantly creating a virtual army of observers and support for law enforcement and emergency response efforts. The shrill alarm you sometimes hear on the radio that is preceded by the phrase, "This will be a test of the emergency notification system," was the predecessor to the current types of widely broadcast crime data available on radio and television.

Cable Television

Public access cable can be a valuable tool in educating the public. At this time, 75% of American households have access to cable and 50% of cable subscribers watch their public access channels regularly. Cable television programs can educate viewers in effective crime prevention strategies for themselves and their communities, as well as disseminating photos and drawings of wanted persons and suspects and advertising rewards for capture or conviction (see Figure 10.6).

FIGURE 10.6: *Local news crew captures up-to-the-minute information.*
Photo courtesy of FEMA News Photo

• The Oxnard, California, Police Department produces a cable TV and Internet series. The show, now called *Straight to You*, has been one of the most popular programs on local cable. Since the show began, Oxnard reports a 50-percent decrease in burglaries despite population growth of more than 20,000 people.

• The Hawaii Attorney General produces a television talk show for teens. *Bridging the Gap* provides a platform for teens to voice their concerns about an array of prevention-related topics.

• In Louisville, Kentucky, the Louisville Metro Police Foundation, a non-profit organization that raises money to support the police, has launched a series of public service announcements on local television. *Could You Do It?* aims to raise awareness of the dangers of police work.

YouTube

YouTube, often referred to as part of the "New Media," has proven to be a valuable investigative tool. Criminals have filmed themselves committing crimes and then posted the videos on YouTube for bragging rights, so much so that, in the United Kingdom, random assaults for the purpose of collecting video footage now has its own name in the urban lexicon, "happy slapping."

Here in the United States, we have our own people with rather peculiar ideas about what to post on the Web for public consumption:

- Oklahoma Highway Patrol officers arrested a man who posted videos of himself speeding down freeways in the Oklahoma City area.

- Domino's Pizza filed criminal charges against two former employees in North Carolina who videotaped themselves contaminating pizza with their own bodily excretions.

- A Eureka, California man was arrested after posting a video of himself looting an archeological site.

- A Connecticut man was arrested for "impairing the morals of a child" after posting video of himself coaching his neighbor's 8-year old son into uttering a stream of profanity for the camera.

Apart from utilizing information provided by criminals, police are using the New Media to reach out to an increasingly wired population:

- In Ontario, Canada, police posted surveillance footage on YouTube in hopes of solving a nightclub murder. A week later, driven in part by the additional publicity, the suspect turned himself in.

- The U.S. Immigrations and Customs Enforcement (ICE) have a YouTube channel devoted to public outreach on a variety of topics including drug smuggling and human trafficking.

• The Baltimore County, Maryland, Police Department produces a 30-minute monthly show called Police Report. The show features department members providing valuable information to county residents.

• The New York City Police Department maintains a YouTube channel, "Inside the NYPD."

Effective use of YouTube and other social media will become even more important with the wide use of smartphones, tablet computers, and ebook readers (see Figure 10.7).

FIGURE 10.7: *Person getting up-to-the-minute traffic information on a smart phone*

CASE STUDY

Smart Phone Leads to Arrest

Claire Blevins, of Denver, Colorado, never thought $4.99 could be so well spent. That it was spent well illustrates the effective use of new technology in fighting crime.

Blevins had purchased an iPhone application that streams motion-activated snapshots from webcams. Blevins bought it to keep an eye on her Wheaten Terrier puppy, Callie, when Blevins was away from home. Blevins logged on from work late one afternoon and noticed a high photo count. She was surprised to see, not her dog or her roommate, but a strange man picking up items from her room and placing them into the shoulder bag he wore.

Police released footage from the phone to a local television station that same night. A viewer recognized the intruder and tipped off the police, who promptly arrested the suspect.

The suspect, on parole at the time of the break-in, denies stealing anything. He says he went into the house, "just to look around."

Summary

The changing face of communications technology, and the social changes that accompany it, create new challenges and opportunities for law enforcement.

Technology, properly applied, can ease the burdens of law enforcement. Increasing use of the Internet for surveillance, reporting, and other forms of communication have made the demise of Plain Old Telephone Service a question of "when", not "if". As consumers drive improvements in both fixed and mobile Internet connectivity, law enforcement agencies must look for ways to leverage those developments to better serve their communities, from education and prevention to arrest and conviction.

Discussion Questions

1. How has technology changed the way you communicate? How do you do things differently now and what changes can you foresee in the future?

2. Have you, or has anyone you know, given up landline phone service for mobile or Internet telephony? Why or why not? Discuss.

3. Is law enforcement making the best use it can of current communications technology? Discuss.

4. How can law enforcement leverage current and future communications trends to improve community outreach?

5. What are the implications for civil liberties of the new wave in communications? Are there dangers in large-scale surveillance and data mining? Does the "eye-in-the-sky" model differ from the "cop-on-the-beat" approach? Discuss.

Key Terms

ANSI/SIA DC-09-2007: A standard developed by the Security Industry Association (SIA) for Internet Event (alarm) Reporting. Approved by the American National Standards Institute (ANSI).

Community Corrections: A broad category of alternatives to incarceration such as parole, probation, house arrest, electronic monitoring, work furlough, etc.

Global Positioning System (GPS): A space-based global navigation satellite system that provides reliable time and location information to Earth-based fixed and portable receivers.

Internet Protocol (IP): The primary communications protocol for relaying data across the Internet.

Long Term Evolution (LTE): An emerging standard in mobile network technology, endorsed by public safety agencies in the United States as the preferred technology for the new 700MHz public safety radio band. Due to roll out in 2011.

N-DEx: A national criminal justice database, operated by the FBI's Criminal Justice Information Service, designed to unify and share law enforcement data from agencies throughout the United States.

National Suspicious Activity Reporting Initiative (NSI): A United States Department of Justice program to collect and share reports of suspicious activity. Unlike N-DEx, which is a criminal justice program, NSI is an intelligence-gathering program aimed primarily at thwarting terrorism.

Probation Kiosk: An automated check-in system for supervision of probationers.

RFC 4783: A protocol for alarm communications over IP, developed by the Internet Engineering Task Force.

YouTube: A video-sharing website (subsidiary of Google) where users can upload, share, and view videos.

References

Reentry, U.S. Department of Justice, Office of Justice Programs

Special Report: The California Department of Corrections and Rehabilitation's Supervision of Parolee Phillip Garrido, Office of the Inspector General, State of California (November, 2009)

Strategic Design in Social Issue Media Keynote address, 2010 "Making Your Media Matter" conference, American University School of Communication (Podcast/downloadable video)

LTE Home Page, Motorola Corporation

Averting an Alarm Communications Gap, Security Sales & Integration (September 1, 2010)

Monitoring America, Top Secret America: A Washington Post Project (December 20, 2010)

The Rafael Resendez-Ramirez Case: A Review of the INS's Actions and the Operation of Its IDENT Automated Fingerprint Identification System, *USDOJ/OIG* (March, 2000)

Case Studies: Crime Prevention, Public Service Advertising Research Center

You're Grounded! How Do You Qualify for House Arrest?, *Slate (January 28, 2009)*

The Global Positioning System, *GPS.gov*

Washington State's Crime-Fighting Tool: HITS/SMART, *FBI Law Enforcement Bulletin (Feb. 2002) via BNET*

No Soul in the New Machine: Technofallacies in the Electronic Monitoring Movement, *Justice Quarterly*

Technology in the 21st Century Probation Milieu: Some Assembly Required, *Florida Department of Law Enforcement*

APPENDIX A

Report Writing Activities for Criminal Justice

Appendix A: Activities   PAGE

ACTIVITY 1:
Objective Writing vs. Subjective Writing

Key Activity Objectives

- Discern the key differences between objective and subjective writing
- Understand when subjective language is acceptable
- Provide an objective report for a diverse audience

Introduction

Report writing must "tell a story" that complies with certain requirements that are not found in creative writing. One of the most important conditions is that the reporting officer must be "objective," rather than "subjective," in his reports.

Subjective writing is characterized by the author expressing opinions, feelings and, even in some cases, judgments. In objective writing, the author relates facts without imposing his own feelings or opinions into the narrative. When writing an official report, the author needs to be objective, without expressing any personal or professional opinions. Subjective writing has no basis in report writing, be it a news article or a police report, because the audience expects an unbiased account of events. Emotions affect our ability to think and make conclusions rationally. We may hold firmly to how people should be treated when they do something wrong, but when it directly affects us, our opinion of how serious the situation is, or how best to handle the situation is markedly different. Therefore, law enforcement reports in particular must communicate only the facts.

Sometimes it may be appropriate to be subjective and objective in a piece of non-fiction writing. If the author is writing an editorial piece about the effects of war, he may communicate objective information by providing statistical information concerning the cost of war in terms of money and lives. To make or emphasize a point, the editorial author may be subjective in adding how war had a devastating emotional effect on him or someone he knows. However, an editorial piece is, by design, based on one person's opinion and/or experience, and is not held to the same factual standards of a news or police report.

For the purposes of report writing, individuals in the criminal justice field are expected to provide facts while withholding emotion. This allows the reporting officer to effectively provide others with the facts so that they can take the appropriate action.

EXAMPLE

A retired detective is accused of sexual assault. The investigating officer taking the initial report "filtered" out some information or down played the significance of information provided. The actions of others, i.e., supervisors, district attorneys, and judges rely on the information provided to them in reports to help determine that the most appropriate action is taken. If the initial information is faulty, the decisions based upon that information is faulty, and justice is not served.

Sometimes an author may not realize that they are being subjective in their reports. This usually happens with the author makes conclusions based upon observed behavior or information provided.

During the interview, Ms. Wilson did not maintain eye contact and was constantly moving around in her chair. When asked if she could describe the person she saw take the money from the cash register, Ms. Wilson hesitated, took a couple of seconds to respond, and said she doesn't think she can identify the person. When asked if she had seen the person before, Ms. Wilson looked away from me and in a soft voice said, "No."

It was very obvious that Ms. Wilson did not want to be talking to me about the crime and was very uncomfortable. When Ms. Wilson was asked to describe the person she saw take the money from the cash register, Ms. Wilson was evasive and lied to me when she said she could not identify the suspect. It was also obvious that Ms. Wilson knew the suspect because of her reaction when I asked her if she had seen the person before.

When we examine the example, the author is being objective in the first part of the report. He is reporting facts about the physical actions and the subject's responses. But in the second paragraph, the author becomes subjective by making conclusions as to what those physical actions and responses mean. In such situations, the author should describe the facts relating to the subject's actions and verbal responses, and allow the reader to conclude what those facts mean.

There are a couple of key concepts to keep in mind when trying to ensure that the report is objective.

- Avoid making conclusions or inferences
- Do not address emotions, thoughts, or feelings. Stay with the facts.
- Don't try to convince the reader of anything. Let the reader make conclusions based upon the facts in the report.

Report writing is not the place to be creative or make an emotional plea. Only by being objective can we have the best chance of rational, fair decisions being made.

Sample of an Objective Report:

> I bought a puppy yesterday. He is a purebred American Eskimo. He is only seven weeks old and has very white fluffy hair. When we first brought him home, he spent the first couple of hours lying in one of the corners of the kitchen. After that, he jumped on the couch and lied next to my wife and fell asleep.

Sample of a Subjective Report:

> I bought a puppy yesterday. When we went to look at the litter, the one I picked out had a fantastic personality. He ran up to me and acted as if we were long lost friends. When I got him home, he was a little afraid and spent the first couple of hours shivering in one of the corners of the kitchen. It was obvious that he was afraid and uncertain of his new surroundings. I had no doubt that he would become comfortable in a short period of time. Sure enough, a couple of hours later he jumped up on the couch and lied next to my wife. He was so content he fell asleep on her lap. He is going to be a fantastic dog.

Activity

Go to "YouTube" and type in "Job Interviews." Click on the link for "Two Sample Interviews." Review one of the interviews and write two summaries of the interview you watched. One report should be objective and the other should be subjective. Remember, in the subjective report, you are free to use emotions, conclusions, and opinions, while the objective report contains facts.

In class, be prepared to discuss which of the two styles was easier to write and what made the other style harder. Present what you did in the objective report to lead the reader to a specific conclusion or if you simply reported the facts.

Discussion Questions

1. What are some consequences that may result from a subjective report?

2. What are some situations, if any, in which the author can make conclusions in an objective report? (Example: Expert witness) How is this different from being subjective?

3. Are there any situations in which a subjective report is appropriate to be used in an investigation, administrative case, private investigation's report, or a probation report?

ACTIVITY 2:
Using Active Voice in Police Reports

Key Activity Objectives

- Understand the importance of clear, concise writing
- Develop basic report writing skills
- Demonstrate the ability to write incident reports using active voice

Introduction

Police officers and security personnel write reports for many types of events, from non-emergencies to violent crimes such as homicides. Whenever an officer is dispatched to a scene, a clear, concise, accurate incident report must be completed and filed, because the report may be used as evidence in the future. If used as evidence, lawyers, judges and juries will review the officer's writing as part of a case. Therefore, the report must be immediately accessible and easy for civilians to understand.

Many CJ students are uncomfortable with writing; after all, they are looking for a career in criminal justice or security, not journalism or publishing. Frequently, these students write long, expressive sentences with a high word count because they think it makes them look "smarter." This is usually not the case; in fact, longer sentences that mix verb tenses and use unnecessary vocabulary are simply harder to follow and make the writer's point vague and awkward. This is especially true in police reports. No matter what type of incident is reported, whether criminal or civil, it is essential that report writers use active voice. The use of active voice helps to make a report clear and concise, which is beneficial in the long run.

Reports that use proper, active verb tenses and that clearly describe subjects and actions lead to less confusion during the investigations process and ultimately at trial. Use of active verbs is called using "active voice." Once you get into the habit of using active voice in your writing, it will become second nature to use it in your reports.

As writers, when we use active voice, we make the subject (in the case of police reports, a person) the main actor in the situation. This means we make the subject the focus of the sentence. In short, active voice tells you "who" did "what." In a police report, this subject ("who") may be the officer, suspect, victim or witness. The verb ("what") is often, but not always, in the present tense, and indicates some form of action or movement. For instance, the following sentences use active voice. The subject is underlined, and the action is italicized.

- "The witness saw the accident."
- "The victim answered all our questions."
- "Mr. Jones drove the car that night."
- "I spoke with the witnesses and took their contact information."

Passive voice can make a sentence longer, but that does not necessarily make the sentence better. In fact, passive voice makes a sentence weaker, because the subject is acted upon, putting more importance on the act than the person. In fact, in some cases, the subject of the sentence is not even revealed, as in "Two kids were seen spray painting the wall of the city library."

An easy way to recognize use of passive voice is to look at the content of the sentence itself. Instead of using verbs that denote some sort of action, passive voice usually use some form of "to be," such as "are," "is" "was" or "were." Compare the following statements, as written in passive voice, to the ones written above. Again, the subject is under-lined, and the action is italicized.

- "It was stated by the witness that she saw the accident."
- "Questions were answered by the conscious victim."
- "The car was driven by Mr. Jones that night."
- "The witnesses were spoken to and their contact information was taken by me."

Sometimes the passive voice is unavoidable; for instance, you may take a quote from a witness who is speaking in passive voice, and you must directly relate what she said without changing her words. However, use the active voice whenever it is within your control. When compiling your incident report, remember that less is more. Try to analyze your writing for situations where the active voice is more appropriate for your purposes than the passive voice.

Sentences using active and passive voice are listed below.

EXAMPLES OF ACTIVE VOICE	EXAMPLES OF PASSIVE VOICE
"I interviewed Mr. Smith"	"Mr. Jones was interviewed by me."
"Laura obtains statements quite easily."	"Statements are obtained quite easily by Laura."
"He cooperated fully with our investigation."	"He was cooperative with our investigation."
"The suspect denies any wrongdoing."	"Wrongdoing is denied by the suspect."
"The officers canvassed the neighboring houses for information."	"The neighboring houses were canvassed by officers seeking information."

Activity

You and your partner are dispatched to the scene of a purse snatching. During the course of your initial investigation, you interview the victim, who was crossing the street at the time her purse was snatched, and three witnesses to the event. One of those witnesses tripped the suspect as he tried to get away with the victim's purse. The suspect was knocked unconscious and is still on the scene, and conscious, upon your arrival.

While filing your case, you come across your partner's report. It reads as follows:

> **My partner and I were dispatched to the scene of a purse snatching. 8:00 p.m. was our arrival time at the scene on Mulberry Street. A middle-aged man was observed on the ground; a large bruise was forming on his forehead. Three people were comforting an elderly woman on the ground; the contents of her purse were scattered on the sidewalk. The middle-aged man was assessed by me; the other individuals were interviewed by my partner. The following events were recounted by the victim and corroborated by witnesses.**
>
> **The elderly woman was taking a walk when the middle-aged man grabbed her purse and began to run away. He was tripped by one of the witnesses, a teenage boy who was nearby. The actions were observed by the other two witnesses, sisters who were aware of other purse snatchings in the area. The elderly woman was comforted by the women, while 911 was called to the scene by the teenage boy.**
>
> **The suspect was disoriented, and said he could not recall any of the events that were communicated by the other individuals. It was stated by the suspect that he did not know about any such crimes in the neighborhood. His residence is in another neighborhood; there was no reason provided for his presence on Mulberry Street.**

An ambulance was called to attend to both the victim, who seemed to be in shock, and the suspect. The paramedics released the victim, who was fully alert and aware. An assessment was made of the suspect, who was then transported to the emergency room for care. Upon his release from the ER, the suspect was arrested by myself and my partner, and taken into custody.

Rewrite this report so that it uses more active language, but the integrity and meaning of the report does not change.

Discussion Questions

1. Why might using passive voice be a hard habit to break?

2. Can you think of any situations, other than direct quotes, where using passive voice might be unavoidable?

3. What are some tricks or reminders you might use to help keep your writing more active?

ACTIVITY 3:
Chronological Writing in Police Reports

Key Activity Objectives

- Develop a working knowledge of what constitutes a "chronological order style report"
- Demonstrate how a chronological order style report is an effective means of communicating what was done during the course of an investigation
- Evaluate the strengths and weaknesses of a chronological order style report.

Introduction

The primary purpose of investigative reports is to effectively and accurately convey information from the officer (the author of the report) to the reader, who may be any number of people, including other officers, lawyers, paralegals and jury members. Quite simply, it is the author telling a story, but the story is restricted in ways that a novel is not. Effective report writing is comprised of several steps:

1. An incident occurs that required an officer to respond or take action

2. The officer responds, conducts an investigation, and takes notes

3. The officer writes a report and provides the report to specific audiences; such as supervisors, detectives, and fellow officers

4. The "audience" reads the report and is able to obtain a "picture" of what occurred

The investigative report must be factual, be devoid of bias, and provide detailed information concerning what the author saw, heard, and did. The report must also document how and from whom the information was obtained. The goal is to convey the information in such a manner that the reader can fully understand and follow along with what the author wrote. How that information is conveyed can be accomplished in a number of ways.

The two most common methods of investigative reporting are chronological order and logical order. Both are effective means of communicating with an audience, but each have different strengths and weaknesses. Logical order is an analytical approach. The logical order is divided into "topics," such as how the crime was discovered, what was done during the course of the investigation, how the suspect was identified, and what evidence was seized. The logical order approach emphasizes what was done and learned, rather than what action occurred first.

Chronological order is the style that is most frequently used in report writing. There are several benefits to using chronological order. We are used to giving and receiving information in a chronological manner, starting with what occurred first and continuing until the conclusion. Because of this structure, people are used to information that starts at the beginning and concludes at the end. Not only is it easier for the reader to follow; it is also easier for the author to write, because the information flows with each section tying to the preceding section.

EXAMPLE

"I pulled up to the residence and got out of my vehicle. As I approached

the residence, John Wilson, who identified himself as the person who

called the police, came up to me. After speaking with Mr. Wilson, I went

into the residence and contacted Janice Adams, the victim."

If the officer started his report with the information he received from Ms. Adams, the audience will wonder what the officer did prior to meeting with Ms. Adams and how the officer learned of Ms. Adams in the first place.

When we talk about chronological order as it relates to investigative reports, there are two chronologies that come into play: the chronology as it pertains to the investigation, and the chronology as it pertains to the crime. The investigation chronology sets forth what first occurred in the investigation and follows through to the end. The crime chronology emphasizes the criminal's actions from start to finish. It is important to keep in mind that either type of chronology can be effective, depending on what the author wants to emphasize. The other important consideration is that the author is not tied to only using one of the two types of chronology, but must choose which of the types will be the predominant style in the report.

Many police supervisors and prosecutors do not advocate use of the chronology order   style. An officer using this style may write too much detail concerning aspects of a case that are not critical to the investigation. Police supervisors and prosecutors are more concerned with the "topics" of the investigation: what the responding officer did, what evidence was obtained, how did the investigation establish who the suspect was. Another criticism of the chronological order style is that the reporting officer has a tendency to start sentences with "I," which strikes many readers as too informal for a legal document.

EXAMPLE

"I got out of bed at 6 a.m. and went downstairs. I put on a pot of

coffee and went outside and picked up the newspaper. I then came

back into the house and I ate a bowl of cereal."

With practice, the writer can overcome both these obstacles by realizing that using the first person, or "I," simply cuts down on the number of words the reader has to cover. Learning to use transitional words, such as "immediately," "after," and "soon after," also helps place

events into perspective. Using transitional words, the sentence now reads, "Immediately after getting out of bed, I went downstairs. After putting on a pot of coffee, the newspaper was retrieved from outside. Sitting down at the kitchen table, I ate a bowl of cereal."

Since chronologies deal with the order of events, they can be presented forward or reverse. When writing an investigative report, "going forward" starts with the discovery of the crime and proceeds from that event, while "going backward" starts with the investigation and goes in reverse to explore how the crime occurred.

Chronologies, as they pertain to the recording of investigative activities, shows a clear picture of an investigator's actions and provides some insight as to why the investigator did what he did. In turn, they give the audience a chance to see how events evolved and the explanation behind certain actions.

EXAMPLE

As read in court proceedings, an investigator filed a written report that, upon arrival at the scene, he spoke to a witness who saw the defendant threaten the victim. The officer wrote that he then obtained evidence that he submitted to the crime lab, and that the lab proved the evidence to be associated with the defendant. The reader of the report can readily understand why the officer concluded the defendant was the person who committed the crime.

To summarize, either the logical order style or the chronological order style may be used when submitting written reports, though the chronological style is more commonly utilized. It is important to remember that the report writer is not restricted to using only one style during the entire report. The overall style of the report may utilize the logical order style, but when the author describes the actual crime, such as a homicide, the chronological order style may be more effective. No matter which style is used, the ultimate goal is to effectively convey accurate information to the reader.

Activity

The following activity allows students to practice reporting in a chronological order. It also provides opportunities to use transitional words, first person narrative.

You are the training officer for new patrol officers assigned to the burglary unit. Using the chronological order style, describe how to teach a new patrol officer to investigate a burglary. Remember one of the criticisms of the chronological order style was that too much information might be provided. Attempt to convey the information in such a manner that the essence of the activity is conveyed, but the report isn't bogged down with information that is irrelevant to what you are trying to convey to your audience.

To help you get started, the following is offered as the first step:

1. You would read the offense report to learn what the patrol officer discovered when he responded to the scene of the burglary.

Discussion Questions

1. After completing this exercise, what do you think are advantages and disadvantages of the chronological order style of report writing?

2. Do you think the chronological method is an effective method of conveying information? Why?

3. What types of reporting would not call for the chronology method?

ACTIVITY 4:
First Person Narrative and Other Pronoun Issues

Key Activity Objectives

- Recognizing the importance of first person pronouns in report writing
- Understanding the relationship between pronouns and antecedents
- Developing the skills to use proper pronouns in official reports

Introduction

One of the most important qualities an officer can bring to the report writing process is clarity, or clearness. Because the report can be read by a wide variety of people who have different experiences with police activities, it is best to be as clear and precise, using everyday language, as possible. One way to guarantee that your report is easy to follow is to use proper pronouns, including the first person pronoun ("I"). Many people feel awkward about using "I" in their writing, because they have been taught in school not to use personal pronouns such as "I" or "you." For most academic papers, this is true. However, because an offense report is directly related to your personal observations and ac-tions, it is completely appropriate to use the first person. You do not need to refer to yourself in the third person, such as "this officer" or "this writer." In fact, referring to yourself as "I" makes your report much easier to follow. Compare the following two examples:

EXAMPLE

Upon arrival at the scene, this officer approached the suspect and ordered the suspect out of the house. He failed to comply and became increasingly verbally uncooperative. For officer safety reasons, this officer physically removed him from the house, read the Miranda Warning and placed him in the back of this officer's police vehicle.

Upon arrival at the scene, I approached the suspect and ordered him out of the house. The suspect did not comply and became increasingly verbally uncooperative. For officer safety reasons, I physically removed the suspect from the house, read   him the Miranda Warning and placed him in the back of my police vehicle.

The second report is briefer and more to the point than the first example. The average reader or speaker does not refer to himself in the third person ("this officer"), so the use of "I" will be much more accessible to jury members. Since the reporting officer signs his or her name to the report, it will be clear to the reader who is speaking to when "I" is referenced.

Other pronoun issues may come into play when writing reports. It is important to make clear connections between pronouns (which take the place of a person or object) and their antecedents (the object that has a relationship with the person or object).

In the English language, there are three cases of pronouns:

SUBJECTIVE PRONOUNS (PRONOUNS AS SUBJECTS)	OBJECTIVE PRONOUNS (PRONOUNS AS OBJECTS)	POSSESSIVE PRONOUNS
I	Me	My/mine
You	You	Your/yours
He/she/it	Him/her/it	His/her (hers)/it (its)
We	Us	Our/ours
They	Them	Their/theirs
Who	Whom	Whose

For instance:

Laura gave her car to Richard.

Written when substituting pronouns, the sentence reads:

She (subjective pronoun) gave the car/it (antecedent) to him (objective pronoun).

Writers commonly make errors when using pronouns; these must be avoided for clarity. The most frequent errors involve incorrect pluralization when combining pronouns and antecedents. Remember that these words indicate one person, and need to use singular pronouns: everybody, anybody, anyone, each, neither, nobody, and someone. Here are some examples of incorrect phrasing, followed by the corrected phrase.

INCORRECT: Every known individual must have their fingerprints taken.

CORRECT: Every known individual must have his or her fingerprints taken.

***This is correct because "individual" is singular, while "their" is plural. Therefore "his or her," which also is singular, matches "individual."

INCORRECT: Each suspect must submit their alibi.

CORRECT: Each suspect must submit her alibi.

***Again, the second sentence is correct because "suspect" is singular, while "their" is plural. Therefore "her," which also is singular, matches up with "suspect."

INCORRECT: Bob and me saw the crime occur.

CORRECT: Bob and I saw the crime occur.

***It is grammatically incorrect to say "Me saw the crime occur;" the same rule applies when there is another subject.

When in doubt, say the sentence out loud to see if it sounds right before you write it in your report.

Like any other skill, using pronouns and first person narrative correctly requires practice; as you become more comfortable with these concepts, your report writing will become more refined.

Activity

You have been dispatched to the scene of a domestic violence call. At the scene, which is a residence, you find a man, woman and child; each is upset, and each has sustained some sort of injury. The residence is in disarray. The man is verbally threatening the woman and child, who are visibly frightened. Using first person narrative and proper pronouns to indicate the people present and the objects in the surroundings, write a report detailing the scene and your actions. You have the freedom to describe the state of the residence, the type of injuries and the actions taken upon your arrival.

Discussion Questions

1. What reservations do you have about using first person pronouns in your report writing? What steps can you take to eliminate those reservations?

2. Why do you think so many people are confused by proper pronoun use? Why is it important to use proper pronouns in your police reports?

3. Can you think of any tips or devices to help you remember how to use pronouns with their antecedents?

CPSIA information can be obtained
at www.ICGtesting.com
Printed in the USA
FFOW02n0702040416
22912FF

9 781938 087066